Dialogues wi...
and S...

Renée Weber was educated at t...
Sorbonne and Columbia University, where she g...
philosophy. She is currently Professor of Philosophy at Rutgers
University in New Jersey, where she was awarded the Rutgers
College Outstanding Teacher Award for 1979. A former editor of
ReVision Journal, she has published numerous interviews and articles
on science and mysticism in journals. Her work has also appeared in
eight anthologies, including *The Metaphors of Consciousness*, *The
Holographic Paradigm and Other Paradoxes* and *David Bohm: Quantum
Physics and Beyond*. She lives in Princeton, New Jersey.

DIALOGUES WITH SCIENTISTS AND SAGES

The Search for Unity

RENÉE WEBER

ARKANA

ARKANA

Published by the Penguin Group
Penguin Books Ltd, 27 Wrights Lane, London W8 5TZ, England
Penguin Books USA Inc., 375 Hudson Street, New York, New York 10014, USA
Penguin Books Australia Ltd, Ringwood, Victoria, Australia
Penguin Books Canada Ltd, 10 Alcorn Avenue, Toronto, Ontario, Canada M4V 3B2
Penguin Books (NZ) Ltd, 182–190 Wairau Road, Auckland 10, New Zealand

Penguin Books Ltd, Registered Offices: Harmondsworth, Middlesex, England

First published by Routledge and Kegan Paul plc 1986
Published by Arkana 1990
3 5 7 9 10 8 6 4 2

Printed in England by Clays Ltd, St Ives plc

Dedicated to

FRITZ KUNZ

who opened the doors to a world of meaning and beauty

Contents

Acknowledgments

THANKS are due to the many people who helped make this book possible. Although he does not appear in the volume, I owe the greatest debt to one man: Fritz Kunz. I attended his New York lectures while an undergraduate at the University of Pennsylvania, and recognized their rare value. He was the earliest pioneer of the current movement that tries to reconcile science and mysticism, and the first to call attention to what he felt were remarkable similarities between western science and the wisdom traditions of India and Greece.

In the 1920s, 30s and 40s, his was the lone voice in the wilderness. An American educator who had lived long years in India and Ceylon (where he was principal of Ananda College), Kunz related how, on first coming across Einstein's epoch-making equation $e = mc^2$ in 1922 while in India, he recognized in a flash that "here were the ancient *darshanas* of India [i.e., the perspectives on the universe] in modern dress."

The realization that twentieth-century science could be mapped on to these ancient systems changed Kunz's life. For fifty years, until his death in 1972, his work revolved around the exploration and integration of these ideas. He already possessed a vast knowledge of philosophy and religion, especially their mystical traditions, and was also at home in science to the point where he knew and could converse with many of its great minds. Commenting, decades later, on the roots which this movement had struck, Heisenberg told Kunz: "We are on an island, but it is getting wider."[1]

On his return from India, Kunz resolved to commit his life to this work. He established the Center for Integrative Education in New York, which became the base of operation for his many activities. A brilliant and witty speaker, Kunz attracted intellectuals from a variety of fields. The Center drew such prominent scholars as Henry Margenau and F.S.C. Northrop from Yale, Kirtley Mather from Harvard, Donald Hatch Andrews from Johns Hopkins, and many others who debated these ideas at the conferences, lectures, and seminars which it organized. In 1940, Kunz founded a journal, *Main Currents in Modern Thought* which—together with Emily Sellon—he edited for decades. It was to

FRITZ KUNZ

have a quiet but decisive impact on American culture for over thirty years. Its purpose, summed up in its masthead, was "to promote the free association of those working together towards the integration of all knowledge through the study of the whole of things: nature, man, and society, assuming the universe to be one, dependable, intelligible, harmonious."

Main Currents drew high-powered contributors, many working at the frontiers of their fields: Heisenberg, von Weizsäcker, Eugene Wigner, H. S. Burr, Buckminster Fuller, von Bertalanffy, Dobzhansky, G. C. Amstutz, Jean Gebser, Jean Charon, Stockhausen, Adolph Portmann, Lancelot L. Whyte, Gardiner Murphy, William Irwing Thompson, and of course Margenau, Northrop, and the core group. In 1972, it published an article by an unknown young physicist, Fritjof Capra, an excerpt from a forthcoming book, *The Tao of Physics*.

After *Main Currents* ceased publication in 1975, a young biophysicist named Ken Wilber founded *ReVision Journal* (1977), modelled after *Main Currents*, but also expressing the unique outlook and formidable talents of its new editor-in-chief. He is one of the people whom I would like to thank. He was a gifted editor, and ours an harmonious working relationship during the seven years in which I published interviews in *ReVision*. Even where we disagreed, Wilber was supportive of my work, and his brilliant challenges concerning the relationship between science and mysticism often forced me to rethink my position, a process from which I invariably benefitted. Working with Rachel Gaffney, who succeeded Wilber as editor, was a consistent pleasure.

A word about the dialogues in this book. Six of them (and my own essay) have not been published before; six originally appeared in *ReVision Journal*. These have been cut, re-edited, and at times re-titled for this volume, given thematic coherence by their focus on issues that recur in all the figures I interviewed. In a few places I have re-edited relevant passages from several dialogues, and combined them, where this would provide greater detail and depth. With their permission, I have inserted several passages of the Bohm-Sheldrake discussion into my dialogue with Sheldrake on a similar topic; and combined several passages from my first Bohm interview on the implicate order with another dialogue on that subject that we did at a later date. In all the dialogues—except for stylistic editing—the words are the person's own. To ensure verbatim accuracy, the dialogues were conducted with a tape-recorder runnig, but the recorder was soon forgotten in the atmosphere of spontaneity which prevailed.

For me, these were real learning experiences and I feel privileged to have participated in them. I am deeply grateful to the people who allowed me to share their insights and who gave so generously of their time and energy, and wish to thank them for making this book possible.

The colleague to whom I am most deeply indebted is Dr. John

Briggs, who read and edited several chapters, and whose many constructive suggestions have greatly improved the organization and integration of the book. He was the first to urge me to publish this material, and his friendship and encouragement have meant much to me.

There are a number of colleagues whom I want to thank for their interest and help, either by reading one or more chapters or by sharing their knowledge and good judgment with me in a variety of ways: Dr. Patricia Hunt-Perry of Ramapo College; Dr. Robert Matthews and Prof. Mary Frances Egan of the Rutgers Philosophy Department; Dr. Robert Weingard of the Philosophy Department and Dr. Terry Matilsky of the Rutgers Physics Department, both of whom generously allowed me to consult them on various technical points; and also Dr. John Bronzan of the Physics Department, with whom over the years I have had exciting discussions on some of these issues; Paul Weber, M.D. who made invaluable critical comments and helpful suggestions and whose unfailing support and enthusiasm for my work over the years have significantly contributed to it; and Dr. Richard A. Falk of Princeton University, for his perspicacity and directness, leading to welcome improvements.

My appreciation goes to Saral Bohm for her warmth and friendship, which enhanced the setting of many of these dialogues; and to Dr. Janet Macrae of New York University, whose interest in my work and supportive attitude were real morale boosters.

Without the good offices and participation of Mrs. Emily Sellon, the dialogue with Lama Govinda would not have taken place; but quite aside from this, her knowledge of eastern philosophy, generously shared in discussions over the years, has greatly enhanced my perceptions of the subject.

I owe a special debt to Mrs. Dora Kunz whose teachings and rare personal insight into the realities that form the subject of this book have been a source of unfailing inspiration.

There is one person without whose help this volume could not have been prepared. No conventional acknowledgment of thanks can possibly capture my gratitude to Mrs. Loretta Mandel of the Rutgers University Philosophy Department, for the indefatigable energy and rare skill which she brought to the typing of this book and the many varied editorial tasks involved in its preparation, all of which she undertook with her customary enthusiasm, fine judgment, and remarkable steadiness even under pressure.

My thanks to Mrs. Margaret Melton of the Philosophy Department for her cheerful and tireless typing help.

Finally, thanks are due to Mrs. Eileen Wood Campbell, my editor at Routledge & Kegan Paul, and her staff, for providing a supportive and harmonious atmosphere in which this book could grow.

Renée Weber
Princeton, New Jersey
November 10, 1985

The following originally appeared in *ReVision Journal*:

"On Poverty and Simplicity: Views of a Post-Industrial Christian Sage," a Dialogue between Fr. Bede Griffiths and Renée Weber (1983).

"Of Matter and Meaning: The Super-Implicate Order," a Conversation between David Bohm by Renée Weber (1983).

Bohm and Weber "Nature as Creativity" (1982).

Sheldrake and Weber "Morphogenetic Fields: Nature's Habits?" (1982).

"The World-View of a Mahayana Buddhist," a Conversation with Lama Govinda (Renée Weber and Emily Sellon) (1971).

"The Enfolding-Unfolding Universe," a conversation with David Bohm by Renée Weber (1979).

"Field Consciousness and Field Ethics" by Renée Weber (1978).

Sheldrake and Bohm, "Morphogenetic Fields and the Implicate Order" (1982).

Reprinted by permission of the *American Theosophist*.

Excerpts from "On Compassion," Essay on and an Interview with His Holiness, the Dalai Lama (copyright 1981).

Acknowledgments are also gratefully made for the use of the following photographs:

Cover photos: Spiral Galaxy NGC 5457 in Ursa Major, 1983 Copyright California Institute of Technology; David Bohm and the Dalai Lama photograph by Brian C. Beresford.

Text photos: Krishnamurti, photo by John Briggs; Fr. Bede Griffiths, Templegate Publishers; Ilya Prigogine, News and Information Service, University of Texas; Lama Govinda, Li Gotami; His Holiness, the Dalai Lama, J. Treasure; Renée Weber, Patricia Hunt-Perry; Rupert Sheldrake, Harald Laabs; David Bohm, the Dalai Lama, and Renée Weber, Brian C. Beresford.

The scientist does not study nature because it is useful; he studies it because he delights in it, and he delights in it because it is beautiful. If nature were not beautiful, it would not be worth knowing, and if nature were not worth knowing, life would not be worth living.

HENRI POINCARÉ

Science is reticent also when it is a question of the great Unity—the One of Parmenides—of which we all somehow form a part, to which we belong. The most popular name for it in our time is God.

ERWIN SCHROEDINGER

We thus arrive at a conception of the relation of science to religion very different from the usual one.... I maintain that the cosmic religious feeling is the strongest and noblest motive for scientific research.

ALBERT EINSTEIN

RENÉE WEBER

1
The search for unity

RENÉE WEBER

> Science is the attempt to understand reality. Science is a
> quasi-religious activity in the broadest sense of the term
>
> GEORGE WALD

THEY have tried to talk me out of it repeatedly and over many years and from both sides of the spectrum—scientists and mystics—but it will not take root. At times my mind—trained for years in the rigors of philosophy—is nearly convinced, won over by some argument whose validity I cannot help but grant at the moment. But after a while this leaks off again because it does not go deep enough, does not touch the core of me which stubbornly holds out for *that*. Sometimes, listening to my colleagues talking about philosophy in the measured and modest style which has become the official way of doing American philosophy—taking on small problems that lend themselves to solution—I realize that I am a maverick, for I can settle for nothing less than the whole. It is a feeling deep in my bones and blood. It has been there since my childhood and has accompanied me through all the years of education at elite universities, where it stayed underground for the sake of prudence. But it only went into hiding. It is still there and has been in the background all along, the scale against which every particular truth I have met with is weighed.

It is the sense of the unity of things: man and nature, consciousness and matter, inner and outer, subject and object—the sense that these can be reconciled. I have never really accepted their separation and my life—personal and professional—has been spent exploring their unity in a spiritual odyssey.

I have finally come to ask these scientists and sages themselves. The question that continues to preoccupy me will perhaps be answered here, for these are the people whose work is at the center of the search for reality. Talking to the more conventional scientists and religious figures has proven to be a dead-end; they are not synthesizers and thus do not understand my question. They suspect it is the result of confusion about the nature of science or the nature of mysticism. As for philosophy itself, it has long ago given up such pursuits as hopeless, leading neither to a philosophical nor to a professional "pay-off"—a poor investment of one's time. Nevertheless, it is what matters most to me. I have struggled to balance the productivity and integrity of the scholar with the search for wholeness. It is a priority with which nothing else can compete. To explain this to others borders on spiritual auto-biography, which I have resolved to keep to a minimum.

The fact, nevertheless, is that my odyssey takes me from one end of America to the other, three times to Europe, and finally to Asia, south-ward into India and northward into Nepal. I carry my search to Bohm and Krishnamurti amidst the orange groves of California; to Fr. Bede Griffiths at his Christian ashram in the parched Indian countryside; to the halls of Cambridge University and its leading astrophysicist, Ste-phen Hawking; to Nobel laureate Ilya Prigogine in the bustle of New York City; to the Dalai Lama's peaceful monastery in Switzerland and an alpine retreat and renewed meeting with Krishnamurti; to more ordinary settings like Princeton, Westchester County, Syracuse, and London, where I converse with Sheldrake, Lama Govinda, and Bohm on various occasions.

But my deepest dialogue takes place in silence. It happens in Nepal, to which I travel to see the Himalayas. Their grandeur, stillness and preternatural beauty affect me so powerfully that these mountains be-come my symbol of spiritual aspiration. Seeing them evokes a sense of awe unlike anything else I encounter, except perhaps the sight of a galaxy teeming with hundreds of billions of stars.

All my life I have felt close to nature. Her presence was real to me long before I knew anything of the laws by which she works—a child's pre-reflective though definite awareness of nature's being. Looking back, I realize that since my earliest childhood I have sensed "some-thing" in nature's background and even in the foreground. The beau-tiful and lavish variety of her forms has been a source of real meaning in my life, and from the beginning I felt a kinship with nature's off-spring—animals, plants, rocks, forests, water, earth, the sky, and even with remote stars and galaxies. No one taught me this; I simply awoke to the world with the conviction of my relatedness to these things. This feeling, common in childhood and often lost as we grow up, has re-mained with me.

It is only much later that I learn the names for these feelings—the immanence and transcendence of a force in nature—and learn, as well, that others before me have had these feelings and have written of them. This pursuit of the source has shaped my life and work. Everything of importance that I have done has been done in the hope of penetrating the veils covering nature's face.

I take up the study of philosophy in college because philosophy seems to hold out the promise of getting beyond these veils, the reality behind the appearances. In this belief I am encouraged by Plato, the first philosopher I ever encounter. It is the beginning of an intellectual and spiritual journey.

But philosophy, it turns out, cannot by itself fulfil what it seems to promise. It departs too far from the study of nature's ways and, in its modern guise, philosophy ignores nature altogether, leaving that task to the scientist. I seek the deep-structure of things which—though it was once the province of philosophy—has for the last century become the province of science. Physics, a step closer to nature, seems bent on getting to the deep-structure, but I discover some years later that mysticism comes closest of all, for it is still more abstract and also more inward than science, more obsessed with simplicity and unity. This fact is captured in Meister Eckhart's austere command: "To find nature herself, all her forms must be shattered."

Each of these domains holds its own rewards, each offers a part of what I seek, yet by itself each reveals gaps. None can singly create the coherent vision of things. It is Fritz Kunz (as noted in the credits) who makes me aware that I seek the integration of all these—philosophy, science, and mysticism—and that my quest is not hopeless but merely too early. Only in the last decades does the movement towards the unity of these domains flower in American culture, and at that only in a minority, though it is a large and steadily growing minority.

Since they form the basis of this book, I want to characterize philosophy, science, and mysticism more closely. My aim here is not an exhaustive nor even primarily a "professional" perspective, but a personal one. (The reader who looks for my scholarly views on this subject can find them in my other writings.) Here I offer a distillation of my personal search—what attracts me to these fields and what they mean to me.

Philosophy, during the years in which I study it (at the University of Pennsylvania, Columbia, and the Sorbonne) has almost completely abandoned its original quest—"love of wisdom"—the one for which it was named. For the last three centuries, that conception of philosophy has gone steadily out of style, and in my own century it has become nearly extinct. Any professional philosopher caught in the act of "searching for wisdom" becomes suspect, is subtly ostracized and viewed—I exaggerate only slightly—as a danger to (the career of) his students.

Contemporary Anglo-American philosophy is chiefly "analytic philosophy" which seeks to clarify the meaning of small questions. It has given up on wrestling, as philosophy did since the Greeks, with life's great questions: Truth, God, the Good, the soul, man's fate after death, enlightenment, the source of the universe, the immanence and transcendence of something beyond ourselves. In the twentieth century, all these are considered meaningless questions, to be rejected along with the suggestion that "Truth" may actually exist and be accessible to man. Since the days of its great holistic practitioners—Pythagoras and Socrates, Plato and Spinoza, Hegel and Whitehead—philosophy has narrowed itself to a small compass. Thus, mine is basically a solitary journey, shared only occasionally by a handful of other philosophers who still pursue the vision of the whole, and by people outside my field like the ones who appear in this book. In seeking them out, I have in fact ventured into a territory that is forbidden by the conventional canons of my profession.

For reasons too complex to enter into here, my reservations extend even to existentialism, where the grand philosophical questions still flourish. After nearly a decade immersed in it, I conclude that existentialism can provide no more than sporadic spiritual nourishment because it entirely dismisses nature from its concerns and has—like all philosophy since Kant—given up on the search for the deep-structure.

Thus, between my M.A. and Ph.D. in philosophy, for several years I turn away from philosophy altogether. What I turn to is science. I seek it out in a rigorous form, for I do not want small snatches of predigested conclusions in "physics for poets" courses, but want to experience the actual life of the scientist. This I find in a premedical curriculum which requires lab-work and problem-solving. After all the years of philosophical theorizing about nature, immersion in the concrete details is exhilarating.

For two spellbinding years, plunging into the minutiae of physics, chemistry and zoology, I finally see at first hand the scientific method which until now has been acquired only in philosophy of science courses. Science, I have been taught, stands and falls with the empirical method. This involves formulating one's hypothesis, subjecting it to empirical experiment via carefully collected data that verify or falsify the hypothesis, in order to draw conclusions that will become a theory or perhaps even a law. Entwined with this process are the equations empowered to bear the message of science—mathematics, its language and handmaiden. Science is thus the interplay between the concrete details and abstract reasoning, between the inductive and the deductive way, between the senses that register the data and the abstract mind that orders it into meaningful patterns of relationships. Science is of course more than this rudimentary characterization; it is a highly sophisticated structure too complex to do full justice to here.

The leitmotif of this book—the integration of science and mysticism—becomes the leitmotif of my life during this period. I discover that, contrary to what I have been taught, I do not have to choose between them. Science and mysticism may have a common pursuit and may even enrich one another in ways that we have ignored. I see this possibility at work in my own experience.

In a brief earlier encounter with science (as an undergraduate, for whom it was a compulsory requirement for graduation), I approach it with a kind of lockjaw of the mind. The course is a burden to be endured, the data to be memorized, the lab chores to be disposed of as quickly as possible. My attitude (generally shared by my classmates) strikes me in retrospect as bored, blasé, turned-off.

Almost a decade later, in the two-and-a-half-year pre-med course to which I now refer, science is meaningful and exciting to me. How does this change come about? It is largely due to the fact that I have meanwhile studied mysticism, which speaks of a single spiritual principle both in nature and behind nature. It is this idea which pervades the background of my mind as I study the specific details, and these now take on a double meaning. The thing at hand is both itself and something beyond itself which it expresses.

Statistics about the diameter of the sun, the mass of the proton, the precipitate in my test-tube, and the brain-stem of *Rana catesbiana*, (the frog which we dissect) no longer produce a shrugged "so what?" This is of course also true of my classmates, most of them embarking on careers in science or medicine. Still, I notice a difference. For me the scientific details acquire meta-scientific meaning; they glow with another reality.

This lesson is etched into me through one particular image which powerfully captures my changed attitude. To demonstrate Newton's law of gravitation—that an unsupported mass is drawn toward the earth with ever-increasing velocity, i.e., the law of falling bodies—we perform an experiment in our physics lab that records the body's position as small dots on a paper strip. The object of this experiment is to demonstrate that these dots get farther and farther from each other as the body nears the earth. Millions of students have performed this demonstration, but for me it takes on the meaning of a sacred act. I cannot bring myself to throw away the strip of paper which my classmates so casually toss out at the end of our lab session, for it feels like nature's signature, one of her many messages. It is the same with other experiments; they take on a meaning that overflows their empirical one.

This episode and others like it convince me that the mystic can contribute something to science, namely the sense that nature is not a mere collection of sense data but a single reality of grandeur and beauty which can be experienced on multiple levels. Perhaps numberless scientists already feel this, but only a handful—Einstein and the "mystical scientists"—have expressed it publicly.

I have offered a definition of science, but as yet none of mysticism. Simply stated, mysticism is the experience of oneness with reality. As I reflect on their essence, I perceive science and mysticism as two approaches to nature. Their history is like the proverbial dance of Shiva, the resilient energy entwining and separating. Science was not born only of the utilitarian side of man's nature—the need for mapping navigation or agriculture—but from curiosity, man's need to know. In the beginning there was wonder and awe. These inspired the search with which science and religion began. Originally they were one, untroubled by the modern separation that would develop to decree that they become distinct domains with uncrossable borders. In that separation, the sense of wonder became science, the sense of awe, mysticism.

During most of their history, science seemed guided by the maxim "God is in the details," mysticism by the maxim "God is the circle whose center is everywhere and whose circumference is nowhere." To this day, science seeks the boundaries of nature, mysticism its unboundedness, science the droplet of the ocean, mysticism the wave. Science works to *explain* the mystery of being, mysticism to *experience* it. They share the search for reality because, in their own way, both science and mysticism look for the basic truth about matter and the source of matter.

The question of the source, though crucial to mystics, has been pushed into a corner or out of the picture altogether by scientific officialdom, but it is the question that interests me the most. I have been drawn to science because it wants to understand the phenomena of nature in all their details and to unify them within one all-encompassing equation. This drive for unification is a further link between the aims of science and mysticism. It is what attracts me to both. Unification is, at least in theory, the scientist's aim, embodied in the quest for simple and elegant laws. But I soon discover that there seem to be two kinds of scientists. For most scientists the search for coherent laws ends in equations. However, for the greatest scientists, equations alone are not enough to satisfy the scientists' wonder. It is to this second kind that I am drawn.

For those rare minds, the equations merely tantalize and point to something else, the reality which the mathematics express, and it is this that these great minds seek. Thus, equations for people like Kepler, Galileo, Newton, Schroedinger, deBroglie, Planck, Einstein, Eddington, Jeans, Heisenberg, Bohm and others, appear to be something of a code word, a disguise for their desire to display the source behind the equations. It was this that Pythagoras may have had in mind when he claimed that "God geometrizes," and Galileo when he said that "God's book of nature is written in the alphabet of mathematics." Is it this that Richard Feynman is after when he writes: "To those who do not know mathematics, it is difficult to get across a real feeling as to the beauty, the deepest beauty, of nature."[2] This point is the key to the scientific dialogues in this book, where science is represented by a reverential attitude toward nature rather than a ruthless one. This distinction may also summarize the contrast between the two kinds of scientists. Francis Bacon, in the sixteenth century, wrote "We must put nature to the rack and with screws secure her secrets." Einstein wrote: "The longing to behold harmony is the source of the inexhaustible patience and perseverance with which Planck has devoted himself to ... science.... The state of mind which enables a man to do work of this kind is akin to that of the religious worshipper or the lover."[3] Science as it is used in this book stands for the attitude of Einstein rather than of Bacon: an attitude of kinship with nature rather than of exploitive power over her.

Mysticism, too, begins in awe and wonder. But unlike science, it ends in union, the "Thou Art That" of Indian philosophy. I have encountered the object of this union under many names: the dharma, the dharmakaya, Brahman, the Tao, the One, the Good, emptiness, the void, the Abyss, God, and even the Godhead who stands behind God. For the mystics all the names are wrong in any case and in that sense names do not really matter. This is brought home in a sentence of singular beauty in the *Bhagavad-Gita* when Krishna tells Arjuna: "By whatever name you call me, it is I who will answer you," and voiced in Meister Eckhart's blunt remonstration: "Why do you prate of God? Don't you know that whatever you say of Him is untrue?" All mystics agree that language and schema attempt in vain to translate that ineffable domain into our feeble symbols. They are all shadows on the wall in Plato's Cave, though to different degrees. Eckhart in fact places the reality behind the shadows quite beyond verbal reach, saying "There is nothing in all the universe so much like God as silence."

Even so cautious a characterization as "the unconditioned" can only approximate to the reality to which it refers. Therefore all schemas, words, concepts, formulae and formulations, whether scientific or mystical, suffer from the flaws of the Cave. [See my "The Good, the True and the Beautiful: Are they Attributes of the Universe?" (1975) and Ken Wilber's "Introduction" in *Quantum Questions* (1984) for a fuller discussion of this issue.] These designations have a relative reality and a relative usefulness, but mystics caution against taking them too literally and against confusing the names with the reality. Hence Eckhart's earnest prayer of protection from this fallacy: "I pray to God to keep me from 'God.'" Granting this limitation of language, the one word repeatedly used by mystics to describe their experience is *unity*.

Unlike science, which turns to the world outside the seeker, mysticism turns within, to the laws that govern the seeker himself. Science is outer empiricism, mysticism inner empiricism. But doesn't such a dichotomy violate the mystic's claim of a unitary reality? There is no contradiction, since for the mystic the inner and outer are reconciled through the hermetic dictum: "As above, so below."

For mystics like Hermes Trismegistus of Egypt, Parmenides, Pythagoras, Plato, Spinoza, and virtually all the eastern sages, the quest for outer being is bound up with the quest for inner being. The hermetic dictum that links the microcosm with the macrocosm, links nature with man, and the observer with the observed. In turning within, the mystic reads the selfsame laws that operate in the world of nature, though he reads them from a different perspective. This perception is not restricted to the mystics. The scientist, in this case Max Planck, acknowledges it as well. "Science cannot solve the ultimate mystery of nature. And that is because, in the last analysis, we ourselves are part of nature, and, therefore, part of the mystery that we are trying to solve."[4]

This principle is stated with clarity by David Bohm in this volume: "You can overcome that problem [i.e., of unifying the laws of the inner and the outer] only if you accept the premise that in some sense man is a microcosm of the universe; therefore what man is, is a clue to the universe." Bohm, in fact, is a good example of the scientist who understands and appreciates the relationship between science and mysticism. But all the scientists in this book accept the hermetic dictum to some degree. It is what makes them post-quantum mechanical scientists. It may be part of what they have in common with mystics and suggests a re-emergence in a modern form of the ancient relationship between the two approaches. But whether or not there really is such a relationship is a subtle issue. It requires a closer look at the differences and similarities of science and mysticism.

The most obvious difference is methodology. Science is quantitative, mysticism qualitative. Science has a rigorous and formalized methodology, mathematics. The methodology of mysticism is meditation. Science seeks mastery over gross matter, mysticism over subtle matter, which is said to have its own laws, analogous to those in science. Science has amassed impressive insight into the inner workings of matter and energy. The esoteric tradition—especially in the east, where it merges with the mystical tradition—has given us in the *Upanishads*, and the teachings of Patanjali, Buddha, Nagarjuna and others, detailed accounts of the subtle matter which constitutes the inner bodies of man, the energy fields or "auras," to use archaic language. In these pages, subtle matter reappears in the theories of a twentieth-century physicist.

Despite these similarities, science cannot and should not be conflated with mysticism. The domain and style of science are the cognitive and, unlike mysticism, science asks its questions mainly with the mind. In the differences named, there are obvious similarities, but other differences appear more severe. Science, as I have observed for myself, studies things by taking them apart into smaller and smaller components. In some way, this painstakingly precise, piecemeal analysis has been the great strength of science. It may also constitute its weakness. By fragmenting nature, science loses a sense of the whole. An even greater price is the loss of meaning—of the whole and sometimes even of the details. This is an issue the scientists in this book are trying to contend with, as they are with the pretense that science has made of being "objective" and "value-free." As if the demand for objectivity were not a value! It says that "to be value-free is good." But this judgment is man-made and subject to the imperfections of human judgment.

Nevertheless, I reject the stereotype of the scientist as necessarily cold, remote, and mute on the question of human values. The great-souled scientist contributes richly to our search for ourselves, as we can see from these dialogues. Most of the mystics in these pages embrace science as another perspective on their path—that laboratory within, which to them is as real and familiar as the physical laboratory is to the scientists. One perennial danger to mysticism is the temptation to lose itself completely in the *ground*, shortchanging the *figure* (to borrow from Gestalt terminology) in the foreground—to favor transcendence over immanence. Science can re-enlist the mystic's interest in the daily world and make him see the particular thing in all its intricate beauty.

The relationship between simplicity and multiplicity, the universal and the particular, is a fundamental issue in this book. I have been struggling with the question of what the scientist and the mystic can learn from one another. Some sort of answer comes to me in a rather personal way during the odyssey I am describing. It suggests that just as science can become deepened through our acquaintance with mysticism, so mysticism can become clarified through science. I learn this lesson in a most unexpected way. After I have been teaching eastern philosophy for some years, I perceive a recurrent metaphor in the *Upanishads* in a new light because of my experience with chemistry. It concerns identifying an "unknown" (element) in qualitative analysis.

The object of this pursuit is to extract a solid, the precipitate, which dwells hidden in the clear colorless liquid handed me by the lab-instructor and which—by the appropriate chemical steps—can be coaxed forth and made to reveal itself at the bottom of the test-tube as a characteristically colored element—chromium, for example. Invisible until now, it has been there all along in that homogenous solution. Now, as I teach the *Svetasvatara Upanishad* with its enigmatic metaphor of creation, it brings back my experience in the chemistry lab with particular vividness. "Like the butter hidden in cream is the [source] which pervades all things."[5] Here is a creation myth of surprising elegance. It accounts for all diversity by means of one principle, transforming itself out of its own ground. In Indian cosmology, the phenomenal world is the solid, the precipitate which becomes crystallized in space and time by the cosmic consciousness in which it floats. I am struck by the economy of this model, which accounts for all the diversity in the universe by evoking one single principle, transforming itself into density and visibility out of its own subtle and invisible ground. When, a few years later, I come across David Bohm's implicate order cosmology, with its schema of dense and subtle matter, I recognize its close kinship with Indian mystical cosmology.

Indian mysticism centers on the reunification of man and nature, man's actual experience of the single principle—and source—that underlies the universe. It is a heady claim, puzzling even to one familiar with mysticism. The price for experiencing this union of the finite with the infinite is self-knowledge and self-deconditioning. When all our masks have been stripped away there remains only *that* and—as the Upanishadic sage tells his student—"Thou *art* that." This emphasis on immanence is appealing—divinity in everything—but it will take me some years to understand why self-deconditioning should be the gateway to union with the infinite. Oddly, what helps me to grasp it better than the study of mysticism is the study of science.

Again the metaphor from the *Upanishads* is the catalyst. It furnishes a plausible model for visualising the relationship between the finite self and cosmic consciousness. The postulate that allows for their identity rests on the equation of Brahman with Atman, the asserted identity of field-consciousness with our localized individual consciousness. Since matter, in the Hindu model, is crystallized energy, matter is a manifestation of infinite mind. The universe is materialized Brahman.

> Like the butter hidden in cream, pure consciousness resides in
> every being. It is to be constantly churned, with the mind serving
> as the churning rod.... Knowledge of the [cosmic] Self is gained
> through meditation. (*Amritabindu* and *Svetasvatara Upanishads*)[6]

This theory of consciousness encompasses cosmic creativity on the one hand—Brahman precipitates itself as matter—human creativity on the other. Through the churning rod of meditation, the bonded ego goes back into solution, reunited with its source. Such a reversible equation recalls Einstein's equivalence of matter and energy, and the particle and wave identity of quantum mechanics.

I reflect on the irony that, if the search for unity is intrinsic to science, an unsettling possibility suggests itself. By the criterion of unity, science may be less "scientific" than mysticism, which aims at a more comprehensive unification. It is mysticism, not science, which pursues the Grand Unified Theory with ruthless logic—the one that includes the questioner within its answer. Although the scientist wants to unify everything in one ultimate equation, he does not want to unify *consistently*, since he wants to leave himself outside that equation. Of course, with the advent of quantum mechanics, that is far less possible than it was in classical physics. Now observer and observed are admitted to constitute a unit. But the full meaning of this has not yet caught up with most of the community of scientists who, despite quantum mechanics, believe they can stand aloof from what they work on. In one sense, this is of course true.

In splitting the atom, as we know, the physicist releases vast amounts of energy that was needed to hold the core of the atom together, its "binding power." The operation requires the physicist's intelligence, effort, time, and commitment, but not his very self, which can remain fundamentally unchanged. Of the mystic, more is required. He is engaged in deconstructing and reconstructing not some neutral external reality, but himself.

Like most people, I find this hard to follow until one day during my study of physics, it is suddenly borne in on me that a remarkable likeness exists between the work of the mystic and that of the physicist.

By analogy with the physicist's splitting of the atom, the mystic is engaged in splitting his self-centered ego and the three-dimensional thinker that sustains it. The ego, like the atom, coheres in time through its "binding power," what Buddha called "the aggregates" (*skandhas*) that make up our personality.

When the binding power of the physical atom is released in an accelerator, the resultant energy—staggeringly huge—becomes freed. Analogously, huge amounts of binding energy are needed to create and sustain the ego and its illusion that it is an independent, ultimate entity. That energy is tied up and thus unavailable for the "high energy state" that mystics like Lama Govinda, Fr. Bede, and the Dalai Lama assert in these pages is necessary to reach inner truth.

Energy thus preempted cannot flow into other grooves. The sage who has seen through this principle and understood it, no longer fragments and exhausts himself trying to hold his bounded self together, but lets go of the ego and releases its energy, opening a channel to the limitless universal energy. The clearer and less obstructed the channel, the greater the free-flowing energy available. Though it is difficult for the layman to follow, this principle underlies all mysticism and it is repeatedly invoked by the sages in these dialogues. It may also explain why so many mystics seem imbued with exuberance and joy, which underlies their strength and integration. Spinoza—the most mystical of modern western philosophers—observes that this high energy state is the true unfoldment of the human potential, a health-giving mode of being he terms "blessedness." Merely to be in that state is its own reward. Spinoza observes that nothing need—or can—be added to it.

There are evident similarities between atom-splitting and ego-splitting. The mystic is said to need a high energy, focused and intense, in order to accomplish the task of getting his ego out of the way and becoming transparent to the source. From the point of view of the ordinary person, this requires courage and risk-taking, although mystics like Lama Govinda, Krishnamurti, and Fr. Bede reject these terms on the grounds that they imply calculation and, therefore, a spiritual hedonism that invests itself in a pay-off. For this reason, most mystics have insisted on the purity of motive for sacred ego-splitting—to distinguish it from the schizophrenic variety.

This distinction is important. Sacred ego-splitting demands a strong and originally integrated person to withstand this arduous path, a balance and toughness which the pathological ego-splitters simply do not possess. But the most significant difference lies in the fact that sacred ego-dissolution is a skilled practice that lies within the practitioner's voluntary control. Pathological (clinical) ego-disintegration is involuntary, beyond the person's control [For a further discussion of these differences see my "The Reluctant Tradition" (1975) and Ken Wilber's "The Pre-Trans Fallacy" (1980).]

Sacred ego-deconstruction is a difficult task for the ordinary person, who contends with the demons of fear and other conditioning. The most obvious is the fear that, in becoming a universal vessel, we will be washed down the cosmic drain and somehow cease to be. This fear the physicist cannot possibly experience when he works on demolishing his particles. Despite the "observer effect" which has modified the remote role of the classical scientist, by comparison with the mystic, even the work of the contemporary physicist is external to himself, and unlike the mystic, he seems invulnerable. The mystic, in changing himself, changes the subtle matter within in some radical way for which no scientific explanation is at present adequate.

But I can conjecture. One interesting possibility is that, in his altered state of consciousness, the mystic has learned to harmonize his awareness with the sub-atomic matter of which he is composed. In this process, he aligns himself with the deep-structure of nature, where flux and transformation are the rule. As quantum mechanics teaches, this is how matter operates on the micro-level, by contrast with the macro-level, where we function mostly as isolated, separate units stuck in our Cartesian space-time grids and inflexibly hanging on to our patterns and time-bound personalities. We do not let go and transform ourselves afresh each moment in the manner of the quanta, in the manner the mystics have urged—living in what Buddha called the ceaseless flux. The mystic, a true alchemist, brings micro-level and macro-level together. He lives psychologically in the mode of creation, manifestation, and dissolution of every particle of subtle matter and energy. He can let go of and die to each moment, and therefore be constantly reborn. In short, he lives in the timeless present, like the medieval monk who said "The man who dies before he dies, does not die when he dies." Interestingly, this way of life is the one advocated by both the sages and scientists in this volume, though not always for the same reasons.

Despite the analogies I have drawn thus far, the differences between science and mysticism seem to outweigh the similarities, so why can I not rest content with their separation? This question of the parallels or lack of them in science and mysticism has generated considerable debate in a remarkable and growing literature. In spite of my appreciation of the many solid arguments offered by those who deny any similarities between science and mysticism, my position has not really been changed by the arguments. If I did not see a connection between science and mysticism, there would have been no need for this book. The connection I perceive is this: A parallel principle drives both science and mysticism—the assumption that unity lies at the heart of our world and that it can be discovered and experienced by man.

I believe that this one similarity is so powerful that it transcends the many differences which divide science and mysticism.

The commitment to simplicity and unity in science is especially striking since a comprehensive unity is not necessary for prediction and control, which are the stated and utilitarian aims of most scientists. These aims could as well be achieved without the "simplicity," "elegance" and "beauty" for which the greatest scientists strive.

Obvious examples of this commitment are Newton's grand schema unifying all masses in the universe through his Law of Gravitation, Maxwell's unification of magnetism and electricity, Einstein's unification of matter and energy, and of space and time. His intuition about this was so strong that Einstein pursued the Unified Field Theory to the end of his life, though it tragically eluded him. Now scientists are working to unite into one force the present four known basic laws of nature—gravitation, electromagnetism, and the strong and weak nuclear forces within the atom. A single comprehensive law remains the current ideal.

The drive of scientists to achieve this ideal cannot be "scientific" in the conventional sense. It seems closer to an aesthetic demand, the sense that unity is somehow truer, more beautiful and *better* than multiplicity. The scientific drive seems to me to border on Plato's vision that the good, the true, and the beautiful are the fabric of reality. Such terms as "elegance" and "beauty" recur regularly in philosophical scientists like Einstein, Heisenberg, Eddington, Jeans, Schroedinger, Bohr, Feynman, Wald, Bohm, Prigogine, Hawking, Sheldrake and others. Behind the aesthetic demand, I believe, lies a spiritual one.

But *is the search for unity in science itself a spiritual path*? My hypothesis is that it is.

Behind the intellectual drive of the great creators in science, a deeper force seems at work. I believe that at some intuitive level of his awareness, the scientist senses that nature is simple, subtle, interconnected, and one. Without this idea or something like it, it is difficult to account for the way scientific genius operates. Why should one equation expressing nature's workings be truer and better than four, three, or two? The drive to unveil this inner structure and to express it in the beautiful and elegant language of mathematics seems similar to the mystic's insistence that behind the multiplicity of appearances there lies the unity of reality.

Sheldrake and Bohm readily assent to this interpretation of their work. However, few other scientists will admit to it. Comparison with the mystic is offensive to them, and they strenuously deny any similarity between their vision and that of the mystic. This is particularly true of Prigogine and Hawking, to whom such comparisons actually appear odious. One can speculate about the reasons for many scientists' hostility to mysticism. As these dialogues make clear, it is not a hostility modern mystics (with the possible exception of Krishnamurti) seem to share. Most of them easily accommodate and even embrace scientific cosmology as an alternative glimpse into things or, as the Dalai Lama, Fr. Bede Griffiths, and Lama Govinda suggest, as a move towards balance.

But most scientists want to dissociate themselves from mysticism, and this may have a historical basis. The scientist perceives himself as the defender of truth against superstition, and may remember the hold that *religion* had over science before it shook off theological authority, a hold that cost people like Giordano Bruno his life and Galileo his freedom. The confusion between mysticism and religion is an easy one. The irony is that the mystic, no less than the scientist, often suffered at the hands of institutionalized religion, and was in many cases hounded and endangered—Bruno and Eckhart are memorable examples—for his vision of unity.

Two important issues arise in comparing science and mysticism: their content and their form. The form concerns theory-formation, the question: when is a theory complete? For mainstream scientists, a theory is complete when all its equations add up consistently, give a full description of the phenomena, and allow it to make observable predictions. But for scientists like Bohm a theory is complete only if—in addition—it integrates the observer and the observed, subtle matter and dense matter, and both of these with their source—i.e., if the theory is comprehensive. Lastly, for the mystic no theory can be either complete or comprehensive because it imposes boundaries on the unbounded.

But, of course, it is the similarity of their content that is the most interesting question of all. How alike are science and mysticism in this? That is the question I have travelled to three continents to ask of the figures in this book. All scientists postulate the unity of matter at an initial point before the Big Bang, when everything in the universe was in contact—condensed and united into one infinitesimally small point—the singularity. The search for "the singularity" before time was born is linked with the search for who we are, common to both science and mysticism. Stephen Hawking makes this link explicit in our dialogue. When I ask him why he is interested in the "early universe," he tells me that we all want to know where we come from, and that whatever happened in the first second after the Big Bang holds the answer to that question. In that sense, his quest and my own are alike.

It differs in one fundamental respect. Along with the mystical tradition, I want to push this puzzle of my origin back one step further. The difference between Hawking (I use him as a symbol of the non-mystical scientist) and myself on this issue is one of degree. I have asked many scientists "Where did the singularity that became the Big Bang come from?" "What happened before the Big Bang?" "What lies beyond the edge of the universe?" and—most important—"What started it all, and why?" Science cannot answer. Mysticism at least points to a direction.

It forms part of a theory known for millennia and presumably verified by the mystic's experience. This theory proposes that the universe originates in consciousness. Subtle matter gives birth to and governs dense matter, but all matter forms a continuum. The subtler the matter, the closer it gets to what we call consciousness. At its most subtle and inward point (if there is such an end point) matter and consciousness become indistinguishable. This is the docrine of the ancient wisdom traditions.

Finally, neither matter nor consciousness are ultimate. Both have their source in something beyond themselves of which they are the outcome and expression, in which they are rooted and reconciled. This unknown reality cannot become an object of knowledge. My quest here hits bed-rock. There is nothing more to say of it. There is only silence, as Eckhart—and, for that matter, even Wittgenstein—knew.

But subtle matter and n-dimensional space can be approached through non-ordinary states of consciousness. A traditional meditation in Tibetan Buddhism enables the meditator to experience the unity of space, matter, and consciousness. The tool for this practice is light, an energy whose material and spiritual role is repeatedly debated in these dialogues. In the Tibetan practice, the meditator visualizes a beam of light slender as a single strand of hair, deep within the center of himself. Gradually he widens its magnitude to the breadth of one finger, one hand, and finally extends it to his whole body, which he now visualizes enveloped in light. Thereafter he projects the light-energy outward into the surrounding space until this sea of light extends into the infinite sea of space. Inner and outer space, self and nature, consciousness and matter have lost their distinction. In the Buddhist tradition, this is no mere epistemological exercise but a method for radiating the energy of compassion to all corners of the cosmos.

The clearest explanation of how the integration of matter and consciousness might work appears in Lama Govinda's seminal book, *Foundations of Tibetan Mysticism*:

> The fundamental element of this cosmos is space. Space is the all-embracing principle of higher unity. Space ... therefore, is not only a *conditio sine qua non* of all existence, but a fundamental property of our consciousness.
>
> Our consciousness determines the kind of space in which we live. The infinity of space and the infinity of consciousness are identical.

In the moment in which a being becomes conscious of his consciousness, he becomes conscious of space. In the moment in which he becomes conscious of this infinity of space, he realizes the infinity of consciousness. If, therefore, space is a property of our consciousness, then it may be said with equal justification that the experience of space is a criterion of spiritual activity and of a higher form of awareness. The way in which we experience space, or in which we are aware of space, is characteristic of the dimension of our consciousness. The three-dimensional space, which we perceive through our bodies and its senses, is only *one* among many possible dimensions.[7]

To summarize: All mystics seek the depths, as do the greatest creative minds in science—and implicitly, perhaps, all scientists do. For both scientists and mystics unity remains the ideal. For both, matter is a mystery: it is more than "mere matter," the billiard balls of eighteenth- and nineteenth-century physics. Both scientist and sage are transformers of energy, involved in the dance of Shiva. The scientist makes the dense matter dance to produce pure energy, the mystic—master of subtle matter—dances the dance of himself.

In emphasizing the greater wholeness of mysticism, I do not devalue science. It is an endeavor whose value and power are enormous. Along with scientists, I feel that its autonomy must not be jeopardized and would defend it from regression to the days when it was bound and gagged by religion. For me, both science and mysticism are unique and irreplaceable perspectives on reality. I cannot do without either of them.

In the quantum and post-quantum era science and mysticism, the long separated siblings, seem to be drawing closer together. Consider what has happened to the concept of time, for example. Time is crucial to both science and mysticism. The mystic's denial of time's reality has always troubled those who live in ordinary clock-time. Yet in seeking to understand the Big Bang, science draws close to the mystic's paradox. In pushing back the universe to its first moment, does science seek the beginning of time or does it seek the timeless? If science finds its Grand Unified Theory will it have to contend with the question of the source of that, too, or will it have come upon the ultimate source of things? Through these and similar problems created by relativity and quantum physics, the line between science and mysticism has grown thin, and each of the scientists in this volume seems to respond to this line in different ways.

Reflecting on the progress of science, I come upon a surprising conclusion, faintly reminiscent of a Zen koan. As science unravels more and more of the puzzles, the mystery of nature does not diminish but deepens. This is as illogical as it is unexpected. The more science learns, the greater nature's mystery grows. By contrast with the positivist scientists, who settle for prediction and control and for whom the ability to quantify nature's phenomena lessens the enigma, for the mystical scientists this is not the case. Increasing their knowledge of nature's laws paradoxically preserves and even deepens the sense of mystery. Although the mystery of the details gives way before science's scrutiny, the overall mystery does not seem to yield to it. Niels Bohr observed that "Those who are not shocked when they first come across quantum theory cannot possibly have understood it."[8] Still, it may be too much to expect that science, even in the character of its most visionary practitioners, can go all the way to the mystic's cosmic "oneness." Perhaps science can at best take us to some rim, and from there we must make a further leap by ourselves.

One of these is the leap into ethics. The awareness of the unity and interconnectedness of all being leads—if it is consistent—to an empathy with others. It expresses itself as reverence for life, compassion, a sense of the brotherhood of suffering humanity, and the commitment to heal our wounded earth and its peoples. All the mystics (and virtually all the scientists) in these dialogues draw this connection between their vision of the whole and their sense of responsibility for it.

Einstein writes, "I maintain that the cosmic religious feeling is the strongest and noblest motive for scientific research" and hereby interfuses the sacred and the secular, just as Eckhart does when he writes, "If the soul could have known God without the world, the world would never have been created."[9] This shows that certain spirits do bridge the gap created between the known and the mystery that remains unknown.

The known and the unknown, the spirit of wonder and awe evoke the famous Zen parable which seems to unite them. "Before I studied Zen, mountains were just mountains and rivers just rivers. When I first took up the study of Zen, mountains were no longer mountains and rivers no longer rivers. But now that I've really got some understanding of Zen, mountains are once again mountains and rivers once again rivers." Even as I struggle with the many interpretations to which this parable is open, I know that I cannot exhaust them all. But it triggers the image of a spiral, a path whose perspectives change as we change. It points to a dialectic—or better yet, to dialogue.

There are few final conclusions in dialogue because it is, by definition, open-ended, flowing, and tentative. It explores rather than settles questions, and allows for—demands—a participatory mode, ideally something akin to Buber's I-Thou experience. Dialogue reflects the insights of each partner at *this* moment in time, and does not negate the fact that another moment may call forth another response. In this sense, dialogue is creativity.

I think once again of an analogy from science. In physics, the "world-line" of a particle refers to its path in spacetime, to the history of all the energy exchanges which the particle has undergone since its birth, and which it brings to bear on *this* moment. By analogy, dialogue is like the world-lines of two people intersecting at this given moment of spacetime, exchanging their energies and insights, adding something fresh and thereby changing—however modestly—the happenings of the universe through their encounter. The mystic has always known of this possibility. For him, everything is dialogue, every encounter—even with what is inert—is with a living presence. This experience is preserved in such Zen dicta as "The eye with which I see is the very eye which also sees me," and "It is difficult to know whether I am seeing or being seen, knowing or being known."

In the post-quantum mechanical world, many scientists, too, have found dialogue an apt analogy for describing their work. Heisenberg comes to mind, as does John Wheeler with his concept of the "participatory universe." So does Ilya Prigogine for whom the model of dialogue is so important that it appears in the sub-title of his latest book. Prigogine conceives his work as "a new dialogue with nature," one which reintroduces a lost enchantment into our lives. I savor his phrase yet notice that it embeds a tautology, for dialogue is always new. It cannot be rehearsed or rerun. Participants in dialogue, besides using their own intelligence and insight, seem to draw on some insight beyond themselves.

It is this factor which elevates dialogue to the sacred for Socrates—its originator—and makes him link it with a divine presence within, his *daimon* or inner voice. Even in its absence, dialogue can be interesting and informative. But when that dimension is present, it releases a greater—perhaps a more subtle and high-powered—energy in the participants that distinguishes dialogue from debate and other sorts of discourse. This deeper dimension can be activated in all the participants in dialogue, including the reader, whose own world-line intersects with and forms part of the process, which he continues and carries into his own spiritual journey.

My journey has led me—through this lattice-work of world-lines that began with the Big Bang—to the scientists and sages who are at the center of the dialogue with the cosmos. In these pages they take a stand—at times factual and sober, at times speculative and intuitive—on the question that informs this book—the possibility of a synthesis between two modes of approaching the universe. How do the insights of my partners in dialogue fit into my quest for a bridge between science and mysticism?

One suggestion comes from David Bohm, who proposes that *meaning is a form of being*. In the very act of interpreting the universe, we are creating the universe. Through our meanings we change nature's being. Man's meaning-making capacity turns him into nature's partner, a participant in shaping her evolution. The word does not merely reflect the world, it also creates the world. This is the deeper message of

Prigogine's work. Bohm goes even further. In one of our sessions, he suggests that what the cosmos is doing as we dialogue is to change its idea of itself. Our doubts and our questions, our small truths and large ones are all forms of its drive toward clarity and truth. Through us, the universe questions itself and tries out various answers on itself in an effort—parallel to our own—to decipher its own being.

This, as I reflect on it, is awesome. It assigns a role to man that was once reserved for the gods.

I think it's a cop-out. If you find theoretical physics and mathematics too hard, you turn to mysticism.

STEPHEN HAWKING

We could think of the mystic as coming into contact with tremendous depths of the subtlety of matter or of mind, whatever you want to call it.

DAVID BOHM

We still believe that the universe should be logical and beautiful; we just dropped the word "God."

STEPHEN HAWKING

I would put it another way: people had insight in the past about a form of intelligence that had organized the universe and they personalized it and called it "God."

DAVID BOHM

DAVID BOHM

2

The implicate order and the super-implicate order

DAVID BOHM

I do not know why matter should be unworthy of the divine
nature, since outside God no substance can exist from
which the divine nature could suffer.... Therefore in no
way whatever can it be asserted that ... substance extended
... is unworthy of the divine nature, provided only that it
is eternal and infinite.

SPINOZA

I T is fitting that these dialogues begin with David Bohm, for he is
a rare combination of the scientist and the mystic combined in one
person. My first conversation with him in 1977 led to several more and
subsequently to a series with other scientists and with sages.

David Bohm is considered one of the world's foremost theoretical
physicists and one of the most influential theorists of the emerging
paradigm. His *Causality and Chance in Modern Physics* (1957) has become a classic in the field of quantum mechanics and is widely used at
universities, as are his books on quantum theory and relativity. Bohm
was born in 1917 and educated at Pennsylvania State College. His
graduate degree is from the University of California, Berkeley, where
in 1943 he got his Ph.D. in physics, the last graduate student to study
with J. Robert Oppenheimer before the latter went off to Los Alamos.
Bohm's thesis was on "Neutron-Proton Scattering." He taught at
Princeton, the University of São Paulo in Brazil, and at the Technion in
Haifa before becoming Professor of Theoretical Physics at Birkbeck
College of the University of London, where he is now Professor
Emeritus.

During the war Bohm worked on plasma in magnetic fields; along
with others, he worked out a theory that plays an important part in
fusion studies—a phenomenon now called "Bohm-diffusion." At
Princeton he extended the plasma-theory to metals, which is part of
solid-state physics (the study of the properties of matter at very low
temperatures). Bohm also worked on the design of instruments such as
the cyclotron and the synchro-cyclotron. In Bristol, England, in 1960,

23

Bohm worked out the effect that bears his name, the "Bohm-Aharonov effect." This holds that an isolated line of magnetic force is able to affect electrons that pass around it without contacting it—which is impossible according to classical physics but is predicted by quantum physics.

Bohm's work over the past four decades has been primarily concerned with the fundamentals of quantum theory and relativity and their philosophical meaning, and it includes research at the Lawrence Radiation Laboratory in Berkeley. His books include *Quantum Theory* (1951), *Causality and Chance in Modern Physics* (1957), *The Special Theory of Relativity* (1966), and *Wholeness and the Implicate Order* (1980), his most recent work, which deals with physics, the philosophy of physics, and with Bohm's revolutionary views on consciousness.

His explorations into the nature of consciousness were in part stimulated by the dilemmas he found in quantum mechanics, in part by his discovery of the Indian philosopher-sage, Krishnamurti. One day Bohm's English wife, Saral, brought him a book she had chanced upon at the library, which she took to be about quantum physics, since it centered around problems created by the observer/observed relationship. It turned out to be a volume by Krishnamurti, with whom Bohm from then on became closely associated. Asked about their relationship, Bohm said: "We are friends and have had a close relationship, formed around questions of mutual interest that we've explored together for many years." Two of their dialogues appeared as books, *Truth and Actuality* (1978) and *The Ending of Time* (1985).

Because of Bohm's international fame, I was quite unprepared for the unusually modest and unassuming, gentle person he turned out to be. He is the paradigm of the committed searcher and researcher, intensely absorbed in his philosophy of the implicate order, on which he lectures all over the world. Bohm looks like the proverbial professor, dressed in casual tweeds and almost always wearing a sweater. He is of average height, with brown hair, hazel eyes, a rather pale face, inward and intellectual in expression, a captivating smile and a quiet, low-keyed manner except on discussing physics, when he becomes animated and almost transformed, punctuating his points with vivid gestures.

As I look back on this meeting, I am struck by the synchronicities that led to it. Two of my articles in *Main Currents in Modern Thought* had caught David Bohm's attention, and I was invited to a small conference of scholars and scientists hosted by Krishnamurti and Bohm in Ojai, California in the Spring of 1976. Meeting Bohm was memorable for two reasons. Not since Fritz Kunz had I come across someone who—*through science*—perceived a universe of truth, beauty, meaning, even the good, and who made his perceptions come so convincingly alive to others. And—like Fritz Kunz—David Bohm seemed imbued with a feeling that whatever lies behind nature is holy. Our dialogue at Ojai was the beginning of many others. There is aesthetic closure for me in the fact that Fritz Kunz, who began it all, led me to David Bohm, the *ReVision* dialogues, and to this book.

The implicate order grew out of Bohm's earlier work on hidden variables and the causal interpretation of quantum mechanics. Like Einstein—though for different reasons—Bohm has never been reconciled to current interpretations of quantum theory, and proposes that a hidden order is at work beneath the seeming chaos and lack of continuity of the individual particles of matter described by quantum mechanics. That hidden dimension became Bohm's implicate order, the source of all the visible (explicate) matter of our space-time universe. The implicate order has infinite depth; Bohm proposes that in its inward recesses both matter and consciousness have their source and become unified.

In this first dialogue, Bohm outlines his basic theory. He suggests that the world we live in is multidimensional. The most obvious and superficial level is the three-dimensional world of objects, space, and time which he terms the *explicate order*. Its matter is composed of a dense grade, and although it can be *described* by reference to itself alone, Bohm feels that it can neither be explained nor clearly understood in this way. Unfortunately, he says, this is the level on which most of physics operates today, presenting its findings in equations the meaning of which is unclear.

A clearer understanding becomes possible only by going to a deeper level—the *implicate order*, which is the all-encompassing background to our experience: physical, psychological, and spiritual. This source lies in a yet subtler dimension called "the super-implicate order." Beyond this we can postulate many such orders, merging into an infinite, n-dimensional source or ground.

This dialogue was held in Ojai, California in 1978 and at Syracuse University in 1981. In Ojai, in the bungalow amidst the orange groves in which Bohm always stays during his visits with Krishnamurti, Bohm seemed particularly taken with the giant live oak trees, which he said symbolized the constant movement in nature that his "holomovement" theory tries to express. This first dialogue raises many questions that will be taken up in later ones, both by Bohm and the other figures in this book, i.e., our notions of space, time, matter, energy, consciousness, finitude and the infinite. His viewpoint as a physicist conjecturing about the mystic's recurrent use of light to express his experience is especially intriguing because Fr. Bede Griffiths, in Chapter 9, rejects light and suggests that "the divine darkness" is a better symbol.

In this present dialogue, Bohm also mentions for the first time a seed idea that he went on to develop in the 1980s, and which has become central to his recent work, namely the idea of soma-significance and the sigma-somatic. This theory, which he takes up again in Chapter 6, postulates meaning and therefore consciousness throughout nature, even at the level of the electron.

WEBER   Can you explain the basic idea of the implicate order?

BOHM   Ordinarily the whole enfolded order cannot be all made manifest to us, only some aspect of it is manifest. When we bring the enfolded order into that manifest aspect, we get an experience of perception. But that doesn't mean that the whole of the order is just what is manifest. That would be the Cartesian view: that the whole of the order is at least potentially manifest though we may not know how to make it manifest on our own. We might need microscopes and telescopes and various instruments.

In the implicate order what is going to be visible is only a very small part of the enfolded order, and therefore we introduce the distinction between what is manifest and what is not manifest. It may fold up and become non-manifest or unfold into the manifest order and then refold again. The fundamental movement is folding and unfolding. Whereas the fundamental movement of Descartes is crossing space in time, a localized entity moving from one place to another.

WEBER   Is this like Einstein's field theory?

BOHM   In the implicate order we not only always deal with the whole (which the field theory also does), but we also say that the connections of the whole have nothing to do with locality in space and time but have to do with an entirely different quality, namely enfoldment.

WEBER   In other words, what is significant here is that it's not crossing or traversing certain places?

BOHM   In these earlier models, either a particle crosses certain places or a force of an energy field crosses that place and therefore from the point of view of the implicate order we don't have a fundamental distinction between Einstein and Newton. We say that they are different, but they both differ equally from the implicate order.

WEBER   You have called this vast and dynamic background "the holomovement."

BOHM   The holomovement is the ground of what is manifest. And what is manifest is, as it were, abstracted and floating in the holomovement. The holomovement's basic movement is folding and unfolding. Now, I'm saying that all existence is basically a holomovement which manifests in relatively stable form.

WEBER   The flux arrested for the time being?

BOHM   Well, at least coming to balance for the time being, coming into relevant closure, like the vortex which closes on itself though it's always moving.

WEBER You said these would be denser forms of matter rather than subtler and less stable ones.

BOHM Yes, they are more stable forms of matter, let's put it that way. See, even the cloud holds a stable form so the cloud can be regarded as a manifestation of the movement of the wind. Now, in a similar way matter can be regarded as forming clouds within the holomovement and they manifest the holomovement to our ordinary sense and thought.

WEBER If all entities are forms of the holomovement, that would obviously include man with all his capacities.

BOHM Yes, all the cells, all the atoms. I should add that this begins to give a good account of what quantum mechanics means: this unfoldment is a direct idea as to what is meant by the mathematics of quantum mechanics. What's called the unitary transformation or the basic mathematical description of movement in quantum mechanics is exactly what we are talking about. It is just simply the mathematical description of the holomovement.

WEBER How, exactly, does the holomovement relate to present quantum theory?

BOHM If you follow through the mathematics of the present quantum theory, it treats the particle as what is called the quantized state of the field, that is, as a field spread over space but in some mysterious way with a quantum of energy. Now each wave in the field has a certain quantum of energy proportional to its frequency. And if you take the electromagnetic field, for example, in empty space, every wave has what is called a zero point energy below which it cannot go, even when there is no energy available. If you were to add up all the waves in any region of empty space you would find that they have an infinite amount of energy because an infinite number of waves are possible. However, you may have reason to suppose that the energy may not be infinite, that maybe you cannot keep on adding waves that are shorter and shorter, each contributing to the energy. There may be some shortest possible wave, and then the total number of waves would be finite and the energy would also be finite.

Now, you have to ask what would be the shortest length and there seems to be reason to suspect that the gravitational theory may provide us with some shortest length, for according to general relativity, the gravitational field also determines what is meant by "length" and metric. If you said the gravitational field was made up of waves which were quantized in this way, you would find that there was a certain length below which the gravitational field would become undefinable because of this zero point movement and you wouldn't be able to define length. Therefore, you could say the property of measurement, length, fades out at very short distances and you'd find the place at which it fades out would be about 10^{-33} cm. That is a very short distance because the shortest distances that physicists have ever probed so far might be 10^{-16} cm. or so, and that's a long way to go. If you then compute the amount of energy that would be in space, with 'hat shortest possible wave length, then it turns out that the energy in one cubic centimeter would be immensely beyond the total energy of all the known matter in the universe.

WEBER   In one cubic centimeter of space.

BOHM   Yes. And therefore, how is one to understand that?

WEBER   How *do* you understand it?

BOHM   You understand that by saying: the present theory says that the vacuum contains all this energy which is then ignored [by physics] because it cannot be measured by an instrument. The philosophy being that only what can be measured by an instrument can be considered real, except that physics also says there are particles that cannot be seen in instruments at all. What you can say is that the present state of theoretical physics implies that empty space has all this energy and matter is a slight increase of the energy, and therefore matter is like a small ripple on this tremendous ocean of energy, having some relative stability and being manifest. Therefore my suggestion is that this implicate order implies a reality immensely beyond what we call matter. Matter itself is merely a ripple in this background.

WEBER   In this ocean of energy, you are saying.

BOHM   In this ocean of energy. And the ocean of energy is not primarily in space and time at all. It's primarily in the implicate order.

WEBER   Which is to say unmanifest.

BOHM   Right. And it may manifest in this little bit of matter.

WEBER   The ripple.

BOHM   The ripple.

WEBER   But the source, you're saying, is in the implicate order and that's this ocean of energy, untapped or unmanifest.

BOHM   That's right. And in fact beyond that ocean may be still a bigger ocean because, after all, our knowledge just simply fades out at that point. It's not to say that there is nothing beyond that.

WEBER   Something not characterizable, or unnamable?

BOHM   Eventually, perhaps, you might discover some further source of energy but you may surmise that that would in turn be floating in a still larger source and so on. It is implied that the ultimate source is immeasurable and cannot be captured within our knowledge. That really is what is implied by contemporary physics.

WEBER   Can you now clarify the relationship between wholeness and relatively independent sub-wholes? Is there any justification for claiming that I am an individual and you are an individual or is it pure illusion, what the east calls *maya*?

BOHM   It depends on the level at which you operate. Clearly the body has a certain individuality, it's a relative sub-whole which has its own self-referential order but it's also highly dependent on the environment in order to exist. Any person has some degree of difference from another—his own background, ideas, tendencies. So in a relative sense we have some individuality. But the question is how deep is it, what is the ground of it all?

WEBER   I'm postulating, along with you, that the ground of it is one. Accepting that as given, that the ocean is one, is there a genuine working sense in which the droplet is *itself*, and is not the next droplet on the surface?

BOHM   There is, certainly, on the surface. Everybody has got his own interests and background, and his own special way of putting everything together, which may have its value. I think this is a problem of language and dialectic. If we were to discuss the whole and the parts, or the whole and the sub-wholes, we could look at the wholeness of the whole and the parts, which says the parts are there and that they help enrich the whole towards a higher unity. But we have another principle, which is the partiality of the whole and the parts. Which do we emphasize? Let me make an analogy. When you're playing music it is very important which theme is given the dominant role and which the secondary role. If we reversed their roles, it would be an entirely different piece. What has happened is that the dominant role has been given to this theme, namely the partiality of the whole and the parts. I'm proposing that we keep this as a secondary role and assign the other a major role.

WEBER   The major role, the real music of the universe, for you is the *unity* of unity and diversity or the wholeness of the whole and the part. That is what must always be in the foreground.

BOHM   Yes, and given the major stress.

WEBER   Although they share your assumptions, many philosophies, especially in the east, nevertheless assign a weighty role to the part, even though they assert the unity of the whole and the part. This comes out in ethical and social ways, especially in the notion that each person has a unique role to play, that he's sounding a unique note in the whole symphony. That is the *dharma* in your life that you must uniquely find and live, or you'll have missed your chord. What do you feel about that?

BOHM   Everybody has some unique potential. You can't state what his unique role is because he has a range of potentials. Given another circumstance he could probably have carried out another role, but he has a certain potential that is different from anybody else's. While you have a special potential, the energy doesn't come from your predispositions. They must serve the whole. The energy comes from the whole, basically from the insight.

WEBER   Why does the energy that comes from the whole take on different aspects in different individuals?

BOHM   I propose that the whole is enriched by introducing diversity and achieving the unity of diversity.

WEBER   That's where the relative role of the sub-whole comes in. Even though we are one in the implicate order, we are not inter-changeable with others like bees in a beehive.

BOHM   No, each one is different, though perhaps not as different as we'd like to think. Under the present circumstances people are not realizing their potential for uniqueness, but in so far as they follow their predispositions they're part of the mass. Each person in his being has a particular unique character and quality, but its whole meaning is to unite with all the others into something greater.

WEBER   It would resolve one cliché that holistic theories often gener-ate, namely that everything is one big cosmic mush and it does not reflect individual contributions. In a sense, finitude also contributes by "re-injecting" its contributions back into the whole.

BOHM   Yes. But of course all opposites are one in the ultimate ground.

WEBER   It's a dialectic: the more the sense of the whole is alive in us, the more we feel responsible to express that as individuals in our daily lives.

BOHM   The point about dialectic is the ultimate identity of the uni-versal and the individual. The individual *is* universal and the uni-versal *is* individual. The word "individual" means undivided, so we could say that very few individuals have ever existed. We could call them *dividuals*. Individuality is only possible if it unfolds from wholeness.

WEBER   That is a corrective to rampant ego-centeredness, which is not true individuality.

BOHM   Ego-centeredness is not individuality at all.

WEBER   Can you make the distinction?

BOHM   Ego-centeredness centers on the self-image which is an illu-sion and a delusion. Therefore it's nothing. In true individuality a true being unfolds from the whole in its particular way for that particular moment.

WEBER   Oddly, one's sense of being rooted in this whole is what permits true individuality.

BOHM   Yes. It is impossible to have true individuality except when grounded in the whole. Anything else is egocentrism.

WEBER   Most people think these are synonymous.

BOHM   Anybody who is self-centered must be divided, because in order to become self-centered he must establish a division between himself and the whole.

WEBER   He has not even understood himself.

BOHM   Not only that, he's fragmenting himself, shattering his individuality, and turning it into a collective mish-mash.

WEBER   By contrast, the true individual understands that he is an outgrowth of the whole at every moment.

BOHM   There's nothing fixed about him. He is eternally unfolding his potential as the ancient saying goes, continually flowering as Krishnamurti likes to say, revealing more and more deeply what he is.

WEBER   This is analogous to your cosmology. If one understands that, one has to conclude that there are no events in the universe, that time is not a river, that nothing happens, because everything just *is*.

BOHM   Time is another way of looking at it. Nicholas of Cusa said that eternity unfolds in time. That time is the same as the particles; in a way, time is an enrichment of eternity. But we can't understand it except from the standpoint of the ground of eternity. If we attempt to make time self-referential it is going to lead to chaos.

WEBER   Using your vocabulary, if in this unity of unity and diversity, one looks at the diversity, one can talk about history, change and events. But from the point of view of the unity, one has to conclude that nothing happens, that everything just *is*.

BOHM   Yes. That is clear in the case of time. Past and future are always present as overtones of the present. We may be remembering the past but the memory is present, and we're expecting the future, but the expectation is present. The future might be simply the depths of the implicate order which *is* and which is unfolding.

WEBER   If the future is the depth of the implicate order which *is*, then that would also point to the relativity of time from the human, commonsensical view, because one is not completely separated from one's future; one *is* already its potential.

BOHM   You *are* your future, but not yet unfolded. You're still enfolded.

WEBER   The mystic (it's a term I like, though I understand your reservations about it), has actually experienced the unity of those moments. So perhaps what we call "time" is space for him, a depth of penetration within the implicate order.

BOHM   Nicholas of Cusa is reputed to have been a mystic, and that's what he saw. I take it that he didn't get this out of his mathematics, but that it was probably the way he experienced it.

WEBER   If you wanted to eliminate the term "time" in this description, could you use spatial metaphors like "depth of implication" as an equivalent to time?

BOHM   Yes, I think depth of inwardness, a certain kind of inwardness. But how to do that hasn't been worked out. Time is succession, it is the aspect of succession, and succession in depth of inwardness.

WEBER   If you go far enough inward into the implicate order, what will "later" appear as succession is still co-present.

BOHM   Yes, you could almost say that things may be organized in a hierarchy (though I have reservations about the word), that any particular level of time may have its level of eternity. For certain purposes, a long period of time functions as the eternity of our age. In turn, the age of ages has a higher eternity, leading up to the ultimate, which is ineffable. Any eternity that we could get hold of would still be a relative eternity. The Greeks had the view, as did other ancient peoples, that each age had its characteristics of time and was, as it were, the eternity of that period. That's why this eternity can be affected by what happens in time.

WEBER   Its residue—what has been achieved in that time period— can be the seeds of a whole new epoch.

BOHM   A whole new age.

WEBER   Do you mean a new age historically or cosmologically?

BOHM   Both. The cosmos may be a certain age. The present idea of the universe may represent some age of this universe of light. The universe of light is eternal as far as we are concerned, but at a certain stage some of these light rays got together and made the Big Bang. And that unfolded into our universe, which will have its end. But the universe of light is beyond time, and therefore there could be other universes. There may be many ages, not necessarily in succession.

WEBER   Hindu cosmology has a model of *pralaya*, a rest period, and *manvantara*, the active period—they call it the night of Brahman and the day of Brahman. There is a huge astronomical time scale in both these cosmologies (I discussed this with John A. Wheeler in 1976 by the way, and he was interested). They say when the universe goes to sleep, everything is dormant in it and aeons pass before it starts up again; nevertheless, the *essence* of what was learned before carries over as a seed. Do you claim anything like that?

BOHM   In the concept of this projection and introjection [i.e., of implicate order philosophy] there might be something like that.

WEBER   Contrasted with traditional systems in which a God directs the world like a stage director, your system seems really serious about its view that the whole acts together. That implies that we also are contributing to the deeper inward nature because we've contributed to what is re-injected into the implicate order from the explicate order.

BOHM Yet, it contributes in some way and we could say that we ourselves maybe can bring order to what we're doing, we can play a functional role in producing a higher order than would be possible without us. We do not merely modify it somewhat, but rather although we make a very tiny change in the whole thing, nevertheless, it may be crucial in allowing this higher order to come to something new to realize its potential.

WEBER One creative aspect of nature is evolution and you're saying that we are not just being shaped by that, but that we can help shape it.

BOHM We're part of the movement, there's no separation between us and it, we are part of the way in which that shapes itself.

WEBER So what is introjected back into the implicate order is not lost, but its essence is in some way preserved.

BOHM There may have been something out of which the Big Bang came.

WEBER You've recently proposed a super-implicate order. How does it differ from the implicate order?

BOHM If you apply this model, the enfoldment is now seen on two levels: first, an enfolded order of the vacuum with ripples on it that unfold; and second, a super-information field of the whole universe, a super-implicate order which organizes the first level into various structures and is capable of tremendous development of structure. The point about the super-implicate order is that if we take the holographic theory, though we have an implicate order, nothing organizes it. It is what's called "linear," and it just passes through itself and diffuses around; special devices can unfold it but it does not have an intrinsic capacity to unfold an order. The super-implicate order, which is the so-called higher field (the implicate order would be a wave function), would be a function of the wave function, a higher order, a super-wave function. The super-implicate order makes the implicate order non-linear and organizes it into relatively stable forms with complex structures.

WEBER Is there a super super-implicate order?

BOHM There might be an implicate order even beyond that one. I'd like to propose that we are making a series of abstractions and any level of thought must cut off somewhere. Even if we put more in, there is still more left out. It's inherent in thought that it is not going to grasp the actual totality. But the holistic part of thought would be thought which does not make a break, thought which is unbroken.

WEBER It's a continuum of ordering principles?

BOHM That's right. Even when we say that we have made a break, we realize that it really shades off into the unknown. That's essential for this quality of wholeness.

WEBER   It has no endpoint and no origin?

BOHM   We produce an arbitrary distinction, merely for the sake of thought.

WEBER   But the reason for postulating a super-implicate order is that you want an organizing and active principle.

BOHM   I don't need to postulate it. As soon as you make this model of de Broglie and extend it to the quantum mechanical field, you've got it.

WEBER   In physics?

BOHM   That is exactly what is implied by quantum mechanical field theory. When seen in this way and through this model, this theory is exactly what I have described.

WEBER   Would conventional physicists accept that?

BOHM   They *have* accepted it, but they say, "What is the use? It does not produce anything different from what we've already done. We only care about the empirical results." The other is philosophy and poetry as far as they are concerned.

WEBER   They are only attuned to the explicate and not to the enfolded source of it.

BOHM   Yes, of course, that's the whole purpose of the operation. They say "The essential thing of truth is to produce theoretical, mathematical ideas which actually predict the results of experiments, and in that act you are grasping truth."

WEBER   How it got there is irrelevant?

BOHM   They say that's not interesting, and they dismiss it.

WEBER   One of your reservations about the direction of contemporary physics is that it does not tie its findings enough to the philosophical meaning.

BOHM   The imaginative side, the intuitive side.

WEBER   Making models?

BOHM   Not necessarily new models, but new forms of imagination. I regard the implicate order as a new form of imagination. They would say "It's no use if it doesn't produce an empirical pay-off. We will look at that as soon as it is producing an empirical pay-off—we'll look at anything." That's one of the errors of science, which is just part of the error of our society, that the empirical pay-off is the main point of the operation, that it is truth. They feel that the empirical agreement is what is meant by truth, provided that you have a logical mathematical argument behind it.

WEBER   You are saying that an imaginative model like the implicate order may, in fact, get us closer to the truth of things, even though at the moment we may not be sure what the empirical pay-off is.

BOHM   Yes. In fact, I think any new idea must involve the free play of the mind without thinking too much about the empirical pay-off.

WEBER   Einstein got to the idea of relativity because as a child he imagined what the universe looked like riding on a beam of light.

BOHM   That's right. It took him ten years even to work out the theory of relativity.

WEBER   So you are endorsing that as one possible avenue to discovering physics. When I asked a colleague in physics for his reaction to the implicate order, he said: it is an interesting idea, but does Bohm have any shred of evidence for it?

BOHM   I would say, what shred of evidence is there for the present interpretation as opposed to the one I propose? I have heard that argument before and I say it is fortuitous that this interpretation of quantum mechanics and this way of doing it have developed. For example, de Broglie proposed quite a different approach which was squelched by the leading physicists of the time. Had that been adopted and had people got used to that, then people would have asked the same question, "What is the point of this present approach?" It is nothing different from de Broglie.

WEBER   You are saying that the accepted model of quantum physics is accepted because of familiarity?

BOHM   Yes, and that it was chosen for reasons that are fortuitous as far as science itself is concerned.

WEBER   The implicate order, as you said elsewhere, is highly compatible with the equations, more so perhaps.

BOHM   Yes. Even de Broglie's idea extended in the way I did it would have been a more imaginative way of looking at the thing and it would have been easier to reach. Had people adopted it, they would have regarded this current way [of interpreting physics] as terribly obscure.

WEBER   Is it too technical to give a brief picture of de Broglie's theory?

BOHM   It was the idea that basically an electron is a particle (I'll simplify it very much) and that it has a field around it, a new kind of quantum mechanical field which in some ways is similar to old kinds of fields, in some ways different. The key difference was that its activity did not depend on its intensity. That's like saying that it did not act by mechanical pressure on the particle, but it acted from the information content which carried information about the whole experimental arrangement. So the meaning of an experimental result and the form of the experimental conditions were no longer separable, they were a whole, as even Bohr said. This was immediately obvious in de Broglie's interpretation, whereas it's a deep, impenetrable mystery in Bohr's language.

WEBER   Did Bohr not accept it?

BOHM   Bohr did. Bohr had the insight to see this, and this is the basis of his work on interpretation, that the form of the experimental conditions and the meaning of the results are a whole, not further analyzable. He has a very complex way of putting it which very few physicists understand. In fact, one of the points is that the only consistent interpretation of that kind is Bohr's, and the number who understand it is very small. Most physicists are just using it, taking it for granted that Bohr has done it right.

WEBER When you say "he," you have been referring to Bohr, not to de Broglie.

BOHM Yes, de Broglie, even before Bohr, had proposed another interpretation. What happened was that scientists ignored his picture and just took the mathematical formula.

WEBER If the community of physicists had taken the de Broglie model, would that have moved them closer to an awareness of the unity of things?

BOHM Yes, because nowadays no physicist understands this at all except by very complicated mathematical arguments which are so distant from his intuition that he regards it as significant only in connection with his work, but not connected with anything else. It's so complicated that very few physicists hear about it and each time new textbooks are written, more and more of it is lost so that by now textbooks don't refer to it all; they just present quantum mechanics as a set of formulae you've got to learn how to use. Because of the lack of imaginative understanding, this result was very likely to come about.

WEBER You are assigning a creative and constructive role to imagination, whereas earlier you cautioned against its abuse.

BOHM Coleridge has proposed two kinds of imagination, primary and secondary. The primary imagination is the direct expression of the creative intent within, what we may call the display in the mind. The imagination is an unfoldment of some deeper operation of the mind which is displayed as if coming from the senses, and you can grasp it as if looking at it directly as a whole.

WEBER It reveals.

BOHM Yes. Reveal and display have much the same meaning here. But the secondary imagination arises when you keep on repeating an image from the primary display and it becomes automatic.

WEBER It becomes self-referring. It no longer reveals but becomes a fantasy.

BOHM That's exactly what Coleridge called it. He called it "fancy," which is the same as fantasy.

WEBER Imagination, then, in the creative scientific sense, is our attempt to verbalize deep insights about nature.

BOHM Or make a picture.

WEBER So you are arguing for imaginative models that would be multi-leveled, mutually supportive, and, most importantly, show their interconnectedness. That is not being done in physics?

BOHM   Well, they simply ignore it and say that that it's out of date. It doesn't produce an empirical pay-off.

WEBER   This model would produce only understanding!

BOHM   Yes. But they say, "What does it mean to understand unless you can predict something empirically?"

WEBER   So they have equated understanding with empirical prediction and control and you are diverging from that. You are saying to understand means to grasp it clearly and to see it connected to everything else. Is that right?

BOHM   That's right. Comprehension is the word. To comprehend, to hold it all together.

WEBER   Is talk of a super-implicate order something new, or was it already implied in the implicate order?

BOHM   In talking of a super-implicate order, I am not making further assumptions beyond what is implied in physics today. Once we extend this model of de Broglie to the quantum mechanical field rather than just to the particle, that picture immediately *is* the super-implicate order. So this is not just speculation, it is the picture which is implied by present quantum mechanics if you look at it imaginatively.

WEBER   Including the claim that there is an ordering principle?

BOHM   That's right. Mathematically it is called non-linear equations.

WEBER   When you say we should look at it imaginatively, let's be clear: you are not proposing that we introduce vague fantasy.

BOHM   No.

WEBER   You mean imaginative interpretations and models for the mathematical equations, creative imagination.

BOHM   Imagination which directly displays the meaning of the mathematics, the mathematics which is being used by all the leading physicists now in whatever they are doing.

WEBER   You are drawing out the consequences of quantum mechanical mathematics.

BOHM   Yes. Further, I am saying that by not doing this you fail to see the full meaning of that mathematics and are able to restrict it to making empirical predictions.

WEBER   This super-implicate order is not the end. It can go as far as thought can take it, a super super-implicate order, and so on?

BOHM   That's right. That was one point I wanted to make. The second point is that if we remain with the holographic model, this essentially sticks to the implicate order and leaves out the super-implicate order. In other words, it's a tremendous simplification of quantum mechanics to make the holographic model; that is good enough in the classical sense where you use the holograph. But as a model for organizing the implicate order through the informational field—the quantum information potential—it leaves out what is very interesting, namely that this implicate order now actively organizes itself. This is crucial to understanding thought and the mind.

WEBER   So it's the self-organizing universe, and it makes clear that consciousness can't be divorced from matter because it resides within it in some way.

BOHM   Yes, that's right. The relationship of the super-implicate order to the implicate order is similar to the relationship of consciousness to matter as we know it. There is a kind of analogy.

WEBER   The super-implicate order would be the conscious aspect and the implicate order would be the material aspect?

BOHM   The neuro-physiological aspect, which is still enfolded relative to what we ordinarily see.

WEBER   So these pairs occur on many different levels.

BOHM   Yes, in fact there is a principle I once thought of, I called it "soma-significance." Instead of "psychosomatic." The word psychosomatic emphasizes two entities, mind and soma (or body), but I want to emphasize two sides of *one process*. Any process can be treated either as somatic or as significant. A very elementary case is the printed paper: it's somatic in that it's just printed ink; and it also has significance. I say all along the line any part of the body or the body processes is somatic, it's the nerves moving chemically and physically; and in addition it has a meaning which is active. The essential point about intelligence is the activity of significance, right? In computers, we have begun to imitate that to some extent. I am trying to say that all of nature is organized according to the activity of significance. This, however, can be conceived somatically in a more subtle form of matter which, in turn, is organized by a still more subtle form of significance. So in that way every level is both somatic and significant.

WEBER   That is very much like Spinoza. Would you extend this all the way into the heart of matter to the atom and the sub-atomic particles?

BOHM   Yes, because what we call the atom is organized by the super or the quantum field of information, which gives it its significance.

WEBER   Is the significance something that *we* impute to an otherwise neutral domain?

BOHM   No, the essential point is that if we merely imputed significance to it, it wouldn't be *active*. Do we impute significance to the activity of the computer? There is information-content stored in a program. That significance is active because it determines the activity of the computer and all sorts of activities that flow out of it.

WEBER   One might question that analogy because the significance of the information-content in the computer is what we've put in and then we read it back out. But here we're dealing with nature as a whole.

BOHM   But quantum mechanics is indicating that that order of activity or that order of relationship is what is actually present, and that we are merely imitating nature.

WEBER   We're imitating nature in our cognitive processes and creative acts?

BOHM   Yes, and extending it in some ways.

WEBER   But are these processes truly similar?

BOHM   If we take the basic structure as similar, we can say that the super or information-potential is related to the implicate order of matter as the subtle aspects of consciousness are related to the material movements of hormones and electrical currents in the nerves.

WEBER   It's almost the old hermetic principle, "as above, so below." We're the mirror image of larger processes.

BOHM   Yes, you could say that essentially it's the principle of what we call similarities and differences: the differences within one field are paralleled by similar differences in the other field. The quantum field contains information about the whole environment and about the whole past, which regulates the present activity of the electron in much the same way that information about the whole past and our whole environment regulates our own activity as human beings, through consciousness.

WEBER   Is that like saying that nature thinks?

BOHM   Not exactly, but nature has active information as we have; at least at the level of *unconscious* thought it's similar.

WEBER   And part of that active information is derived from its own past?

BOHM   Yes, or from elsewhere.

WEBER   Is the super-implicate order a euphemism for God?

BOHM   I don't know what the meaning of the question is since the super-implicate order is in turn part of a still greater implicate order. It's not a euphemism for God because it's limited.

WEBER   Then let's shift the question to the ultimate super super-implicate order.

BOHM   But we can't grasp that in thought. We're not saying that any of this is another word for God. I would put it another way: people had insight in the past about a form of intelligence that had organized the universe and they personalized it and called it God. A similar insight can prevail today without personalizing it and without calling it a personal God.

David Bohm

WEBER Still, it's a kind of super-intelligence and you've said elsewhere that that is benevolent and compassionate, not neutral.

BOHM Well, we can propose that.

WEBER To you the notion of creativity entails building larger wholes.

BOHM We cannot in the end do anything but destroy if we have a fragmentary approach.

WEBER How do you order these various levels?

BOHM To say that the higher level simply transcends the lower level altogether. It's immensely greater and has an entirely different set of relationships out of which the lower level is obtained as a very small part, in an abstraction.

WEBER It has wholeness, more power, more energy, more insight?

BOHM Yes, and it contains the lower level in some sense.

WEBER And not vice-versa?

BOHM The lower level will be the unfoldment of the higher level.

WEBER In space and time.

BOHM Yes.

WEBER So in a sense they contain each other but in another sense the higher one contains the whole and the lower one is more linear.

BOHM Yes. The higher one is called non-linear, mathematically, and the lower one is linear. That means of course that the linear organization of time and thought characteristic of the ordinary level will not necessarily be characteristic of the higher level. Therefore what is beyond time may have an order of its own, not the same as the simple linear order of time.

WEBER In that case we have this all upside down: we foist our limited version of space and time on these higher levels and think that's the only ordering possible.

BOHM This higher order is not basically the order of space and time, but the order of space and time unfolds from it and folds back into it in the way we've been discussing.

WEBER Our kind of space and time is one among perhaps infinitely many orderings possible in the universe yet we think that it's the only way and in fact the necessary condition for understanding. Kant almost said that and could not conceive of an alternative arrangement. The super-implicate order proposes an alternative to current narrow western epistemology.

BOHM Yes, it says that the information content out of which the implicate order unfolds is not determined in an order of space and time as we know it, but it contains that order within it.

WEBER We might say this is the creative play (*lila* in Sanskrit) of the universe, where from its deep recesses it evolves different combinations.

BOHM Yes, and through that it's unfolding and developing and flowering (if you want to use that word as Krishnamurti does) and therefore evolution is fundamental. This involves both space and time. Time itself is an order of manifestation, you see. We are going to say that it is possible to have an implicate order with regard to time as well as to space, to say that in any given period of time, the whole of time may be enfolded. It's implied in the implicate order when you carry it through: the holomovement is the reality and what is going on in the full depth of that one moment of time contains information about all of it.

WEBER   You've said that the moment is timeless.

BOHM   Yes, the moment is atemporal, the connection of moments is not in time but in the implicate order.

WEBER   Which you said is timeless.

BOHM   Yes. So let me propose that also for consciousness; let me propose that consciousness is basically in the implicate order as all matter is and therefore it's not that consciousness is one thing and matter is another. Rather consciousness is a material process and consciousness is itself in the implicate order, as is all matter, and consciousness manifests in some explicate order, as does matter.

WEBER   The difference between what we call matter and consciousness would be the state of density or subtlety?

BOHM   The state of subtlety. Consciousness is possibly a more subtle form of matter and movement, a more subtle aspect of the holomovement. In the nonmanifest order there is no separation in space and time. In ordinary matter this is so and it's even more so for this subtle matter which is consciousness. Therefore if we are separate it is because we are sticking largely to the manifest world as the basic reality where the whole point is to have separate units, relatively separate anyway, but interacting. In nonmanifest reality it's all interpenetrating, interconnected, one. So we say deep down the consciousness of mankind is one. This is a virtual certainty because even in the vacuum matter is one; and if we don't see this it's because we are blinding ourselves to it.

WEBER   Your implicate order philosophy treats space very differently from the usual way.

BOHM   Yes. There are two views of space. One view is to maintain that the skin is the boundary of ourselves, that there's the space without and the space within. The space within is the separate self, obviously, and the space without is the space which separates the separate selves, right? And therefore to overcome the separation you must have a process of moving through that space, which takes time. Is that clear?

WEBER   That's how human beings have always thought of it.

BOHM   That's right. But if we looked at it as a holomovement with this vast reserve of energy and empty space where matter itself is

that small wave on empty space, then we should really say that the
space as a whole is the ground of existence and we are in it. So
the space doesn't separate us, it unites us. Therefore it's like saying
that there are two separate points and a certain dotted line connecting them, which shows how we think they are related; or to
say there is a *real line* and that the *the points are abstractions* from
that.

WEBER   Demarking the boundaries of the line.

BOHM   Yes.

WEBER   You turn the whole thing around.

BOHM   The line is the reality and the points are abstractions. In that
sense we say that there are no separate people, you see, but that
that idea is an abstraction which comes by taking certain features
of the whole as abstracted and self-existent.

WEBER   So space is more fundamental and more real than the objects
in it. Applying your theory to time, we would have to say that the
interval between the moments is the real.

BOHM   It could be considered to be that. But see, if we take the view
that the space is what is real, then I think that we have to say that
the *measure* of space is not what is real. The measure of space is
what matter provides. So space goes beyond the measure of space.

It's the same with time. If we want to say that the interval is
real, then the measure of time cannot be taken as fundamental.
Therefore we are already outside of what we ordinarily would call
time. But rather, if we have silence and "emptiness," it does not
have the measure either of space or of time. Now in that silence
there may appear something which is a little ripple which has that
measure. But if we thought that the little ripple was all that there
is and that the space between was nothing, of no significance, then
we would have the usual view of fragmentation.

WEBER   Taking what we call events as the points.

BOHM   Yes. Events are like the points.

WEBER   But if you don't allow time to be measured by events, the
line then....

BOHM   Then it's flowing movement, right?

WEBER   Well, then in a way it's silence.

BOHM   It's just flow. If you look at nature and say, there's no event
in nature, really, then it's just flowing. It's the mind that abstracts
and puts an event in there.

WEBER   But doesn't it follow that the flow or the silence cannot be
broken up by any distinguishing characteristics?

BOHM   Yes. Except that's what thought puts in, the distinguishing
characteristics. The distinguishing characteristics have their place
in a certain limited domain of the explicate order and of the
manifest.

WEBER   Still, I think to some people all this is going to seem very strange. First of all, it challenges everything we've known or been taught. Second, it appears to be counter-intuitive, certainly to those who have been trained in modern science. Third, it may appear frightening or threatening. So let's spell it out. You're saying that the events are always distinguishable, they have characteristics, they are what we call happenings, and they're the ones we've seized upon as what transpires in the world, as the world's business, so to speak. Those—you're saying—are secondary, derivative, and less important than the absence of all that. And the absence of all that is emptiness, silence.

BOHM   It would be the holomovement, you see, the flowing movement. But it goes beyond that. We could say that even at this level of thought there is a way of looking at it in which emptiness is the plenum, right? I'm saying that what we call real things are actually tiny little ripples which have their place, but they have been usurping the whole, the place of the whole.

WEBER   By "emptiness" we don't mean a substantive emptiness like an "empty" box. We're talking about a plenum.

BOHM   It's emptiness which is a plenum. Yes.

WEBER   An emptiness which is a plenum. What does that mean?

BOHM   This is a well-known idea even in physics. If you take a crystal which is at absolute zero it does not scatter electrons. They go through it as if it were empty and as soon as you raise the temperature and [produce] inhomogeneities, they scatter. Now, if you used those electrons to observe the crystal (e.g. by focusing them with an electron lens to make an image), all you would see would be these little inhomogeneities and you would say they are what exists and the crystal is what does not exist. Right? I think this is a familiar idea, namely to say that what we see immediately is all there is or all that counts and that our ideas must simply correlate what we see immediately.

WEBER   From that, of course, it would follow that history and all multiplicity of objects and events are just ripples.

BOHM   Yes. They're merely ripples and their meaning depends on understanding what underlies the ripples.

WEBER   And you're saying what underlies the ripples is the true and profound source.

BOHM   Yes.

WEBER   And you've also said that man can connect with that emptiness.

[Bohm then makes the point that the human mind as it ordinarily functions cannot understand "emptiness," which lies beyond three-dimensional consciousness.]

BOHM   It's not enough to say we are going to consider a consciousness which is more than this limited three-dimensional kind. The trouble is that we are still using the three-dimensional consciousness to guide us in that.

WEBER   To talk about it?

BOHM   To talk about it. The point of meditation would be to stop doing that.

WEBER   What you have been saying sounds like mysticism—that we are grounded in something infinite. How does it differ from what the great mystics have said?

BOHM   I don't know that there's necessarily any difference. What is mysticism? The word "mysticism" is based on the word "mystery," implying something hidden. Perhaps the ordinary mode of consciousness which elaborately obscures its mode of functioning from itself and engages in self-deception might more appropriately be called "mysticism." Or we could call it "obscurantism," and say there's an opposite mode that we could term "transparentism" (although I don't really like the suffix "ism" in any form).

WEBER   A transparence with respect to the whole.

BOHM   Yes, as opposed to obscuring the whole.

WEBER   Kierkegaard had a wonderful phrase for that. He said true religion is "to be grounded transparently in the power that constitutes one."

BOHM   Yes, that's exactly what it would mean.

WEBER   Speaking of mysticism, there is one important idea that I would like to discuss and understand and that is the idea of light. That is especially important to me because you are a physicist. Light has been used as *the* privileged metaphor in the language of mysticism and experimental religions, going back to the Greeks and the east. In all these, light is the symbol of our union with the divine. They talk about a light without shadow, an all-suffusing light, and it comes up as the central metaphor in near-death experiences. Do you have any hypothesis as to why light has been singled out as the privileged metaphor?

BOHM   If you want to relate it to modern physics (light and more generally anything moving at the speed of light, which is called the null-velocity, meaning null distance), the connection might be as follows. As an object approaches the speed of light, according to relativity, its internal space and time change so that the clocks slow down relative to other speeds, and the distance is shortened. You would find that the two ends of the light ray would have no time between them and no distance, so they would represent immediate contact. (This was pointed out by G. N. Lewis, a physical chemist, in the 1920s.) You could also say that from the point of view of present field theory, the fundamental fields are those of very high energy in which mass can be neglected, which would be essentially moving at the speed of light. Mass is a phenomenon of connecting light rays which go back and forth, sort of freezing them into a pattern.

So matter, as it were, is condensed or frozen light. Light is not merely electromagnetic waves but in a sense other kinds of waves that go at that speed. Therefore all matter is a condensation of light into patterns moving back and forth at average speeds which are less than the speed of light. Even Einstein had some hint of that idea. You could say that when we come to light we are coming to the fundamental activity in which existence has its ground, or at least coming close to it.

WEBER Why is speed the determinant?

BOHM Well, let's turn it around. If you look at Piaget and young children, movement is primary in perception. They see movement first and its unfoldment as time, and only perceive distance later. They have a tendency to say that if something went further it must have been going faster. They only learn later how to do it right. They are carrying some deeper perception into the ordinary explicate level, where it is inappropriate. In the deeper perception, movement is the primary reality in perception. The thing that is not moving is the result of the cancellation of movement. We say that there is no speed at all at light. To call it speed is merely using ordinary language. In itself, when it is self-referential, there's no time, no space, no speed.

WEBER What is it?

BOHM It's just a primary conception. As you move faster and faster according to relativity your time rates slow down and the distance gets smaller, so as you approach very high speeds your own internal time and distance become less, and therefore if you were at the speed of light you could reach from one end of the universe to the other without changing your age at all.

WEBER Isn't that saying that it's approaching a timeless state?

BOHM That's right. We're saying that existentially speaking or logically speaking, time originates out of the timeless.

WEBER This is primary and time is derivative of it, cutting it down, freezing it, arresting it.

BOHM Yes, arresting it to a certain extent, not absolutely, but to a large extent.

WEBER When mystics use the visualization of light they don't use it only as a metaphor, to them it seems to be a reality. Have they tapped into matter and energy at a level where time is absent?

BOHM It may well be. That's one way of looking at it. As I've suggested the mind has two-dimensional and three-dimensional modes of operation. It may be able to operate directly in the depths of the implicate order where this [timeless state] is the primary actuality. Then we could see the ordinary actuality as a secondary structure that emerges as an overtone on the primary structure. It's again the business of what is emphasized and what is secondary—the two kinds of music. The ordinary consciousness is one kind of music, and the other kind of consciousness is the other kind of music.

WEBER The ordinary music can become noise, cacophony and disharmony. The music from the deep-structure cannot.

BOHM The ordinary music is harmonious only in a limited area.

WEBER It's harmonious when it properly expresses this deeper harmony—Pythagoras' harmony of the spheres—but that other music is never disharmonious.

BOHM We might propose that. Let's say there are two poles where we can operate. We could operate from that extreme pole all the way to the ordinary pole, but we have accepted the distorted view that we can only operate at one pole, or very near it.

WEBER We have already closed the gate when we needn't do so.

BOHM Yes.

WEBER For the mystics there is always light. The primary clear light in the *Tibetan Book of the Dead* is the first thing the dying person is aware of. If he doesn't move towards it or away from it or feel awe or fear or manipulate it in any way as if it were outside himself, then he merges with it and is liberated, *enlightened*. Christ says: "I am the light," and so on. I've always asked myself, why light? You're saying that from the point of view of a physicist, it has to do with the absence of speed and the closeness of contact.

BOHM Light is what enfolds all the universe as well. For example, if you're looking at this room, the whole room is enfolded into the light which enters the pupil of your eye and unfolds into the image and into your brain. Light in its generalized sense (not just ordinary light) is the means by which the entire universe unfolds into itself.

WEBER Is this a metaphor for you or an actual state?

BOHM It's an actuality. At least as far as physics is concerned.

WEBER Light is energy, of course.

BOHM It's energy and it's also information—content, form and structure. It's the potential of everything.

WEBER Physicists are not satisfied that they have understood light up to now because of the particle-wave paradox, right?

BOHM Yes, I think that to understand light we'll have to understand the structure underlying time and space more deeply. You can see that these issues are related in the sense that light transcends the present structure of time and space and we will never understand it properly in that present structure.

WEBER How would implicate order philosophy handle light?

BOHM   It could handle it more naturally, mathematically speaking, because it doesn't commit itself to the idea of separate points in space; but it may say that the underlying reality is something which is not localized, and light is also something which is not localized. One view says that light moves from one place to another through a series of positions, and the other view says it doesn't do that at all. Rather, light exists, it just simply *is*.

WEBER   It *is* at all points?

BOHM   Points are defined by the intersections of different rays of light. That's the way we actually do it in perception. We infer a point from the fact that many light rays are coming from it, say a star or any point. In this view, points would be understood as the intersection of many light rays. The light is fundamental, the null ray. That's a technical term that shows the recognition of this fact in ordinary physics.

WEBER   It's where every particle of matter is in contact without the slightest gap between them.

BOHM   Yes, it's possible to have that contact without a gap.

WEBER   So light is one continuous, unbroken, undivided whole?

BOHM   You would have to look at it that way, yes; especially if you consider the quantum theory of it which says the action in it is undivided as well. What G. N. Lewis had in mind was to explain the quantum in that way. It was very mysterious to say that light is a wave which spreads continuously through space and yet that a single quantum of energy goes from one point to another. How could that happen? G. N. Lewis said this wave was some sort of an abstraction, and he said what actually happened in each ray was that there was an immediate contact from the source to the absorber. One understood the quantum in that way, that there was no spreading out of energy.

WEBER   It therefore takes no time, no transmission, no distance. There isn't any, is what you're saying.

BOHM   That is the view I'm proposing. The ordinary view is another map of it. You can take many maps of the world; one of them is Mercator's projection, which is quite good near the equator but it says near the poles that the space is infinite. So maps can have the wrong structure. We can say that the ordinary space-time is a map which holds fairly well for ordinary speeds, but when you get to the speed of light it's as wrong in structure as Mercator's projection is at the pole.

WEBER   We say light is clarity, light illumines, light is energy, some mystics have said light is love, compassion, understanding, light can make whole or heal. If light is the background of everything, what would be its relationship to the foreground?

BOHM   Light is this background which is all one but its

information-content has the capacity for immense diversity. Light can carry information about the entire universe. The other point is that light, by interactions of different rays, (as field theory in physics is investigating today), can produce particles and all the diverse structures of matter.

WEBER You've stressed *information* and that has to do with *knowing* the universe.

BOHM A kind of knowing.

WEBER The other aspect would have to do with its *being*. Maybe there's an undifferentiated realm of light and when it radiates itself as *being*, as particles, those might be its "shadows" or finite expression.

BOHM They are expressions but they are ripples on this vast ocean of light. This ocean of energy could be thought of as an ocean of light. But the information-content may be such as to predispose certain light rays to combine so that they move back and forth rather than moving straight ahead, and thus forming particles.

WEBER Are those ripples, those particles, the silhouette of that light?

BOHM Implicit in the information-content of the light—you could say that. About silhouette, I don't know. Something would have to throw the shadow. What is going to do that? The light, as it were, determines itself to make particles.

WEBER In order to do what?

BOHM I don't know. But we're proposing that this allows for a richer universe.

WEBER To be consistent one might have to say that the light transforms aspects of itself into particles in order that those particles will reveal the light.

BOHM That's right, they will reveal the potential of the light in a new way. So the light and the particles together make a higher unity. Most physicists subtract off this infinity and say it doesn't count and what's left over are the particles, and they claim that these are all that counts.

WEBER But you're claiming that's incorrect and shallow because it's subtracting off the very thing in which these particles have their roots and being.

BOHM That's why I say present physics doesn't understand it, it's merely a system of computing and getting empirical results.

WEBER We've given light a cosmological, a physical, and a metaphysical interpretation. What about the psychological and spiritual interpretation? Why do people who tap into that realm of light feel a rare peace and happiness even though light is considered neutral and value-free by physics?

BOHM The mind may have a structure similar to the universe and in the underlying movement we call empty space there is actually a tremendous energy, a movement. The particular forms which appear in the mind may be analogous to the particles, and getting to the ground of the mind might be felt as light. The essential point is not that it's light but rather this free, penetrating movement of the whole.

WEBER   Somehow the energy it triggers in the experiencer is an integrated whole and that perhaps is what accounts for this profound sense of peace.

BOHM   Yes. The analogy has often been made that even though the ocean is all stirred up and quite stormy on the surface, if you get to the bottom it is peaceful.

When matter is becoming disturbed by non-equilibrium conditions it organizes itself; it wakes up. It happens that our world is a non-equilibrium system.

ILYA PRIGOGINE

The point is that the new raw material doesn't really have to come from anywhere. ... The universe can start off with zero energy and still create matter.

STEPHEN HAWKING

Matter is like a small ripple on this tremendous ocean of energy, having some relative stability and being manifest.

DAVID BOHM

LAMA ANAGARIKA GOVINDA

3
Of matter and maya

LAMA ANAGARIKA GOVINDA

Just as *sunyata* is not only emptiness from all designations
of a limited self-nature, but also an expression of ultimate
reality, in the same way *maya* is not only the negative, the
veiling, the phenomenal form, but also the dynamic principle, which produces all forms of appearance and which
never reveals itself in the single, completed end-product,
but only in the process of becoming, in the living flow, in
infinite movement.

LAMA GOVINDA

THE mystery of matter which Bohm discussed in the last dialogue
is now taken up from the perspective of Mahayana Buddhism,
represented here by Lama Anagarika Govinda, a Tibetan Buddhist who
was both a scholar and a sage.

Lama Govinda was in his seventies when I met him, slim and frail
with large, deep-set blue eyes, a long white beard, wearing the saffron
and red robe of the Vajrayana monk. Despite his still-thick German
accent, he looked like the archetypal image of the eastern sage.

The interview took place in 1979 at the Westchester, New York,
country home of Emily Sellon, the editor of *Main Currents in Modern
Thought* and a student of eastern philosophy in her own right, with
whom Lama Govinda would stay whenever he was in the east.

There was a child-like simplicity about Lama Govinda that struck a
marked contrast to the immense erudition and philosophical sophisti-
cation I had admired in his work. This expression of innocence was
difficult to pin down. Quite aside from a fawn-like face with enormous
eyes, which may have contributed to it, there was also the matter of the
unrestrained delight Lama Govinda took in the simple things of daily
life. I remember him during a music break in the Sellon library sitting
eyes closed, his gnarled hands with long fingers spread wide on the
arms of his chair, totally absorbed in the music of Mahler. Like the
Dalai Lama and Fr. Bede—and by contrast with the much more severe
bearing of Krishnamurti—Lama Govinda gave out the message of simple joy in being.

Lama Govinda was born in Germany in 1898 and died in 1985 in California, where he had been living near the Zen Center in Marin County. He was considered one of the world's leading scholars and interpreters of Tibetan Buddhism, a system that belongs to Mahayana. *The Way of the White Clouds* (1970), an autobiography of his physical and spiritual trek, recounts the search which took him from studies in religion and philosophy in Germany, to the University of Naples and the study of Pali and Sanskrit, and finally to Ceylon, where he studied and taught for some years. His first book on the Buddha (growing out of his studies on comparative religion), was published when he was twenty-one years old. He tells of going northwards into the land of the snows for a scholars' conference in Darjeeling, falling in love with Tibet, her mountains and all-consuming interest in the spiritual life, and of his instant decision to leave his Sinhalese "tropical paradise" behind to settle in the Himalayas.

He lived there as a scholar-monk for two decades, a member of the Kargyupta Order. His studies with masters in Tibetan hermitages and monasteries gave him direct experience of the teachings of Tibetan Buddhism, which he later expressed with the clarity and insight for which his books are famous. After some two decades in Tibet, he and his Indian wife, artist Li Gotami, settled in India in a monastery near Almora high in the Himalayas. He became the spiritual head of the Arya Maitreya Mandala, a Buddhist order of the Tibetan Vajrayana. Lama Govinda, then in his eighties, spent the last few years of his life in the San Francisco Bay area, first on Alan Watts's houseboat near Sausalito, later in Mill Valley.

A scholar of Sanskrit and Tibetan as well as European languages, Lama Govinda published many books on Buddhist philosophy and religion. One of these, *Foundations of Tibetan Mysticism* (1969) has become a classic in the field, cited for its rare insight and beauty. In it he argues that the key to wisdom lies in understanding the relationship of the particular to the universal, to perceive unity in multiplicity, spirit in matter, the sacred within the secular, and the role of individual consciousness within cosmic consciousness. These ideas, partly explored in this dialogue, are parallel to the implicate order philosophy of David Bohm. Like Bohm, Lama Govinda urges the integration of these perspectives, since without this harmony our existence remains truncated.

Lama Govinda's life reflected this drive toward integration; it became the leitmotif of his existence. With astonishing balance he combined the intellectual life of the scholar, the contemplative life of the sage, the meditative life of the mystic, the activist life of the explorer and mountain climber, the artist's life of the painter of the Tibetan landscape, the monastic life in a Buddhist order, the secular life of the husband. He described himself as "an Indian National of European descent and

Buddhist faith, belonging to a Tibetan Order and believing in the Brotherhood of Man."

Like all the sages in this book, Lama Govinda draws contrasts between the ego and true individuality, and like most of the figures here he welcomes the integration of eastern mysticism with western physics. I must confess that I found the frankness of Lama Govinda's comments about Krishnamurti somewhat startling, yet I clearly recall that his tone was characteristically gentle and without any trace of malice. Of all the figures in this book, the one who most closely resembles Lama Govinda is Fr. Bede Griffiths, another western expatriate in India. Chapter 9 draws some further comparisons between the two sages.

WEBER   Can we discuss matter and *maya* in Mahayana Buddhism? *Maya* is often misunderstood as "illusion" (a veil), implying deception and the lack of reality, but I gather that the term really refers to the creative aspect of reality.

GOVINDA   In Buddhism this is a quite typical view. In [Hindu] Advaita, *maya* is regarded as that which prevents you from completeness, but in Buddhism *maya* is something which may even be worshipped! One of the deities is called Mahamaya, because it is a creative force without which we can't exist. In other words, the moment that you understand *maya as maya*, at that very moment *maya* ceases to exist.

SELLON   It's like creative imagination, and it's creative imagination that makes the world.

GOVINDA   Exactly. *Maya*, according to Hindu definition, is a divine force. If this is so, how can it be wrong? Then we should accept it as such.

SELLON   So in that sense, the world is what we have created by the act of imagination.

GOVINDA   Well, we live in a world which we have created or which is created by our senses, or limited by our senses. But since this is not the ultimate world, if there is one, then we should accept the world in its limitations. It's ridiculous to say, "I want to see the world without *maya*." Nobody can see the world without *maya* because everyone is in the world; it is impossible to stand outside. So the idea of a world-in-itself is pure nonsense.

WEBER   Would a Buddha figure be capable of seeing the world without *maya*?

GOVINDA   I think a Buddha is not ominiscient in the ordinary sense of the word, which is "all-knowing." The Buddha, for instance, didn't know anything about science in the modern sense, such as physics. But he was far superior to other people because he saw the essentials of life. And he confined himself to practical knowledge. He said, "How can I be happier? And how can I avoid being unhappy?" That was the problem to which he addressed himself, and he solved it. Later generations tried to make the Buddha into a kind of impossible ideal figure with complete omniscience, complete vision, complete virtue, and other "completenesses."

Therefore the term *avidya* does not mean ignorance in the ultimate sense, but rather the ignorance concerned with one's own ego. An ignorant man is one who takes his ego as ultimate reality, while a person who can overcome the sense of ego is not ignorant. Therefore the word *avidya* is quite wrongly translated as "ignorance" per se. One should rather call it limitation. And the opposite of *avidya* is liberation. Liberation from what? From ignorance, from that wrong confinement in the ego. That means complete openness. Thus I would translate *nirvana* as "openness," because *nirvana* is not a sterile end point. That would be terrible. My idea of *nirvana* is not eternal bliss, but rather an openness which allows us to proceed.

WEBER Is that like the extinction of the illusion of ego, which from that openness leads to other states of awareness?

GOVINDA Yes, that may be. I would not say the extinction of the illusion of the ego entirely, but rather the overcoming of the illusion of the ego as something static and confined. The moment you can see that your ego is only something which you need in order to center your mind ...

SELLON A device?

GOVINDA Yes, a device for action. You need the ego for that. I don't expect a person to be completely egoless.

WEBER It should be in proportion.

GOVINDA Yes, in proportion. The ego shouldn't be too important in one's life. And so I think in Buddhism the middle way really lies between the extremes.

WEBER Do you think that most Buddhist texts bring that out clearly enough?

GOVINDA Three-quarters of Buddhist books are useless! We should take the essence, not the surface teaching. The surface means simply the accumulation of what has happened through the centuries, which may have had some significance in former times—in fact, it probably did. But we should not try to imitate the achievements of other times; we should try to take the essence of the teaching which is relevant for our own present time.

WEBER You said that although the west now has a great interest in Buddhism and other eastern systems, it cannot gain these insights by merely taking over the form, that we must revitalize the inner essence by clothing it in a new form. But do we have the symbols and icons of our own for building new forms?

GOVINDA I think we should apply our intelligence and our own

feeling to the main issues. The important thing is not what oth .
people have to say, but rather what we experience. That means we
should go to the very central question which the Buddha put to
himself. The Buddha was historically the first person who began
to think logically. Before him, it was only a matter of belief, and
one could believe in almost anything. But the Buddha for the first
time said, "It is not what you believe that is important, but what
you do and what you are and what you feel. Only if a teaching is
consistent with your own experience should you accept it. You
should not accept even my own teaching on hearsay, but only if
you understand it from your own point of view." I do not know
of any other religious leader who has had a similarly free attitude,
except perhaps Lao Tze.

WEBER   If we could have a genuine synthesis of eastern spiritual
insight with western science, then we'd create a profound vision of
the universe.

GOVINDA   I think that we should be able to combine our knowledge
in science with our experience of ourselves. This means that we
would make science more "lively," and at the same time our life
more scientific. We need both sides. The west needs the east, and
the east needs the west. If both combine we shall be complete.
East and west are like the two sides of our brain: the one is factual,
the other is imaginative. The imaginativeness of the east should
compensate for the matter-of-factness of the west, and vice versa.

WEBER   There might be an additional meaning to that. As you know,
some writers are now attempting to discern within the content of
the ancient eastern doctrines a parallel to the doctrines of modern
physics regarding space, time, energy.

GOVINDA   Yes. I think that Capra, for example (*The Tao of Physics*)
is quite right. Modern physics is nearer to eastern conceptions
than to mechanistic philosophy. The west, by its own impetus, is
now coming nearer the east; an amalgamation is therefore possible
because there is no longer any contradiction. If one goes deeply
into modern science one finds that it confirms the old experiences.
Even today our idea of the universe is so hazy as to be almost
incomprehensible. We have to admit that we know nothing.

This is very important. Indeed, ignorance is bliss. I must say,
in contradiction to the usual view of *avidya*, that I sometimes like
it! For instance, life gets its meaning and its value mostly through
not knowing what is to come. Take the case of a person who goes
to a football game. If he knew the results beforehand, there would
be little pleasure for him in the game. It is just the *not* knowing—
the tension between the knowing and the not-knowing—which
makes our pleasure. It would be terrible if we were to know what
our life in the future would be.

57

said that a philosophy must spring from the condition
...me. In our own time this is difficult by comparison to
...m of the ancients.

...I think we should be governed by the needs of our time,
...what the ancients did, but rather what we can do now.
...cients lived under very different conditions from ours, and
we must try to find our own way. For instance, if you live in a
great city, you must suffer its noise, its congestion, its turbulence.
But you can be very still even in the midst of noise. For instance,
in Burmese monasteries the monks have a habit, when learning a
thing by heart, of pronouncing it aloud. You have no idea of the
noise! I couldn't imagine anything noisier than a monastery. But
the monks are not disturbed, as a westerner would be, because
they simply don't hear it any more, so it does not disturb their
peace.

WEBER   Is meditation valuable even in the absence of monastic conditions and instruction, in the midst of our hectic western life?

GOVINDA   Yes, I think so. It is really better without instruction
because most instructions are misleading. You see, whatever you
can tell to another is merely your own opinion. It may be all right
for you, but not for the other person. Therefore instruction can be
a very dangerous thing. A real guru is not one who tries to impress
himself on others but rather one who brings out the qualities of
the other person. Only a really good psychologist tries to teach his
pupil to be independent of *him*.

WEBER   That recalls Milarepa, who certainly was given discouraging
tasks over and over again by his master.

GOVINDA   Yes, yes. You know, by the way, the story of how Milarepa
built his different houses: triangular house, round house, square
house, and so on. Now these designs are the forms of the different
chakras in the human body. [*Chakras* are centers of energy in the
subtle, inner bodies that govern our physical and emotional well-
being according to both Hindu and Buddhist philosophy. An interesting possibility is that these *chakras*, said to be seven in number, are composed of what Bohm refers to as "subtle" matter, not
explicate (i.e. visible) but implicate matter.] So Milarepa is made
to build up one *chakra* and then destroy it, and build the next and
again destroy it, and so on again and again. You are free only from
that which you can create and destroy at the same time. This is
very important. It is like the process of meditation, which moves
from the construction to the dissolution of forms.

WEBER   In the west we think of meditation as *alternating* with action:
we withdraw, we meditate, and then we go about our business. Is
it possible to meditate in the midst of worldly action?

GOVINDA   A meditation which cannot prove itself in action is useless.

In such a case you believe that you have achieved something, while you have achieved nothing. But if you prove the result of your meditation in action, then you will gain a kind of control. Meditation should be an opening of ourselves to all the possibilities. Just as a flower opens to let the sun come in, so whatever comes up in your meditation should be accepted. You should become like a vessel which is being filled again. And through the strength which has been accumulated you can perform your actions.

Then it's completely natural. In the Tibetan tradition, for instance, people go about their work: they fill their day, they cook their meal, they do their tasks, they clean their rooms, and make all these actions a part of their meditation. That is really the highest form of meditative accomplishment. Whatever they do, whatever they think, whatever they experience—all belongs to the state of meditation. But these people have very little contact with the outer world.

Actually, meditation is a much more natural thing than we believe. Most people think of meditation as a special state outside life and our usual activities but don't take the time to find out who they are or what is happening to them. Meditation is merely a natural state of quietness in which all those things which are ordinarily suppressed in us are allowed to well up. Today many people are giving out a lot of rules about meditation: what to do and what not to do and how to do it. But I always say, don't try to force anything; simply collect yourself. Simply be centered in yourself for a while. Then whatever comes to you, whatever rises up within you, is significant. And the less you expect, the more you will get. I think the attitude of meditation should be a kind of interested joy. The quality of joy is the best proof of the efficacy of meditation. If it gives you more joy, it is worthwhile. If it doesn't, don't force it.

WEBER   Some people when they first meditate and experience a larger dimension of consciousness feel fear because suddenly they are in such an unfamiliar place.

GOVINDA   I don't see why there should be any fear. I simply feel that human beings should be like a vessel to be filled. Unless they empty themselves first, they can't be filled nor can they enjoy the fullness. Once again, I advocate receptiveness. Make yourself receptive.

SELLON   Don't you think it is fear of the loss of ego, since most people identify themselves through the sense of ego—with the ego? This is the primary illusion. They cling to the idea of the "I" because they feel that without it they're lost. There is nobody there.

GOVINDA   That may be. Here again, the difficulty is due to ignorance of what one's self is. It comes always to the same point.

WEBER   That obliterates the division between the secular and the
sacred, and integrates one's life. It's what we all long for.

SELLON   It makes everything one does have a kind of significance.
So many people today feel that their lives are meaningless. If we
could regain that dimension of consciousness in which we see all
action as significant because it is done in this spirit, meaning would
return to us. It is part of the rhythm of life, isn't it, like breathing
in and breathing out.

GOVINDA   Exactly. Therefore, I think one of the best meditations is
on the breath, it is one of the best ways to convince yourself of the
truth of *anatman* [the doctrine that there is no static self in man].

WEBER   Would that give one experiential conviction of *anatman?*

GOVINDA   *Anatman* does not mean that there is nothing eternal in us
but rather that the eternal consists of a continuous giving and
taking. You draw in your breath from outside yourself, you transform it within yourself, and then return it to nature. You cannot
take anything which you don't give back. Everything in life—
whether your breath, or your food, or your material possessions—
everything which is taken in must be given back.

WEBER   And you've made the point in your book on meditation, that
if you hang on to anything, it's death. [*Creative Meditation and
Multi-Dimensional Consciousness.*]

GOVINDA   I think the impermanence is the one thing which frees us.
Isn't it so? If everything were permanent, everlasting and un-
changeable, it would be a terrible situation , much like those modern plastic substances which cannot be destroyed and which we
can never be rid of.

WEBER   The notion of the *anatman* confuses and troubles people
when they try to relate it to karma. Karma is described as the law
of universal justice, so that everything I sow will I reap: everything
I intend has consequences. The difficulty is reconciling these consequences with the fact that there is no permanent "agent" to do
the reaping.

GOVINDA   There is an agent, but not a static one. This means that
every person is the embodiment of the life-force. But this life-force
is something flowing, something growing, something developing.
So you cannot say that there's a closed agent—something which
abides in itself, separated from the rest. But still, we can speak of
our psyches, can't we?

WEBER   That's the problem, Lama. Even if we accept that
whatever-is-there coheres around intents and purposes and that it
is not a thing or a substance, there is still difficulty reconciling this
with the ascription of karma and responsibility for a past-life—
circumstances which that cluster has set into motion and which is
now working itself out in "my" life.

GOVINDA   What you call your life is, so to speak, your line of successive development. That means you have a different manifestation of your life-energy which goes on in one consecutive line. In this regard it is different from all other lines, but as a force in itself it is not different. What this really means is that it is both different and not different.

WEBER   That's difficult to grasp.

GOVINDA   Well, you can say that all human beings are human beings, but at the same time each human being is different from every other. Therefore there is both unity and diversity. These two poles of existence always co-exist; we can't have the one without the other.

WEBER   You don't see any conflict, then, between the idea of *anatman*—that there is no soul substance such as the Hindus postulate—and ascription of personal karmic responsibility?

GOVINDA   No. You are responsible for your line of action and development which consequently unfolds. But if you want to speak of justice, that is another question. We can speak of justice within our own frame of reference. But it is impossible to moralize about nature or to extrapolate our notions of ethics to the natural world.

WEBER   Earthquakes, for example, can't be "unjust."

GOVINDA   Exactly. And we cannot even say that such an event has anything to do with karma. Natural forces act according to their own nature. They are neither good nor bad, neither just nor unjust.

WEBER   In physics, people now talk about the "world line of a particle," which is the whole history of its exchanges of energy. That sounds similar to what you are saying.

GOVINDA   Yes. I think that the ultimate concepts of physics may lead us to a greater understanding of this whole question. It is very interesting, for instance, that in modern physics the more logical you are, the more wrong you are. This shows very clearly the limits of our logic. Actually, the universe often seems unreasonable to us because we apply our own logic to something which is not of the same category. We never can say where a particle is and what it does, and so we can only guess, or define it as either particle or a wave. Yet it is neither one nor the other, but both.

You asked, for example, about the "logic" of reincarnation. I don't think we can reduce the idea of reincarnation to pure logic. Since our beginnings are infinite, and the causes are also infinite, the combinations must necessarily be infinite. It is impossible to explain such things with our linear logic since the cause and effect, from the universal point of view, are multi-dimensional. For instance in the *Lankavatara Sutra*, I was impressed by the description of karma as "habit energy." Having done something once, we are impelled to do the same thing again under similar circumstances.

Karma is indeed habit energy, and the moment we get out of the habit of something, it is gone.

SELLON   It is a question of perception, too, isn't it? As soon as we perceive things differently, then they are different for us.

GOVINDA   Yes, that also; it is a very subtle thing. And therefore I identify the idea of karma with the idea of character, because our attitude is our character.

SELLON   The law of karma is therefore not mechanical.

GOVINDA   Not at all. You see, most people enjoy the idea that there is a kind of universal revenge.

SELLON   Even if I can't get back at you, the universe will!

GOVINDA   Karma is a very general term which can mean quite different things. In Jainism, karma would mean the effect of an action, whatever that action might be, without taking into account the mental intention behind the action. In Buddhism, however, karma implies volition, and according to this teaching there is no karma without volition.

In modern law one speaks of motive. For instance, wanting to murder someone is not the same thing as actually doing so. Yet the motive is regarded as of more importance than the outcome. Take the example of a man working as a mason on some new construction. He has a brick in his hand that slips from his grasp, falls, and kills a person walking below. That man had no intention of killing anyone; it was a pure accident and therefore he would not be regarded as a murderer according to law. But if he were to have a brick in his hand and seeing his enemy pass beneath the scaffolding he aimed at him and tried to kill him with the brick, even if he missed and failed he would be a murderer, because he *intended* to kill. This constitutes the whole difference between the idea of karma in Jainism and Hinduism (although in the latter there may be different explanations) and in Buddhism. The Buddhist scriptures make it quite clear that karma is identified by volition, for they say, "Cetanaham bhikkhave kamman vadami." ("Volition, O monks, is what I call action.")

WEBER   Can we discuss suffering and compassion as they relate to the ego?

GOVINDA   I think that to have a life entirely free from suffering would also mean a life free from compassion. Because compassion for others is the last suffering of an Arhat, of an accomplished one. Certainly I wouldn't care for a state of existence without compassion. Therefore, in Mahayana or in Vajrayana we regard "saints" as the greatest egoists for the reason that they want liberation for themselves; they want to be left alone in peace; they want to avoid all suffering; they want to escape from the pains and responsibilities of human life. That's egoistic.

WEBER   The ego seems to block this compassion whereas individuality expresses it.

GOVINDA   Individuality is only a focal point of the universe. You see, individuality is not confined to limits. It is rather a focal point of radiation which contains the whole universe. So individuality is no contradiction to universality.

WEBER   But the illusion of ego is.

GOVINDA   The illusion of ego is different.

WEBER   In Buddhist meditation one visualizes a compassionate figure such as a Bodhisattva, and this inactivates the fear of the loss of self?

GOVINDA   Yes, to a certain extent, because you identify yourself with your vision and in so far, you are able to transcend yourself.

WEBER   So what remains is not a nothingness but it is something that pours in.

GOVINDA   Very much so. Therefore I say that *sunyata* is not a negative concept at all. *Sunyata* means the creative void out of which everything comes into existence. This again shows a close parallelism with modern science.

SELLON   It is a plenum as well as a void.

GOVINDA   A plenum-void. This expression, which was created by Evans-Wentz, is quite an accurate description.

WEBER   Can we talk about this emptiness or egolessness?

GOVINDA   I think that in general all religious thinking is founded on this principle. You have to overcome your ego-sense. It is not that you abolish the ego, but that you should not be bound to it or by it. Because at the moment you free yourself from the illusion that the ego is a changeless substance, in that moment you achieve liberation. Originally, in the *Upanishads*, the Atman was conceived as a universal center within the self: Atman is equal to Brahman. In that sense, it is quite acceptable. But the idea of Brahman was not at all popular in the time of the Buddha. When he speaks of Brahma it always means the personal Brahma, never the universal Brahman. This shows that the idea of the Brahman, which had been propagated by the *Upanishads*, probably had not reached the people in the Buddha's surroundings.

WEBER   Can one correlate what the Hindus meant by Brahman with what the Buddha meant by *Dharmakaya* [i.e., truth or law]?

GOVINDA   I think Brahman stands simply for the oneness of the world. One of the associated ideas, propagated mainly by the *Advaita* philosophy, is that the only value in the world is this oneness, and the single central illusion which you have to overcome is that of diversity. But it is naturally impossible to accept oneness and to deny diversity because these are the two poles of the same reality. If oneness and diversity occur together, then I can understand that there can be diversity in oneness. But oneness by itself is meaningless. It is like one big mush—featureless, without any differentiation. Therefore I say that the Buddhist *advaya* is quite different from *advaita*. *Advaya* means "the not twoness," whereas *advaita* means the one against the many—the one and not the many, or the denial of the many. Everything is then the same. This idea nowadays really hampers India because whatever you may discuss, Indians will tell you, "Oh, that's all one; it's the same." Actually, it is useless even to discuss anything if a person doesn't understand the uniqueness and the significance of different things.

SELLON   In the Judeo-Christian tradition, the emphasis is on individuality, the uniqueness of the person. Perhaps it's been overexaggerated in the west, but it does furnish the other of the two poles.

GOVINDA   Certainly. We can be unique within ourselves but this doesn't mean that we are absolutely separated from everything else. It means, rather, that my standpoint is unique for the simple reason that I occupy one particular point in space. I see the world from this point and since everyone else occupies a different point no one can see the same world that I do. Therefore I say there cannot be a reality-in-itself, for where is the person who could experience it? Ego and Atman became more or less synonymous in the popular mind. That is why the Buddha had to speak of *anatman*. He never spoke about the reality of the Atman; he simply said that everything you can think of, everything you can recognize, is certainly *anatman*. The moment you identify it, it is not Atman. So *anatman* is more of a psychological statement than a doctrine. Such a psychological statement is a much safer way to deal with the subject because then, even if you think of the old idea of Atman, which is beautiful, you cannot mistake it for your ego.

WEBER   So you feel there is a danger in generalizing to such a point that one is left with an abstraction.

GOVINDA   Yes. For instance take Ramana Maharshi. He was a wonderful man and I really admire him, but I don't admire his books.

WEBER   Why is that, Lama?

GOVINDA   He says his first question was "Who am I?" But if you start with that as a precondition then you go wrong from the very beginning, because you are searching for an "I" which isn't there.

WEBER   How should he have phrased the question?

GOVINDA   He should have asked "Who am I not?" That would have been more sensible, to my mind—more psychological.

SELLON   If he had asked "What is this I?" that too would have been different?

GOVINDA   Yes. If he had asked "What is an 'I'?" he would have come to the conclusion that nobody really can define it. In the moment when he says "Who am I?" he presupposes a "who" and projects it into the "I."

WEBER   In other words, he set up the wrong equation to begin with.

GOVINDA   He was of course a convinced Vedantist, and so everything that he says naturally fits into the Vedanta. He meant very well, I know that, and as a person I appreciate him very much, but his person was far more important than his teaching. In his person he really embodied some of the greatest religious ideas. But when he tried to put these ideas into words, they seem to be mere repetitions from the *advaita*—nothing really original.

WEBER   What you said earlier about this "mish-mash" of the whole is very interesting. We had a somewhat analogous situation in the west when Hegel objected to Schelling and ridiculed him by terming his Absolute "empty," "the infinite night in which all cows are black," meaning it was so general that it had no content.

GOVINDA   Yes, but Hegel was also one of the great generalizers—a typical logician. He was very logical, therefore very unreal. This represented, so to say, the apex of that kind of European thinking.

WEBER   In your last book you said that once a person chooses a path, whatever it might be, he should pursue it and not mix traditions— taking some Hindu elements, some Buddhist—lifting them from their context. Do you feel strongly about this?

GOVINDA   Yes, I do. Because even if you choose a wrong path, it is better to follow it to the end and realize it is wrong rather than tread no path at all. Eclectic paths lead nowhere because you are continually making false starts—here, there and everywhere. You always have to come back to the starting point in order to begin a new way, so in the end you never get anywhere.

It is just like scaling a mountain. You can approach the mountain from the south or from the east or from the west or from the north. Any one of these points is all right for an attack on the mountain. But what if you start from the north and then suddenly change your mind, go back to the base, and begin your climb from the east? And then, when halfway up, you think "No, no, this is also no good," and so you go back once more and start all over again from the south. Obviously, you will never reach the top from any of these directions because you never pursue one path to the end.

SELLON   Lama, your metaphor involves action, doesn't it? Walking a path. Yet it is possible to study one's route in advance and compare it with other routes. What do you feel about the usefulness of comparative studies?

GOVINDA   I have nothing against them in principle but I have found that most people who study comparative religion have no real knowledge. They come to nothing, because you can go on forever comparing and comparing and comparing, with no results.

SELLON That's true if you only lay them side-by-side without any commitment to pursue them experientially. But if you really are seeking for light on some obscure corner which you want badly to understand, can't this method help?

GOVINDA It's all right to compare different traditions once you have chosen your own way and can no longer be disturbed in your own direction. But if you try to combine many things from here and there and to include everything, you finally end up with nothing.

SELLON In other words, you have to follow one beam of light?

GOVINDA I think so. You should follow your conviction: the way which you feel is good for you. Other people may go other ways, but you can at least pursue your own way with full conviction.

SELLON However, you do feel that a person should make his own choice?

GOVINDA I would say that in the beginning people should look at everything, examine everything. So that they know enough to make a real choice. It is clear that you should know something about Christianity, about Hinduism, about Islam, about Buddhism before you choose, because if you accept one thing without knowing anything else, then it is not choice but chance, isn't it? Therefore one should undergo a certain preparation, make a certain judgment for oneself, but once the choice is made, then one should follow quite consistently the way which one has chosen.

SELLON Some people, such as Seyyed Nasr, the Islamic scholar, hold that you should follow the tradition into which you were born for even though certain individuals may feel alien to it, it is nevertheless the right path for you, part of your cultural and spiritual heritage.

GOVINDA I think that is nonsense. It is perhaps true that most people feel more comfortable within their own tradition. But I disagree that one *has* to follow one's tradition. If one is not convinced of it, one should not follow it.

WEBER The opposite extreme to Nasr would be Krishnamurti, who says if you follow *any* path you're lost, by definition. You can't follow any tradition; that is already poisoning the well. Do you have any reaction to that?

GOVINDA I think that Krishnamurti, who always speaks of the unconditioned, is one of the most conditioned persons in the world. He is so conditioned that he simply can't get out of his own thinking or even his own vocabulary. He is still influenced by the experiences of his youth and early childhood; his tragedy is that he can't rid himself of them. He is an intelligent man, but he is caught in this circular thinking; he goes around and around the question of existence and finally loses himself in pure abstraction. I must say I enjoy hearing Krishnamurti speak; he is a very good speaker, accomplished and pleasant. But when I come away from his lecture, I feel that I have gained nothing. And I have found that he rejects even those who have tried to support him, because he doesn't want to be confronted with his own ideas. Of course, a person without humor has little wisdom, and Krishnamurti is entirely lacking in humor. Also, he is impatient of the slightest contradiction or the slightest question which doesn't fit into his system.

SELLON   I'm certain that he would reject the idea that he has a system.

GOVINDA   Yes, naturally. But actually he tries to follow many of the principles of Zen Buddhism, even though he says he has never read anything in his whole life. I cannot, however, believe this is true or that he has never heard about Zen.

WEBER   He claims that any tradition—any path, even any idea of a path, any ideal—places an obstacle in your way. I gather from what you are saying that you feel quite the opposite: that it can guide and further us.

GOVINDA   Yes, indeed. I believe Krishnamurti would certainly profit from the study of other people's thoughts. He would certainly understand them better. To my mind, it's a kind of self-aggrandizement to say, "I've been influenced by nobody; I'm all and only my own." We are all influenced by many people; we all have to be grateful to many people. Why not admit it? Instead of talking about being unconditioned, one should say, "I have to be *universally* conditioned," that is, conditioned not by one thing or a few things but by all things. We are all conditioned. It is better to admit it. The mistake, or the failure, of most people is that they think only of one or two elements that condition us, not of the infinite conditioning to which life subjects us. But if we could see the whole of our conditioning, then we really would be greater than any of those things. No person in the world can be unconditioned. It's impossible. Nor should he wish to be. For such an idea contradicts the whole of life—renders it meaningless and invalid. Rather, we should always aim that our conditioning be by the whole, which is infinite.

I take the view that the creation ultimately depends on some non-physical or trans-physical reality, spiritual in nature.

RUPERT SHELDRAKE

All of nature is organized according to the activity of significance.

DAVID BOHM

What could be more anthropomorphic in human modelling than to say that everything is a machine? Machines are entirely and specifically human creations.

RUPERT SHELDRAKE

The electron, in so far as it responds to a meaning in its environment, is observing the environment. It is doing exactly what human beings are doing.

DAVID BOHM

RUPERT SHELDRAKE

4

Morphogenetic fields: nature's habits

RUPERT SHELDRAKE

Those who think that form is unimportant, will miss the spirit as well, while those who cling to form lose the very spirit which they tried to preserve. Form and movement are the secret of life, and the key to immortality.

LAMA GOVINDA

THE dialogue with Sheldrake contains the most controversial material in this book. Whether or not this has to do with his age is an open question. In his early forties, Sheldrake is the youngest man in the book and perhaps his daring theories are less surprising in one who grew up in the England of the 1960s, which along with California was the fountainhead of the counter-culture. But meeting Sheldrake shatters all the cliché images of the Beatles era, for in many ways he projects the epitome of British "respectability," with an elite educational background and impeccable manners to match.

It may be important to note this, since Sheldrake's theories have caused a storm. On the publication of his book, *A New Science of Life: The Hypothesis of Formative Causation* in 1981, *Nature*, one of England's most prestigious scientific journals, called it "the best candidate for burning there has been for many years," while the no less eminent *New Scientist* declared, "It is quite clear that one is dealing here with an important scientific inquiry into the nature of biological and physical reality." What was it that so threatened a leading twentieth-century scientific journal that it resorted to language that evokes the Inquisition or a totalitarian bonfire? This question poses itself all the more sharply because of Sheldrake's impeccable educational credentials.

Rupert Sheldrake studied natural sciences at Clare College, Cambridge University. After spending a year studying philosophy and the history of science as a Frank Knox Fellow at Harvard, he returned to Cambridge to take a Ph.D. in biochemistry and cell biology between 1967 and 1973. At Cambridge he was the Rosenheim Fellow of the Royal Society and carried out research on the development of plants and the aging of cells. Sheldrake felt so strongly that he wanted to use his scientific knowledge to help lessen suffering that he decided to work in India. Between 1974 and 1978 he was on the staff of the International Crop Research Institute for the Semi-Arid Tropics at Hyderabad, working on the physiology of tropical legume crops. He still spends four months each year in India as a Consultant Plant Physiologist at the Institute (ICRISAT), living, he told me, not by the lavish standards of the west, but as his Indian colleagues do. His research deals with maximizing the food crops that India and other developing countries so desperately need.

A part of his stay there always becomes a retreat. For Sheldrake this means Shantivanam, Fr. Bede Griffiths's ashram in southern India where Sheldrake spent eighteen months writing his book. In contrast to its stormy reception in scientific circles, *A New Science of Life* was hailed by holistically inclined intellectuals in other professions from California to New York, in Europe and Asia, for whom Sheldrake became *the* biologist, just as Bohm and Capra had become *the* physicists a few years earlier. Scarcely a conference on holistic thought, or on science and mysticism, is held in the world these days without Sheldrake being asked to represent the biological sciences, in which mechanism still largely prevails.

This is due no doubt to the combination of Sheldrake's theories and his attractive personality and style. He is a clear and well-organized speaker and, despite his radical ideas, conservative and careful in his language. He appears, in some ways, like the prototypical Englishman with a ruddy complexion, blue eyes, and fine-boned features. There is a mass of curly brown hair, a tall and slender build, and boyish good looks that belie his age. In the many settings in which I saw him— Princeton, India, Cambridge (Massachusetts), New York and London— there was a sophisticated ease about him, the sense of fitting in any- where, from little bookshops on Harvard Square to a dusty Indian village. Most of the dialogue that follows took place at my home in Princeton, where Sheldrake stayed for several days in 1982; a few brief passages come from a *ReVision* piece which he and Bohm had taped a few weeks earlier in Ojai; a small section was the result of our trans- atlantic telephone conversation last summer.

Sheldrake's hypothesis of a morphogenetic field reintroduces vitalism into biology, but its implications extend beyond biology to the other sciences, to the social sciences, especially psychology; and to politics. One of the recurrent questions in these dialogues is: What, if anything, stands behind our visible world and what governs the creatures in it? Is there a grand principle or are they ruled by the blind, mechanical impulses of inert molecules combining at random? Like Bohm, who addresses this question in Chapter 2, Sheldrake believes that something deeper than blind chance governs the material world. He postulates morphogenetic fields, from *morphe*, form, and *genesis*, coming-into-being. These invisible fields, the matrix for all form, development, and behaviour, can operate across time and space, an "action-at-a-distance" link of organisms that also has implications for parapsychology. In Sheldrake's frequent examples of this, the first bonding of a proton with two electrons created the hydrogen atom and caused later such bondings to be repeated and to establish themselves with fairly well-defined form and behaviour through a phenomenon he terms "morphic resonance." Sheldrake refuses to speculate on where the first hydrogen and oxygen atoms learned to come together as a water molecule, saying it is the proverbial dilemma of the chicken and the egg, whose solution lies outside of science.

In this dialogue, Sheldrake explains his basic theory and relates it to Bohm's implicate order. You may want to note his position on creativity and spontaneity in nature because this issue becomes central in Chapter 10, the dialogue with Prigogine, and to ponder their similarities and differences. Sheldrake is often faulted by scientists for lack of empirical evidence, a topic he tries to deal with in the dialogue. He also has asked the world-wide community of scientists to help him test the presence of his morphogenetic fields by proposing experiments that will put them to the test. The Tarrytown Foundation has offered a prize of $10,000 for the best experimental design to test the fields, to be awarded by the end of 1985; and the BBC in London has made its facilities available to Sheldrake to conduct "learning experiments" with some millions of its viewers. If Sheldrake's theory works, the *rate* of learning should increase exponentially in each new group of participants.

WEBER   Why did you develop your theory of formative causation?

SHELDRAKE   Because biology today s undergoing a major, internal crisis. On the one hand, in the study of modern biology you have chemists and physicists who, in fact, know very little about animals and plants; they wander or wade into biology through biophysics or biochemistry or what's now called molecular biology. Grind organisms up, get crystallized molecules from them, analyze the molecules by x-ray crystallography using standard physical techniques, come up with theories about the structure of molecules, and then start fantasizing about the whole of life. Such people, who are now the most vociferous defenders of this kind of mechanistic approach, are not in fact biologists. They're physicists or chemists who really have not had a classical training in biology.

Those who actually work on truly biological problems, the coming into being of the form of embryos, for example, have all along been the people in biology most prone to dissidence. For example Driesch, one of the first defectors from the mechanistic view, was an embryologist. He went over to the school of vitalism at the turn of the century as a result of his experiments in embryology, where the results again and again showed that the whole embryo was more than the sum of its parts. For example, he would cut bits out and they would regenerate; the whole would be restored.

He thought this showed you could not analyze it or understand it in a mechanistic manner. But vitalism went out of fashion in the 1920s. People began working within the organismic framework, derived partly from Whitehead, which says that there is a definite property of wholeness that enables organisms to develop, and it can't be reduced to an analysis of its parts. That's when in 1922 the idea of morphogenetic fields was first introduced by Alexander Gurwitsch in Russia; independently by Paul Weiss in Vienna in 1925. It was introduced by developmental biologists trying to account for these properties of wholeness which aren't reducible to the interaction of the parts. Von Bertalanffy, in 1933, in his book *Modern Theories of Development*, summarized these various approaches within the organismic paradigm; he went on to develop General Systems Theory. Then Waddington, in a later generation, took the idea of morphogenetic fields further in his concept of the chreode. René Thom begins his mathematical theories of morphogenesis with Waddington's ideas. Waddington had a series of students, one of whom is Brian Goodwin, who has continued developing the idea of morphogenetic fields. He's a developmental biologist. And there are many others. So you see there's a long, dissident tradition within biology which has been groping towards something that goes beyond the mechanistic-reductionist view. This tradition, in which I include myself, has been there all the time. And it's always been strongest among developmental biologists and embryologists, whereas the mechanistic-reductionistic view has always been strongest among physiologists, biochemists, and biophysicists.

WEBER   What's the essence of your hypothesis?

SHELDRAKE   It's easiest to explain the essence starting from the problems that the theory primarily addresses, which are the problems of biological morphogenesis, the "coming into being" of form in living organisms. The task is to explain the development of form in animals and plants. And the reason why it's a problem is that as form develops, as the embryo grows, the complexity of structure gets greater and greater; more form comes from less. This is a problem because there's no clear relation between cause and effect.

Normally, in our physical notions of causality, we have an equivalence of cause and effect. The amount of momentum, energy, and change before a given process is the same as the amount after it. That's why we can construct an equation. All of these things that physical equations deal with are conserved quantities. But forms aren't like that: If you burn a flower to ashes, the mass and energy are conserved, but the form of the flower is simply destroyed. Form isn't a conserved quantity and we can't measure it exactly in terms of mathematical principles. No one can say a chick embryo contains ten to twelve units of form. Attempts to specify quantitative measures of form haven't been successful in biology. So, we're in a position where we can't specify quantities of form, but we *can* see that the complexity of form increases. And this increasing complexity seems to defy all physical explanations.

In biology, the mechanistic (or reductionistic) pitch has been to say that this complexity of form emerges as a result of complex interactions between the parts of the developing organism. But beyond saying that, they haven't said much more. It's simply left as an open question as to how forms appear.

The theory of morphogenetic fields proposes that there's a field, or a spatial structure, which is responsible for the development of the form. And if the morphogenetic field is there and has a pre-existing form, if it shapes the developing organism, there then would be a causal equivalence. You'd have something which already had the appropriate complexity of form molding the developing organism; the morphogenetic field would play a causal role. The developing organism would be within the morphogenetic field, and the field would guide and control the *form* of the organism's development.

The field has properties not just in space but in time. Waddington demonstrated this with his concept of the chreode, represented by models of valleys with balls rolling down them towards an endpoint. This model looks mechanistic when you first see it. But when you think about it for just a minute you see that this endpoint, towards which the ball is rolling down the valley, is in the *future*, and it is, as it were, attracting the ball to it. Part of the strength of this model depends on the fact that if you displace the marble up the sides of the valley, it will roll down again and reach the same endpoint; this represents the ability of living organisms to reach the same goal, even if you disrupt them—cut off a bit of embryo and it can grow back again; you'll still reach the same endpoint.

WEBER   From what I gathered in your book, the morphogenetic field is not a cause in the ordinary sense of the term. It's not the *originator* of the form. In what way, then, can the morphogenetic field be a cause?

SHELDRAKE   The morphogenetic field, I think, is the cause of the specific form. But the problem is why the morphogenetic field becomes associated with that particular developing system in the first place. Why does the morphogenetic field of a chicken become associated with a hen's egg, and not with a partridge's egg or with a human egg? This is tied to the question of origin.

We have two factors here. One is that the field has a causal role in the development of the form. The second is that the field must become associated with a particular system. And that depends on the pre-existing form. So you're never starting from nothing. In biological morphogenesis you always start from an organized system, which is a detached part of the previous organism. Life is always coming from another living organism. You don't get spontaneous generation.

Now in chemistry spontaneous generation does happen: you can have crystallization from a solution without a pre-existing seed or nucleus of that crystal. Of course, the crystallization happens faster if you seed or nucleate the super-saturated solution with an appropriate fragment of the crystal. But it can happen spontaneously. That's probably because in chemistry, thermal motion sooner or later throws up a configuration of the molecules which is sufficiently close to the seed for it to act as a seed. This isn't possible in living organisms because the morphogenetic germ (which is the term I use for this starting point) is so complex that it can't come into being in any feasible time through random fluctuation. It has to be given already and it's given by being part of an already-existing organism.

WEBER   What created the form that's already given and that then connects itself up with the morphogenetic field?

SHELDRAKE   Well, this takes us back to the problem of how we get the first of any given kind of morphogenetic field, the problem of creativity. As you know, this is something I prefer to leave open from the point of view of this hypothesis, because it's really a hypothesis of repetition. And it's not essential for me to answer the question of creativity, although I propose possible answers in my book.

WEBER   A hypothesis of repetition? How does that relate to genetic repetition or genetic inheritance?

SHELDRAKE   Well, I'm saying that heredity in living organisms involves not only genes and DNA but also morphogenetic fields. These fields are derived from past organisms of the same species through the process I call morphic resonance.

The easiest way to understand morphic resonance is in terms of a radio or TV analogy, where the wires and transistors of the radio set act as a tuning device which picks up transmissions from the radio station. The sounds that come out of the radio set depend both on the correct arrangement of the wires and transistors and on the field to which it's tuned, the transmission. If you change the wires and transistors, you'll change the tuning. You may get a different station or a distorted reception of the normal one. Similarly, in the egg, the DNA and the proteins it gives rise to set up the tuning characteristic of that species, and that is what tunes the system in to that particular morphogenetic field.

WEBER Staying with that analogy, what is the transmitter? You would say the morphogenetic field itself is the source of transmission, isn't that so?

SHELDRAKE Yes.

WEBER In your analogy, the field holds the record of the past.

SHELDRAKE Yes. The main purpose of the analogy with a radio or a TV set is to show that there can be two factors involved. You see, the most common kind of objection that the mechanists put forward to any idea that there is something other than DNA or chemicals involved in living organisms or that anything other than the brain is involved in consciousness is that if you change the chemicals or the DNA through genetic engineering or mutation, you change the result. They say this proves that it's nothing but a product of the DNA. We hear this argument time and time again in relation to biology and, of course, in relation to consciousness: consciousness is nothing but an aspect of the brain because if you damage the brain you change consciousness, or if you put drugs into the bloodstream you change the function of the brain. The strength of my analogy is to show that that could all be true—you can affect the system by changing the chemicals or the DNA, proteins and so on—and yet it needn't be *nothing but* that which is responsible for the form.

WEBER The great strength of the analogy is that broadcasting can be going on all the time, but if the receiver has been inactivated, nothing will get through, and that could lead people to infer erroneously that the broadcast originates in that set.

SHELDRAKE If you wanted to carry the analogy a little further you could say the present mechanistic approach to biology is like trying to understand the pictures on the screen of the TV set by more and more detailed analyses of the chemistry of the transistors and condensers and wires and so on, completely leaving out of account the fact that the pictures depend on transmissions coming from somewhere else. The fact is, of course, that neither radio or TV nor living organisms can be explained simply in terms of the chemistry and the arrangement of their components. But the mechanists will then say, "Well, we admit we can't explain it now, but we will be able to explain it in the future." They issue undated promissory notes. It's essentially an act of faith in the mechanistic method, not really a strict scientific hypothesis.

WEBER How does the hypothesis of formative causation differ from that?

SHELDRAKE   The hypothesis of formative causation, unlike the mechanistic theory, is testable. It can be tested through experiments of the kind I propose in the book. One example is based on the idea that if rats learn to do a new trick in one place, that rats of the same breed should be able to learn the same thing more quickly all over the world because of morphic resonance. Rigorous experiments could be done to test this kind of prediction, using normal kinds of scientific procedures.

But even mechanistic biology is forced to recognize something like morphogenetic fields. These are introduced in a disguised form in phrases such as "genetic programs." The genetic program is *not* the same as DNA , because DNA is present in all the cells of the body, and yet the eye and the ears and the kidney and liver all develop quite differently—if they were all following the same program, they wouldn't develop differently. So you have to have something over and above the DNA to structure their development. This concept of the genetic program is, of course, teleological: programming is something that has an end or a goal in view. You see, the mechanistic theory, in so far as it has to postulate genetic programs or genetic instructions, is going beyond the mechanistic approach itself. If you took those concepts seriously, you could say they point toward something like formative causation. These concepts are not thoroughly analyzed and are in fact not mechanistic.

WEBER   You are implying that they make use of the *function* of a field without calling it that and without even being conscious of it.

SHELDRAKE   Yes. I think that many of the things that morphogenetic fields do are the kinds of things that genetic programs are supposed to do, and just as the genetic programs are obviously related to DNA—if you change the DNA, you change the program—so morphogenetic fields are related to DNA—change the DNA and you change the tuning.

WEBER   So heredity is due partly to the genetic seed within the organism and partly to the morphic resonances with the morphogenetic field.

SHELDRAKE   Yes. Heredity has these two aspects, the DNA and something more than the DNA, the morphogenetic field. The morphogenetic field plays a similar role to the genetic program, as I was just saying, and the genetic program, I think, is distinct from the DNA. Mechanists usually assume that the genetic program can legitimately be regarded as an aspect of the DNA. Now the reason I think it can't is that we actually know, as a result of mechanistic research, what DNA does. DNA provides a sequence of chemical letters of the genetic code which spells out the sequence of amino acids in proteins. Some DNA is involved in the control of protein synthesis rather than directly coding the protein itself. This is what's been shown, and it's all perfectly reasonable and very interesting. DNA by providing the code for the sequence of amino acids, enables the cell to make particular proteins. That is *all* the DNA can do.

But the problem with morphogenesis is not just the question of getting the right proteins in the right cells at the right time. It's how, given those proteins, the cells organize themselves into particular forms; how cells group together in tissues of particular forms; and how those are shaped into organisms of particular forms. DNA helps us to understand how you get the proteins which provide, as it were, the bricks and mortar with which the organism is built, but it doesn't explain how these bricks and mortar assemble into particular patterns or shapes. The idea of DNA shaping the organism or programming its behaviour is a quite illegitimate extrapolation from anything we know about what DNA does—it simply codes the sequence of the amino acids in proteins and plays a role in the control of protein synthesis.

WEBER   You're saying it's too *active* a role, which is not warranted by the mechanistic explanation?

SHELDRAKE   That's right. Everything to do with heredity and properties of living organisms is being projected on to DNA within the mechanistic model—all the unsolved problems of biology are being attributed to DNA. DNA, in my opinion, is being grossly overrated. Biologists are forced to project onto DNA roles and possibilities and potentialities which go far beyond anything we know that DNA can do. So what starts as a rigorous and well-defined theory about the way DNA codes the RNA and how RNA codes the proteins, soon turns into a kind of mystical theory in which DNA has unexplained powers and properties which can't be specified in exact molecular terms in any way at all. This is what I mean about the fantasies projected onto DNA, things that DNA is supposed to do which go over and above what we know it does. These extra things that it is supposed to do are, I think, what in fact morphogenetic fields do.

WEBER   What are the characteristics of morphogenetic fields and how do they differ from objects?

SHELDRAKE   In very general terms, fields are invisible and undetectable by our senses. They also have the property of being spatial patterns. The gravitational field is a spatial pattern; in fact, Einstein considered gravitation the very curvature of space itself. Magnetic fields have spatial patterns; for example, iron filings scattered around a bar magnet reveal the spatial pattern of its field. The structure of the field is there whether or not you reveal it: fields involve spatial patterns which in themselves are invisible. They are detectable only through their effects: gravitational fields were put forward to explain gravitational effects, and we know them only through gravitational effects. Electromagnetic fields were postulated to explain electromagnetic effects; we know them through these effects. Now, in a similar manner I think morphogenetic fields are spatial and undetectable directly, and we know them only through their morphogenetic effects.

WEBER   What about the morphogenetic fields themselves? Are they *real* or just nominalistic devices (i.e. real in name only)?

SHELDRAKE   I think they're real in the same sense that we normally consider gravitational and electromagnetic fields to be real.

WEBER   In the book you describe morphogenetic fields as non-energetic. Wouldn't that distinguish this kind of field from the electromagnetic field, which is energetic and can originate events and processes?

SHELDRAKE   Yes. The reason I say that the fields themselves are not energetic is that according to the theory these fields have a non-local character—they are not attenuated by time or space—they act outside of time and space. And if the fields, in their non-local character, involved a transfer of energy, it wouldn't be possible for them to have these properties.

The fields are always linked to energetic systems—they always interact with energetic systems. The reason I say they're not themselves energy is partly because of the way they're transmitted from place to place (non-locally) and partly because the kind of causation they're involved in is distinct from the kind of causation physics deals with, which is always construed in terms of energetic causation. The whole question of form has a curious relationship to energy; it can never exist without energy or activity, because without something having actuality or activity or energy a form can't have any physical reality.

WEBER   Could you go into the idea of morphic resonance?

SHELDRAKE   It involves the idea of an automatic self-selective process. If you have a piano with the loud pedal down, and you make a noise of any particular tone, "A" for example, only the A strings and their harmonics will vibrate, not the B strings. The sympathetic vibration will occur in the appropriate strings. It's an automatically selective process—similarity alone will give rise to this response. Morphic resonance, however, is not exactly the same as other kinds of resonance, all of which are energetic and involve the transfer of energy. The word "morphic" shows that this kind of resonance depends on similarity of form; it's saying that similar forms will influence other similar forms and the criterion for the resonance occurring is similarity of form.

WEBER   Why do you postulate such a multiplicity of morphogenetic fields? Are they really all necessary?

SHELDRAKE   Multiplicity of morphogenetic fields is necessary because of the multiplicity of natural forms. We're dealing with all the different kinds of plants and animals and insects and crystals. The gravitational field is unique in the sense that it's a single field which has this unifying principle—a unifying principle that works for the whole of nature. The kind of forms it gives rise to, left to its own devices, are simple forms like the spherical form—the sun, or the earth, or the planets or the moon. Gravity is a kind of formative field. But it's at a very low level of differentiation and gives these simple unified forms like spheres, and of course also accounts for the spherical flatness of the ocean. That's clearly not good enough to account for all the different shapes of animals and plants that we see around us. So to account for the difference of form, we need more than this very simple kind of field.

Electromagnetic fields are also simple in the kinds of forms they give rise to. And those won't *do* either to account for the multiplicity of forms in the natural world. When we come to the orthodox fields of physics, we find that in fact there is already a multiplicity of fields below the level of the atom, where physicists feel quite free to introduce as many new fields as they feel are necessary. We've got all the fields of quantum field theory: the electron-positron field, the proton-antiproton field, and so on. Each subatomic particle has its own field in quantum field theory. We've already got a plethora of fields there.

Now you might say, on the principle of economy, that you should introduce the minimum number of fields. Pythagoreans, of course, would wish to derive all the forms of things from some basic numerical principles or ratios, and I think there's a strong element of Pythagorean thinking underlying a lot of modern scientific thought. People feel that numbers are somehow fundamental, and that if you can have numerical ratios to explain the diversity of things, this is more satisfactory. That's an opinion I don't happen to share. I think numbers are greatly overrated. The wish to reduce nature to a few rational principles, equations or formulae is something that is very attractive to certain kinds of mathematical minds, but mathematics has been remarkably unsuccessful in dealing with biology and biological forms.

WEBER   So much for Pythagoras. How would your hypothesis compare to Plato's views?

SHELDRAKE   What I'm proposing is closer to Aristotle and his notion of formative or formal causation, as it's usually translated. But what I'm saying also resembles Plato. It's sort of mid-way between the nominalist and realist positions that were debated so much in

the Middle Ages. I'm saying that the form of an organism depends
on a pre-existing archetype which molds or shapes the developing
organism. The idea of a pre-existing archetype is basic to Plato.
But I'm suggesting that this pre-existing archetype derived from
the actual forms, the immanent forms of *previous* systems, which
is closer to Aristotle. So in a sense my hypothesis partakes of both
Aristotelian and Platonic views of form. But it differs from them
in that Plato and Aristotle both thought of the forms as fixed or
permanent.

This idea was then taken up in Christian thought. Augustine,
for example, thought that the Platonic archetypes were ideas in the
mind of God, and since God was the eternal ground of creation,
these eternal archetypes were there before the creation, as the
seminal reasons of things. Certainly in the Aristotelian tradition
the idea was that natural kinds of things were fixed, species were
fixed. That Aristotelian view was also taken over by Christian
theology and combined with the notion of creation from Genesis.
The idea was that there were fixed species, created at the beginning
and not changing thereafter. And of course that's one of the
reasons Darwinian evolution was opposed so much. I'm proposing
an evolutionary view of reality in which these archetypes, the
morphogenetic fields which shape and mold forms, are not regarded as fixed. They are affected by what happens in time, and
past forms have a cumulative influence on them. This is the main
difference from the Platonic and Aristotelian theories.

WEBER   The organisms influence the field to which they are attuned
and from which they take information, patterns, models. You're
saying that the changing organisms change the background, the
morphogenetic field itself, over time. It's more dynamic than in
either Plato or Aristotle.

SHELDRAKE   Yes, it's a two-way process. In the usual view of Platonism or even Aristotelianism you have the fixed form, given *a priori*.
It's given, either because it's just always been there, or because it's
an idea in the mind of God. There's a one-way process whereby
this fixed archetypal form is reflected in the world; what happens
in the phenomenal world is like a shadow of the archetype. The
idea of shadows of archetypal forms doesn't permit a two-way
process. By contrast, I'm proposing a two-way process. The morphogenetic field is built up through what happens in space and
time in the phenomenal world. The morphogenetic field helps
shape and determine things in the world, and then the actual forms
of things in the world feed back, affecting the morphogenetic field
in a cumulative way. So the morphogenetic field itself undergoes
evolutionary development.

WEBER   This reminds me of the theories of David Bohm: his implicate order and its unfolded and enfolded dimensions. The affinity with Bohm is so great that your theory could even be regarded as a subset of his implicate order. How do you see the relationship between them?

SHELDRAKE   When I first read Bohm's work, I also thought that there was a considerable similarity. But I also saw in it a major difference. The implicate order underlying the explicate order seemed to be very like the idea of the Platonic world of Forms underlying the phenomenal world. Bohm's use of the expression "timeless order" made me think his theory was an updated version of traditional Platonism or Neoplatonism. However, the examples he gives of how the implicate order works—for example the one where a drop of ink is folded into glycerin, and then folded out again—are ones where the implicate order is derived from an explicate order.

WEBER   That's true, but he has made it clear that that example is merely a concrete illustration of how an implicate order, invisible to us, could contain what has been enfolded, and what can be unfolded again. But he certainly claims that the explicate order depends upon a prior implicate order that is present before the explicate version displays it.

SHELDRAKE   If there's a continual feedback or introjection from the explicate to the implicate, and then from the implicate to the explicate, as his examples imply, the implicate would be prior only in the sense that it would underlie the first manifestation of any order in the explicate world. The explicate world has a role to play—it would be a two-way process. The implicate would influence the explicate, the explicate would then act back on the implicate. The next time around, when a form was explicated again, it would have the initial impetus from the implicate plus the influence of previous explicate orders of a similar kind. That is quite compatible with what I am saying. It puts the same kind of idea into a very different sort of language, but it is complementary.

You know, if you start framing the whole topic in physical terms, as I do with morphogenetic fields, then you have to speak in terms of morphic resonance, the influence of past forms on present ones through the morphogenetic field by a kind of resonance. If, however, you start using psychological language, and you start talking in terms of thought, then you've got a handier way of thinking of the influence of the past, because with mental fields you have memory. And one can extend this memory if one thinks of the whole universe as essentially thought-like, as many philosophical systems have done. You could say that if the whole universe is thought-like, then you automatically have a sort-of cosmic memory developing. There are systems of thought that take exactly this view. One of them is in Mahayana Buddhism—the idea of the *alayavijnana*, or storehouse of consciousness, rather similar to the idea of cosmic memory. And Theosophists, I think, took over some of that in the idea of the *akashic* record. [The *akashic* record claims that everything that transpires, whether physical or mental, is encoded in subtle dimensions of space, where it functions like a data-bank for karma. This view is also found in Tibetan Buddhism.]

WEBER   Your theory leaves open the origin of forms and takes up their story after they have appeared at least once, but Bohm postulates that novel forms originate in the implicate order, are ejected into the explicate, and then are "reinjected" back into the implicate. That seems the point of departure of these two views.

SHELDRAKE   We're doing rather different things. Bohm is sketching out a philosophy within which modern physics can be seen. It's a highly appropriate metaphysical view that can form a background to modern physics and enable quantum theory to make sense. And I think Bohm's metaphysical view is perfectly acceptable.

But what I'm doing is putting forward a specific hypothesis cast within the framework of natural science, which follows the methodology of natural science, and which is scientific by Popper's criterion of being testable or refutable. The reason I exclude the question of the origin of forms is that I think the question of creativity lies outside the province of natural science. I don't think natural science can explain everything. It can't deal with that which lies behind or beyond nature—with the source of the phenomenal or natural world. That's not the province of natural science; it's the province of metaphysics.

WEBER   If not as a biologist, I would think that as a philosophical human being you'd have some views on the notion of creativity one way or the other, even provisionally.

SHELDRAKE   I do have my own views. I'm much influenced by Bergson in this. As you know, Bergson was very keen to assert the genuine creativity of the evolutionary process. He again and again pointed out that our minds have a tendency to deny creativity. We can't explain creativity. It involves the completely new, the original. So we prefer to say that creativity is not creativity at all but merely the expression of something "archetypal" that already exists in a latent form. That denies true creativity. It's like saying everything is laid down in advance, and that evolution is rather like unrolling a long carpet—it is just unrolled in time.

WEBER   You're saying that creativity, if it's to be genuine and not canned, entails novelty and spontaneity. It cannot just emerge mechanically at a given moment in history, but must be spontaneously flung forth at that moment in history. It's not a choreographed dance that's already been laid out, but more like an improvisation.

SHELDRAKE   Exactly. So whatever view of evolutionary creativity I develop will be one in which I'd like to have some role for genuine novelty. If I agreed with David Bohm in saying that underlying the explicate order is the pre-existing order, I'd then want to ask: where does this pre-existing implicate order come from? Because just taken by itself, with its Neoplatonic overtones, it might imply a static and pre-existing order, which would go right back to St. Augustine.

WEBER   Yet from talking with him, I feel that Bohm believes in a very radical creativity. For Bohm nature is a highly dynamic reality which manifests creativity all along. Would you agree?

SHELDRAKE   Yes. But I'm not sure how much more one can say about it. I agree with you that we're in the realm of mystery when you get to these questions, and that's another reason why I don't speculate about this a great deal: I *think* about it a lot, but I believe it's something where one can never arrive at final, complete, or satisfying answers.

WEBER   The persistence of memory, even on a cosmic scale, is an integral feature of this theory.

SHELDRAKE   Yes.

WEBER   Where is this memory stored? How can natural laws be habits, when you insist on the notion of constant creativity and spontaneity? Can these two views be reconciled?

SHELDRAKE   I do think natural patterns are more like habits than timeless laws. I don't see any conflict between the notion of habit and creativity. We know from our own experience that habits provide the basis on which creativity can act. Most physicists assume that underlying physical reality there are timeless laws. This conflicts with the view we now have of the universe as radically evolutionary. And I don't believe in fact there's any basis for thinking that the laws of nature are timeless. I would suggest that just as morphogenetic fields are built up by habit, so may all the laws of nature be built up as habits—they may have evolved along with nature.

WEBER   Can the laws that govern the hydrogen atom ever change?

SHELDRAKE   Well, I believe once these morphogenetic fields have been set up they can't be abolished, and so I think that once things have got into grooves of habit, they will indeed continue them.

WEBER   In that case, all the fields that have ever been are still there. In order for something else to govern the behaviour of the hydrogen atom, an alternate or competing field would have to be stronger than the present one that governs it.

SHELDRAKE   Yes. It wouldn't be possible for a new field to set up in

the presence of an overwhelming influence from a pre-existing
habit. What *can* happen is that higher level fields can integrate
lower level habits into new syntheses. This is what we get in the
realm of chemistry, where we have hydrogen atoms incorporated
into molecules. The hydrogen atom persists in many of its habits,
but these are subsumed within higher level fields. Evolution pro-
ceeds not by changing basic habits but by taking the basic habits
it's given and building more and more complex patterns out of
them.

WEBER   Since your book stresses that the strength and dominance of
a morphogenetic field is mostly determined by the number of
organisms who have built it up, how would you account for the
power of the rare individual like Buddha or Christ? As far as
numbers go, they have been almost unique, yet the influence of a
Buddha-field or a Christ-field was very great even initially, before
people formed religions around them.

SHELDRAKE   It is probable that there is an intensity-factor here, as
well as quantity. The consistency and intensity of a pattern of
thought or an intention strongly held creates the power in the
field. Presumably, this has its negative side, for example the great
consistency and intensity of a Hitler-field, which mobilized and
virtually hypnotized millions of people. Their own negative impulses resonated morphically with Hitler's powerful field.

WEBER   When I discussed this with David Bohm, he felt that the
power of a Buddha-field, disproportionate to its numbers, came
from the level of wholeness deep within the implicate order from
where the Buddha operated. At that level only compassion and
order are possible, not hatred and disorder.

SHELDRAKE   A Hitler-field tries to make limited wholes, such as his
fanatical and exclusionary obsession with German nationalism.

WEBER   You've made clear that you cannot address the question of
the original creation of forms scientifically. What about the metaphysics of it? In the last chapter of your book you do delineate
four different possibilities and claim that all of them are compatible
with the hypothesis of formative causation.

SHELDRAKE   The four possibilities I propose are not opposed to each
other. They have a nested relationship to each other, each being
included in the following one. In a sense I believe all four of them.
The first is a kind of sophisticated materialism or physicalism
which asserts only the reality of the physical world. This includes
morphogenetic fields, which I think are part of the physical reality—they shape the physical development of material systems. Now
a modified materialist view would stop there, because as a physicalist view it would not be able to answer the question of the origin
of new forms or patterns, or to admit that consciousness

might involve anything more than physical processes going on in the brain. I think that's unsatisfactory because it leaves unsolved the question of creativity and consciousness, so the second view I'm putting forward goes beyond that. It says that in human consciousness there is something that can give rise to new fields and patterns. We know from the history of human invention and human artistic creativity that through our consciousness new forms and patterns come into existence in the world. Our technology is an example of this. If we look around us we see everywhere things that didn't exist in the past—skyscrapers, cars, airplanes, typewriters, computers, and so on. All these are physical things in the physical world which had their origin in human thought. We can say that this consciousness needn't be the same as the physical things of the world that work according to the laws of repetition, but can be a source of new physical forms and patterns.

Thirdly, if we want to say that new actual forms—forms of crystals, forms of plants, forms of animals—are due to creative acts that take place in consciousness, we'd ordinarily have to suggest that it was a consciousness over and above the kind we experience. We could say that in the same way that our consciousness is normally associated with our bodies and is controlling what we experience and do, so an immanent consciousness in nature is associated with nature and what goes on in nature and what nature does next.

WEBER   But it's not *apart from nature*.

SHELDRAKE   It's not apart from nature.

WEBER   It dwells somehow *with* it, if not in it.

SHELDRAKE   Right. This third position embraces the previous two views. The fourth position says all these views are correct, but nature itself has a source *beyond* the natural world. The universe itself has an origin, and both the creativity within the universe and the universe itself require an explanation. And these can only be explained in terms of something which is over and above or beyond the universe—in that sense transcendent. This would correspond to the traditional theistic views of creation, which would have a God who is beyond, above, and in nature. These four views are metaphysical frameworks within which one can see this hypothesis of formative causation. I myself take the fourth of these views. I affirm all four views for each of them includes the previous ones.

WEBER   This still leaves open the question of where the original insight that enabled these higher fields to build themselves up came from; so we're back to the problem of creativity, in this case of the behavioral fields, but it could be asked even of very high-level spiritual fields. At the moment you seem to be taking the position that this problem is insoluble for us.

SHELDRAKE Well, I take the view that the creation ultimately depends on some non-physical or trans-physical reality, spiritual in
nature, to use the traditional terminology, but other people might
take other views.

WEBER There seems to be a confusion today. A number of people,
under the guise of holism, have proposed what look like quasi-
mechanistic theories after all, although subtly disguised. Yet these
may mislead others into passing for genuine holistic models. Can
you clear up this confusion?

SHELDRAKE Theories opposed to mechanistic reductionism are
generally referred to as holistic. Such theories point out, in one
way or another, that as the complexity of systems increases, new
properties emerge which are more than the sum of the parts of the
systems. But there are different ways in which this emergent
wholeness can be understood. Some holistic thinkers see these
properties as somehow latent, as potentialities in matter itself.
They may speak of them as involving a mental aspect, as Gregory
Bateson did, for example, but they do not mean by this that the
mental aspect exists prior to, or is in any way separable from, the
physical system with which it is associated. Such a view is in fact
a kind of sophisticated materialism. By contrast, non-materialistic
holistic thinkers regard the order, purposiveness and creativity of
organisms as directly or indirectly dependent upon a non-physical
source. Holists of the first kind, like ordinary materialists, deny
basic tenets of religion such as the conscious survival of physical
death; whereas non-materialistic holism can harmonize well with
various religious approaches. Much confusion arises from assuming
that all anti-mechanistic and anti-reductionist thinkers are in agreement with each other; they are not. The perennial debate between
atheistic, pantheistic, and theistic views of reality has simply been
transposed to a new level.

For a particular world there is a beginning, but for the cosmos as a whole there is no beginning.

THE DALAI LAMA

I think the universe is completely self-contained. It doesn't have any beginning or end, it doesn't have any creation or destruction.

STEPHEN HAWKING

As far as the implicate order is concerned, every new moment could in principle be entirely unrelated to the previous one—it could be totally creative.

DAVID BOHM

5

Creativity: the signature of nature

DAVID BOHM

Eternity can be affected by what happens in time.

DAVID BOHM

Bohm's philosophy of the implicate order has undergone further development and refinement since his exposition of it in Chapter 2, four years earlier. Ken Wilber's original "Editor's note" prefacing this dialogue when we first published it in *ReVision* will provide a concise summary of Bohm's schema. "[Ed. note: Bohm's theory proposes that, in general, there are three major realms of existence: the explicate order, the implicate order, and a source-ground beyond both. The explicate order is the world of separate and isolated thing-events extended in space and time. The implicate order is a realm in which all thing-events are enfolded in a total wholeness, a wholeness and unity that, as it were, 'underlies' the explicate world of separate things and events. The 'source-ground' (our term) is radically unqualifiable and totally beyond thought-symbols. It is analogous to the Void of Buddhists, the Abyss of Christian mystics, Nirguna Brahman of Vedanta, etc. It is the implicate order that apparently bears most resemblance to morphogenetic fields, and therefore the implicate order is the one most discussed in these interviews.]"[10]

In the present dialogue, Bohm adds a further realm of existence to the three he originally proposed: the super-implicate order. It functions as the organizing principle of all the other orders, is their source, and transcends them. In turn, it may be organized by the super-super-implicate order and realms that shade off infinitely beyond human thought.

I asked Bohm to comment on the similarities and differences of the implicate order and Sheldrake's theory of morphogenetic fields, especially the origin of forms—where do we get the first chicken from that makes the egg that makes a chicken? You may recall that Sheldrake's theory does not, or cannot, account for this phenomenon, but Bohm suggests that the forms of organisms originate in the implicate order.

Bohm, Sheldrake, and Prigogine (in Chapter 10) all are fascinated by creativity in nature and all three try to deal with the relationship be-

tween past and present. Bohm's explanation allows for a genuine dialogue between the finite and infinite realms of existence, each contributing to the other. This view is unusual, for in most conventional
theories eternity can contribute to time (the infinite to the finite), but
not time to eternity. Bohm's explanation uses some technical terms:
projection, injection, re-projection, and re-injection that need explaining. For this purpose, I will again use the original *ReVision* "Ed. note,"
which is clear and concise. "[Ed. note. As a simplistic analogy, take the
ocean and its waves: each wave arises or is 'projected' from the whole
of the ocean; that wave then dips back into the ocean, or is 'injected'
back into the whole, and then the next wave arises. Each wave is
affected by past waves simply because they all rise and fall, or are
projected and injected, by the whole ocean. So there is a type of 'causality' involved, but it is not that wave A linearly *causes* wave B, but
that wave A *influences* wave B by virtue of being absorbed back into the
totality of the ocean, which then gives rise to wave B. In Bohm's terms,
wave B is in part a 're-projection' of the 'injection' of wave A, and so
on. Each wave would therefore be *similar* to previous waves, but also
different in certain aspects—exact size, shape, etc. Bohm is suggesting
that there is a type of 'causality,' but one that is *mediated* via the *totality*
of the implicate ocean, and not merely via the separated, isolated, explicate waves. This means, finally, that such 'causation' would be non-
local, because what happens at any part of the ocean would affect all
other parts. This is according to Bohm's *re-formulations* of present day
quantum mechanics. In the following discussion, Bohm will point out
that present day quantum mechanics, as it is usually interpreted, completely fails to account for the replication of past forms, or the notion
of temporal process, a failure that in part led Bohm to propose 'injection' and 'projection' via the implicate order.]"[11]

Another issue figures importantly in this and several subsequent dialogues (Chapters 6 and 10), namely the status of the laws of nature. Are
these laws eternal or do they change? This question preoccupies not
only Bohm but also Sheldrake and Prigogine. All three lean towards the
dynamic interpretation of laws, though in rather different ways, as you
will see.

This dialogue took place in Spring 1982 near Kennedy Airport in
New York City, where I caught up with Bohm just as he was returning
to London from a stay in Ojai. Since we had each held long conversations with Sheldrake only days earlier, Sheldrake's theory and its meaning were uppermost in our minds, and therefore dominates much of
this dialogue.

WEBER   Let's explore the relationship between your implicate order
   philosophy and Sheldrake's theory of morphogenetic fields. How
   are these alike and how do they differ?

BOHM   The major difference is that the implicate order is more general. It does not require a morphogenetic theory, but it may have room to explain one. The existence of an implicate order would not depend upon whether or not you have a morphogenetic field but through the theory of the implicate order we can give a possible explanation of morphogenetic fields.

The implicate order can be thought of as a ground beyond time, a totality out of which each moment is projected into the explicate order. For every moment that is projected out into the explicate there would be another movement in which that moment would be injected or "introjected" back into the implicate order. Now, if you have a large number of repetitions of this process, you'll start to build up a fairly constant component to this series of projections and injections. That is, a fixed disposition would become established. The point is that, via this process, past forms would tend to be repeated or replicated in the present, and that is very similar to what Sheldrake calls a morphogenetic field and morphic resonance. Moreover, such a field would not be located anywhere. When it projects back into the totality (the implicate order), since no space and time are relevant there, all things of a similar nature might get connected together or resonate in the totality. You see, when the explicate order enfolds into the implicate order, which does not have any special place, all places and all times are, we might say, merged, so that what happens in one place will interpenetrate with what happens in another place.

WEBER   Does this merging happen because their forms make things cohere or resonate?

BOHM   That's right. All basically similar things will be especially closely related inside the totality in the implicate order.

WEBER   They'll somehow attract each other, or resonate.

BOHM   Yes.

WEBER   And in the implicate order you might also get the *genesis* of a form?

BOHM   Yes. Then as that form projects out in different places in the explicate, it would have certain tendencies which are building up constantly through repetition and this would give the appearance of the "causation" of the present by the past.

WEBER   You're saying the implicate order can be the creative source of new forms which then become replicated. I think that's important, because I find a problem in Sheldrake's theory—one he frankly admits he cannot at present deal with and doesn't feel he should deal with—how to account for the origin of form. But you are saying that the implicate order can account for the origin of form?

BOHM   Yes, I think so. The whole notion of the implicate order is, to begin with, a way of discussing the origin of form out of the formless, via the process of "explication" or unfolding. The form is enfolded to begin with, and then it unfolds.

WEBER   Do the forms pre-exist in the implicate order, as in Plato, for example?

BOHM   I think Sheldrake made the point that he differed from Plato in feeling that the forms are not completely pre-existing, but rather that they develop. I agree, and would add that a form develops through the process of projection and injection, re-projection, re-injection, and so on.

WEBER   So there is a developmental process in the implicate order?

BOHM   Yes. A development of form.

WEBER   Where does creativity come into this notion of projection and injection and re-projection?

BOHM   As far as the implicate order is concerned, every new moment could, in principle, be entirely unrelated to the previous one—it could be totally creative. You could say that creativity is fundamental in the implicate order, and what we really have to explain are the processes that are *not* creative. You see, usually we believe that in life the rule is uncreativity, and occasionally a little burst of creativity comes in that requires explanation. But the implicate order turns all that around and says creativity is the basis and it is repetition that has to be explained. That's where the morphogenetic field theory comes in.

Morphogenetic fields are explained in the implicate order theory as due to the constant repetition produced by projection and injection, re-projection and re-injection, and so on. A form emerges or is creatively projected from the whole, then it influences the whole, or is "injected" back into it; in the implicate order it "resonates" with similar forms and then is re-projected back into the explicate order. This whole process—forms ceaselessly emerging and then being reabsorbed—accounts for the influence of past forms on present ones, and also allows for the emergence of new or creative forms. A morphogenetic field is simply a field that, through constant repetition, has become relatively stable.

WEBER   That's clear. But here's my problem: both you and Krishnamurti have constantly emphasized that it is the repetition of the past—thought-forms, habit-patterns, conditioning, past memories—that obstructs present awareness and genuine intelligence. Intelligent living, you have said for years, means living as free from the past as possible. Now it looks as though Sheldrake's theory of morphic resonance, and your own ideas on replication, make the past essential for the behavior and self-maintenance of organisms. This seems contradictory.

BOHM   Well, the point is that we must give the past its due. The past is intrinsically neither good nor bad. But it's necessary. We must have *some* form—we can't live entirely in the implicate order. The problem that Krishnamurti addresses is that the past is overemphasized and becomes dominant, thus resisting creativity where it would otherwise be natural and appropriate. The past must be ready to die when it no longer fits, but it tends to hold on, and that is the trouble. But the past itself, if properly addressed, is useful enough. You see, the past can also have a part in creativity. If you had absolute creativity—absolute novelty with no past—then nothing would ever exist because it would all vanish at the very moment of creation. Nothing could last if everything were entirely new. Therefore, it's a dialectical movement which requires both sides, creativity and stability, the creative present and the relatively fixed past.

WEBER   What, then, is the proper way to relate to the past?

BOHM   Through intelligence. We want neither to ignore the past nor to become attached to it. If something from the past begins to cause conflict and confusion, then that has to be dropped.

WEBER   On the question of how these morphogenetic fields might be affecting the present, Sheldrake delineates four philosophical positions. He says all of them would be compatible with his thesis of a morphogenetic field. One he calls modified materialism; the second is human consciousness giving rise to certain fields; the third is immanentism, where the universe is self-organizing and creative; and the last is a view where the organizing force transcends nature. Towards which of these do you lean?

BOHM   The implicate order would be compatible with immanentism, but it would also be compatible with transcendentalism.

WEBER   Would modified materialism apply?

BOHM   You could use it, but you would have to adopt the attitude that matter is understood in implicate order terms. Hegel took the view that thought was fundamental and that nature was mind showing itself to itself, mind's consciousness of itself through nature. Marx turned that upside down and said matter is fundamental, and consciousness is matter showing itself to itself. Or you could take the view that neither matter nor mind is fundamental, but something unknown, which you could call a deeper or implicate ground. It is this view which I'm inclined toward.

WEBER   Is that deeper ground self-aware?

BOHM   Yes. I would say, since it contains both matter and mind, it would have in some sense to be aware. Let's say it's in the direction of mind, but beyond it. It's not below it, but above it.

WEBER   That distinguishes your view from reductionism or mechanism or materialism, because they would not grant that.

BOHM   No, they wouldn't. You see you could take a kind of mater-

ialistic view that was consistent with this, but it would have to go
very far from the usual form of materialism.

WEBER   To get back to the problem of forms: Are they pre-existing
models?

BOHM   No. A model would be a fixed form, and I don't think it's
necessary to postulate that. Forms may develop out of that which
is beyond form.

WEBER   Is the universe experimenting?

BOHM   Yes, you could look at it that way. Trying out various forms.
You can say that natural selection explains the way things survive
once they emerge or appear, but it doesn't explain why so many
forms *have* appeared. There seems to be a tendency to produce
structure and form, which is intrinsically creative, and survival or
natural selection is merely the mechanism that selects which forms
are going to remain. Any form incompatible with itself or with the
environment is not going to last.

WEBER   So the universe itself is learning?

BOHM   I think so, yes.

WEBER   That makes one feel as if the ground is being pulled away
from under us, as if no one knows the whole picture.

BOHM   I feel that knowledge, or what we define as knowledge, is a
limited category. Therefore it may be that knowledge is too limited
a notion for looking at this thing. Knowledge in our sense of it
involves time, memory, and so on. Yet knowledge of the implicate
order would have to be beyond time. Therefore I don't know if
you would even think of it as knowledge. But it shows itself to us
as if it were experimenting. That is, when looked at from the
limited aspect of time, the structure looks like an experiment.

WEBER   Is there, in your view, solid—I'm inclined to say "scientific"
—evidence for either morphogenetic fields or the implicate order?

BOHM   I think Sheldrake himself admits that the evidence for the
morphogenetic fields is very limited and requires a lot more ex-
perimentation.

WEBER   But he does feel that his theories are testable. Do you see
them as testable?

BOHM   Yes. They are about as testable as any other theories. There
is no way to disprove a hypothesis of this level of generality,
although it's possible to conceive of evidence accumulating which
would make it look unlikely. As far as the implicate order is concerned, since that's even more general, it would be much harder
to discuss evidence. The only "evidence" I can present is that
it's a way of looking at the subject which brings it all together.
And I think that it has a promise of being truthful. That's all I
can say.

WEBER   You pointed to some anomalies in quantum physics and relativity that you felt the implicate order could handle better than any other present theory. Could you go into this?

BOHM Well, in one sense quantum mechanics is not a theory at all—it's just an algorithm for calculating certain results. It does not offer any way of explaining or conceiving these results. In order to assign a meaning to the quantum equation, you say that it gives the probability that something can be observed by means of a piece of apparatus. But that apparatus is supposed to be made of the very same kinds of particles that it's talking about. So you'd need another piece of apparatus to look at that, and so on, which would be an infinite regress of reference. All these problems come from saying that this form of quantum mechanics is an absolute truth—that these general laws of quantum mechanics must not be changed. That seems to be a common tacit or even an explicit assumption in physics today. But the whole thing is a very limited mathematical schema, and why people don't want to change this schema is not clear to me. What is missing is a description of movement and process. In present-day quantum mechanics only one observation can be described, and the successive moments have to be ascertained by means of another isolated observation, and another one and another one. There's no way to discuss what actually happens [to a particle, i.e. continuity] between these moments [of measurement], in reference to the overall process itself, only in reference to what an apparatus will observe or measure at any single moment. By contrast, the implicate order allows you to discuss process, continuity, and context.

WEBER But wouldn't most physicists say that quantum mechanics is a viable theory because it works, whereas other approaches do not?

BOHM Well, nobody has proven that another line of reasoning *doesn't* work. Nobody has tried it. People have jumped on this bandwagon and that's all that's been tried. They don't like to think about other lines of reasoning, that's the main point. It's always taught as though this present quantum formalism were the absolute truth, and for the most part students don't know that anything else would be conceivable.

WEBER Yet physicists point to the prediction and control of nature made possible by present quantum mechanics and claim that that validates the theory itself.

BOHM But surely that doesn't prove the truth of it. It merely proves that we can turn this crank and get the right answers in a certain area. If you restrict yourself to these areas, your theory naturally appears unassailable.

WEBER Then what kinds of areas and questions do you feel physicists ought to be concerned with? What should they ask that they are not asking?

BOHM   Well, some of the questions I've just been posing: questions about self-reference, about movement and process, about descriptions of *sequential moments*. Their primary concern at this point is simply to get numbers that agree with the experimental findings, and that's all. Any question which doesn't lead quickly to that is regarded as having no meaning or significance.

WEBER   Wouldn't they claim that what you're after is not the province of physics but of philosophy?

BOHM   That's another way of saying it has no meaning, because as far as they're concerned, philosophers are just wasting their time.

WEBER   So, as in our earlier discussions, you're really taking issue with physics for setting too narrow a domain for itself.

BOHM   Absolutely. And I think this is a modern tendency. In the past, even as recently as the 1920s and 1930s, physicists had a much larger domain of interest. People like Heisenberg, Bohr, Eddington, and Einstein would have considered much broader questions.

WEBER   You feel that almost no one is doing this now?

BOHM   Very few. I think that on the whole the teaching of physics has degenerated; it has become more and more dogmatic and mechanical, and this is lamentable. All these questions that were so vivid in the 1930s have faded out completely. Students are just presented formulae and told "that's quantum mechanics." Then the next generation writes books on that anemic basis, and they all forget about the profound philosophical questions that have always been underlying the whole approach of physics.

WEBER   I'd like to go back to morphogenetic fields. Sheldrake uses a profusion of morphogenetic fields, even for very specific things—motor, sensory, organs, etc. Does he subdivide too much or are all those fields needed?

BOHM   I don't think that's a real problem. A morphogenetic field is simply the governing form of any organism or entity. Nature is full of a multitude of forms, so naturally there would be this multiplicity of morphogenetic fields. But we can see this diversity in a more unified way if we simply consider the possibility that these fields are arranged in a hierarchical order—the more specific fields are included in more general fields, which themselves are subsets of even more inclusive and general fields, and so on. The diversity is real enough, but there is always a larger and "underlying" unity, as it were. I think Sheldrake would agree with this.

WEBER   But in the implicate order you have kept subdivision to a minimum. You've talked in terms of degrees of implication and unfoldment, of subtlety and density of matter, and in terms of higher energy or power. Other than that, you seem to have resisted subdivision.

BOHM That's because I want to keep it general. But subdivisions can definitely be considered; the point is simply that all subdivisions would be relative, not absolute. That's why we consider the possibility of hierarchy.

WEBER Are morphogenetic fields, as you use the term, actual and concrete forces, or are they nominalistic ways of referring to what happens?

BOHM They are not "mere names." I think that the analogy to the radio receiver is not a bad one. You have a radio wave, sent out from a radio station, that has a form (e.g. music), and this form is carried by a very weak electrical wave that is picked up by the antennae of a particular radio set. When the music comes out of the radio set, almost all of its energy comes from the power plug in the wall socket, but its *form* comes from the very weak electrical wave picked up by the antennae. So here we have a very subtle energy (picked up by the antennae) molding a denser energy (coming from the wall socket). Likewise you could picture a formative or morphic field as a very subtle aspect of the implicate order that would impress itself on denser and explicate energies.

WEBER And ride on it, so to speak.

BOHM Right. As another example, you can look at a seed: the energy and nutrients come from the sun, the air, the soil, the water, and the wind; the seed itself has a very little energy. But somehow the seed possesses the form of the plant, and that tiny energy or form impresses itself on all those other factors and thus produces the plant. That tiny bit of energy somehow governs all subsequent growth so that the whole system is made to produce a plant, instead of producing a dog or a cat or whatever.

WEBER This seems to be a crucial point: Does it matter whether the "molding" energy is intense or weak? To Sheldrake it matters.

BOHM He says that the morphic field has *no* energy at all, but I believe he should say it has a very weak energy, just like the radio wave. At any rate, it would be consistent with my view of the implicate order to say the formative field is (or has) a weak, subtle energy—subtle by comparison with the ordinary standards of mechanical energy.

WEBER We still have to try to understand this notion of "creativity"—the origin of new forms themselves, not merely their replication once they exist. You've said that nature has a deep purpose or intentionality that doesn't necessarily show up in its explicate forms. You suggested that this deep intent, which is creativity, is related to the creation of new wholes. Could you follow through with that idea?

BOHM If you look at nature, you find that elaborate and complex forms appear that are not explained by the mere requirement of survival. If our notion of time postulates that each moment is creative, then at every moment the possibility arises for new structures, along with a continuation of some of the old structure. Therefore you could say that nature is constantly and intentionally exploring new structures, and when these are able to survive (by this process of replication), they will build up and become stable.

WEBER   How does the notion of making greater and greater wholes fit in?

BOHM   The entire notion of wholeness, creative wholeness, is built into the implicate order. What is contained in the implicate order are wholes, or rather potential wholes, that can be realized or unfolded or actualized, depending on the total set of conditions.

WEBER   So nature, in making or realizing these wholes, is having a flash of creative insight, as it were.

BOHM   Yes. It would be similar to the flash of creative insight in our own mental experience. The general tenor of the implicate order implies that what happens in our own consciousness and what happens in nature are not fundamentally different in form. Therefore thought and matter have a great similarity of order; we might extend that idea, so that the creativity and insight that we have may also have its parallel in nature. From this perspective you might transcend the dualism between materialism and idealism.

WEBER   How?

BOHM   By saying that nature, or matter, is also creativity and insight, and the forms of matter themselves are the outcome of this creativity and insight. So in a way nature is alive, as Whitehead would say, all the way to the depths. And intelligent. Thus it is both mental and material, as we are. So there is, in fact, no real dualism.

WEBER   And when nature casts up matter, when it makes forms, that itself is the *evidence* for its creative intelligence.

BOHM   Yes. Even though none of this can be proven in the usual or empirical sense, if you look at it this way, it can explain why we have this richness of forms far beyond what mere survival would call for. It would explain why, for example, such a complex form as the human brain would ever have come about.

WEBER   According to your theory it is the consequence of nature's creative experiments.

BOHM   Yes, nature's intent, its deep intent.

WEBER   You're implying that nature is an organism. An alive organism with a purposiveness?

BOHM   Yes. As we said, deep intentionality, creative and purposeful.

WEBER   You could say nature has made us so as to seek her, and that this is a deep drive in us all. It might even be the basis of our drive for knowledge, including science.

BOHM   We are naturally seeking our source. That's one way to look at it. In that sense, nature is much more than what appears on the surface. That would be a way of expressing a sort of extended form of materialism. But—and this is the point—it could equally well be called idealism, spirit, consciousness. The separation of the two—matter and spirit—is an abstraction.

WEBER   Because at root they are one?

BOHM   The ground is always one.

We understand the laws of chemistry and most people do not feel there's any mystery in that.

STEPHEN HAWKING

I believe that we are living in a world which is not given to us. It is not like an open book which we can read and open at this chapter or that. We have hints, fragments.

ILYA PRIGOGINE

It is implied that the ultimate source is immeasurable and cannot be captured within our knowledge.

DAVID BOHM

6

Matter as a meaning field

DAVID BOHM
AND
RUPERT SHELDRAKE

> In self-transcendence, the opening up of new levels of or-
> ganization – of new levels of the mind – the chord of con-
> sciousness becomes richer. In the infinite, it falls together
> with the divine.
>
> JANTSCH

It is a cold January day in 1985, but my room overlooking Russell Square in London's fabled Bloomsbury district near the British Museum is warm and alive with an atmosphere of expectancy. Sheldrake has come down from his home in Newark-on-Trent, about an hour away, and Bohm from Edgware, the London suburb where he lives. This morning I experience the emotional power of the ideas we are discussing. What begins in an atmosphere of winter-fatigue ends on a note of high energy. We have all met many times before and have participated in a symposium on science and mysticism in Cambridge, Massachusetts, only a few months earlier. But our special harmony this morning goes beyond the friendship of colleagues and seems somehow connected to the grandeur of the ideas we are exploring.

In this dialogue, many of the troublesome problems that have arisen in this book come to a head. Do we live in a meaningless universe where molecules of matter blindly spin along through chance, as mechanists claim? Or is matter alive and—at least minimally—conscious, a participant in the "dance" of meaning, as both Bohm and Sheldrake suggest? The latter view may be the more appealing, but it is unproven. [Sheldrake had earlier told us of his encounter with a famous Harvard scientist who confessed that though he felt Sheldrake still lacked solid scientific evidence for his hypothesis of morphogenetic fields, he (the Harvard scientist) *hoped* the theory would turn out to be true.]

The mortal enemy of many of the ideas presented in this dialogue seems to be Occam's Razor, taught to every undergraduate in science and philosophy. Also known as the Principle of Parsimony, it states that you must not multiply your hypotheses beyond strict necessity. Ergo, do not postulate a vital force in matter (or worse, attribute consciousness to the atom or to the genes!) when a simple mechanistic explanation will do. To violate Occam's Razor, we are taught, is to fall into the anthropomorphic trap feared by both scientists and philosophers.

How surprising, then, that in this dialogue and the next one, Occam's Razor and "Thou Shalt Not Be Anthropomorphic" come under attack by scientists themselves. Both Bohm and Sheldrake question the infallibility of these principles by undercutting their self-evident rationality. They scrutinize not only Occam's Razor but also the feasibility of a science purged of all anthropomorphisms. This paves the way for the tough question at the end: does nature as whole have a purpose and—if it does—are we passive spectators or active participants in it?

But the possibility of a conscious universe with inherent meaning begins to resemble—doesn't it?—the one that Lama Govinda, Fr. Bede, the Dalai Lama and other mystics are trying to describe. The cosmology presented here invites comparison with the one of Ilya Prigogine, who in Chapter 10 shies away from any involvement with mysticism and from all "eternal truths." Though Prigogine, Bohm, and Sheldrake differ in many ways, in others they are unexpectedly similar. Stephen Hawking—who staunchly defends Occam's Razor in Chapter 11—takes issue with most of the views that Bohm and Sheldrake express in this dialogue, and also with those of Prigogine.

WEBER   What is matter? What is a field? What is meaning? How are they interrelated? In what way is matter a field of meaning?

BOHM   It has been commonly accepted, especially in the west, that the mental and the physical are quite different but somehow are related, but the theory of their relationship has never been satisfactorily developed. I suggest that they are not actually separated; that the mental and physical are two aspects, like the form and content of something which is only separable in thought, not in reality. Meaning is the bridge between the two aspects.

WEBER   What is meaning?

BOHM   We can't define meaning directly because we presuppose that we know the meaning of meaning to discuss anything. We will have to unfold what meaning means. The soma is the body so we'll generalize and call that the physical side. The other side, the mental side, is grasped through the significance or meaning of the thing we perceive.

WEBER   That part is not clear.

BOHM   Meaning is obviously subtle. Instead of saying that somebody, having comprehended a meaning, chooses to act or not to act, I suggest that meaning itself acts immediately. There are many experiences of that. For example, if you see a shadow on a dark night, the minute that means an assailant, you have a rush of adrenalin and the excitement of the whole system. You don't will that, it just happens due to the perception of the meaning.

WEBER   The meaning immediately acts on the matter, changes the matter to behave in a certain way.

BOHM   That is very common. Even if you act by will, it is because you see it is necessary. The meaning of necessity leads you to act.

WEBER   If you were to perceive the sketchy outline not as an assailant but as a harmless shadow, matter is relatively quiescent.

BOHM   If somebody is perceived as an enemy, matter is organized differently than if he is perceived as a friend.

WEBER   That would explain in what way matter and meaning are indissolubly connected; they are part of one and the same thing.

BOHM   It is hard for people to think meaning is on the material side. But experience shows that it touches both sides. It is the bridge between the mental and the physical.

WEBER   Do you think that is clear, Rupert?

SHELDRAKE   I'd like to ask David whether meaning is inevitably related to some goal.

BOHM   The relationship between meaning and goal or purpose requires some going into. First of all, meaning is just the activity, virtual or actual, that comes out of whatever is apprehended. That can then be reflected back in thought, reconsidered again and again, building up a kind of meaning that is internal, but it's still activity. In that case it's the activity of thought. Thought is neuro-physiological activity.

WEBER   But does that fully answer Rupert's question whether meaning is always purposive, teleological?

SHELDRAKE   Can we separate this way of looking at a thing from teleology? I suspect we can't.

BOHM   There may not be a conscious goal in the way you act and react to the meanings. It's implicit only in that when you react to the shadow because of past experience, you want to escape the assailant.

WEBER   That would be a kind of goal. There might be such immediate goals that it would be hard to call them teleological.

SHELDRAKE   But we don't have to assume that somebody is conscious of their goal in order to attribute teleology to it. In dealing with the behaviour of animals, say the nesting instinct of the bird, we can clearly say that the bird is building the nest in a purposive way to lay eggs in it. It may well be that the bird building the nest isn't conscious of all these goals and doesn't see it the way we see it, but most people would say that it's purposive behaviour, even the Neo-Darwinians when they talk about adapting and selective advantage. So teleology doesn't imply a sense of conscious purpose.

BOHM   It may be an implicit theme, and in that sense a goal. In some cases the reaction is so fast that we can hardly say it has a goal. If it has been built up very strong, the meaning reacts almost automatically, so the sense of goal is reduced.

WEBER   In the example that Rupert gave, one might want to call it instinct. How does instinct relate to meaning and purpose?

SHELDRAKE   The studies of instinct or innate behavior show that in fact they are related to particular things, to particular meanings. Classical ethology of the type done by Tinbergen and Lorenz has shown that animals react to what we call sign stimuli, namely, particular features of the environment which have a meaning for them. It would be difficult to understand these results without introducing the notion of meaning. A male robin in the mating season will attack other male robins and it has been shown that this is because of their red breasts. The red has a meaning-correlation. It means something like another male intruding on his territory. If you show a stuffed male robin, then it will also attack that—but not as fiercely as a real one. But if you give it a stuffed male robin without a red breast, it is quite indifferent to it. If you take just a bundle of red feathers and nothing else, it will attack the red feathers. So the sign stimulus is this particular feature of the environment which has meaning for it. That's an innate response.

WEBER   In the examples you have given it sounds so automatic that I wonder if the meaning for the robin is anything like the meaning of something for a human being? Are we imputing too much in that example?

SHELDRAKE   I don't think so. The example David gave was one where the meaning is automatic. The idea of the shadow as an assailant in the night is also very immediate in our own experience of the world. The very act of perception involves a kind of implicit naming, a categorizing of our environment, and therefore gives it meaning in relation to other things and to ourselves. Our conscious experience is inseparable from that, and much of our unconscious experience too.

WEBER   But would we be willing to say that the robin is conscious?

SHELDRAKE   I wasn't saying that. I was saying that this thing has a meaning for the robin.

BOHM   We want to distinguish meaning from awareness. Meaning is a form of consciousness but not necessarily aware consciousness. If we say consciousness is knowing in any sense, there is aware consciousness and unaware consciousness.

WEBER   The person who reacts to the shadow with psychosomatic stress symptoms and the robin are examples of unaware consciousness.

BOHM   William James suggested that meaning is in the activity which the sign gives rise to. Immediate activity may be actual but also virtual activity in the sense that it starts as one of many possibilities, only one of which is actually carried out. In the computer, you could say that information in the silicon chips gives rise to further activity in the computer. The activity would be the meaning of that information. The point is you can never fully define the meaning because it depends on the context. So whether a certain set of lights and shade is an assailant or just a shadow depends on the context, which includes the whole background of that person and what he knows.

WEBER   Included in the context is the nature of the individual perceiver?

BOHM   Not only all that he knows, but his whole character.

WEBER   We have been talking about this from the point of view of the individual. But both of you focus on the individual as the expression of a field which is beyond the individual. Let us look at this issue now from the field's point of view.

BOHM   I'd like to mention DNA as an activity of meaning. DNA is said to constitute a code or language. It's read by the RNA. According to the context the RNA reads various segments of the DNA and takes out the meaning, which is to construct various proteins. The whole language of geneticists is such that they're tacitly recognizing the role of information and meaning.

WEBER   When we say "the RNA 'reads' the DNA," is that a standard term?

SHELDRAKE   Yes. The DNA is transcribed into the RNA and the RNA is then translated into protein.

WEBER   So it is really an informational language and a meaning-oriented language.

BOHM   You can't discuss information unless you are discussing meaning. If you want to say what information is, you can use Gregory Bateson's definition, "It's a difference that makes the difference," but that's not enough because every difference makes a difference. I propose that it's a difference of form that makes a difference of content or meaning. On the printed page, differences in form make a difference in the meaning.

WEBER   That is what words are.

BOHM   It makes a difference in the activity to which that page gives rise or the activity to which the computer chip gives rise. Or DNA. So molecular biologists are, at least tacitly, treating meaning and information as real.

SHELDRAKE   More than tacitly because many of them subscribe to the metaphor of a genetic program, where behavior is assumed to be programmed in the DNA. DNA exists before the thing programmed and contains a goal or a purpose. A computer program has a goal and a purpose. The idea of a genetic program means that biology has imported the metaphor of computer programs and informational language. It permeates modern biological theory. Another idea of meaning in genetics comes from the extreme neo-Darwinism of Dawkins and sociobiology.

WEBER   The selfish genes?

SHELDRAKE   Yes. If you read Dawkins's books, these selfish genes think, manipulate, calculate, create bodies and do a whole lot of things which we normally associate with life and mind. Projected on to these inert DNA molecules are all these properties of meaning and purpose. Certainly it's not going beyond current biological theory to attribute meaning to most, if not all, biological phenomena.

WEBER   But what are fields of meaning?

BOHM   I think we should go on to physics here. The first reaction of a scientist might be that this is the sort of language that biologists use, but really everything is made up of little particles which have no meaning if you were to analyze it in enough detail. Quantum mechanics is saying an analysis cannot be made. I've discussed this in terms of the implicate order but also in terms of another model which I've called the causal interpretation of the quantum theory. Those two, in fact, are closely related but I don't think we can develop that here.

WEBER   Could you give a sketch of it?

BOHM   That was a model I've proposed where I said that an electron is a particle, but it has a field around it which obeys Schroedinger's equation, called the wave function. The field and the particle are never separated. The mathematics implies that this Schroedinger-field acts on the particle in a new way. The new way is this: The action depends only on the form of that field and not on its intensity. Therefore it is not a mechanical action like the wave pushing a cork or a ship around. It is more like a radar wave which is guiding the ship on an automatic pilot. That suggests that this wave acts as information, a form that gives rise to an activity which is its meaning.

Somebody might object, "How could you expect an electron to be as complex as a ship or a computer?" It goes against the whole tradition which believes that if you analyze smaller and smaller particles you find simpler and simpler behavior. But it turns out the other way; quantum mechanical behavior is far from mechanical and is very subtle. It's only large masses of things which obey the simple mechanical laws, just as only large masses of human beings obey simple statistical rules. Individually they are far more subtle. One reason people didn't think that we could ever get a physical interpretation of quantum theory was the problem of multi-dimensional space. They said "What does a multi-dimensional space mean physically?" But if we view it as a field of information, it becomes clearer since we know that information is organized in any number of dimensions. Therefore there is no reason why the information field around the electron cannot be said to be in multi-dimensional space. The meaning of this field determines the interrelationships of the particles. It may mean that things which are quite distant from each other are still connected. More than that, it means that the interrelation of these particles depends on the state of the whole in a way which is not a pre-assigned property of the parts. The whole has a certain prior meaning, prior to the parts.

It is like the score of a dance. Electrons in a super-conducting state, for example, move in a regular, coordinated way so they don't scatter. In an ordinary state, they are like a disorganized crowd of people. Now if you compare this to the ballet, you could say that in the super-conducting state, the wave function is like the *score*—it's a kind of information—and the dance is the meaning of the score. It is possible for the wave function to have a special form—mathematically called *factorize*—where the various dancers are independent. Generally they are not. This explains why at higher temperatures we get independence and classical behavior. But the lower the temperature, the less the independence. There are other conditions which favor quantum mechanical behavior, but in general high temperature favors independence of the various dancers, so the system falls into independent parts. The meaning of the whole score is such that it determines how many independent dances are going on and what they are. To make this ballet dance analogy better, let's say the wave function score is not fixed, but it's a score which depends on the initial configuration of the particle. The dance would vary according to the initial configurations of the dancer.

WEBER Improvisation, not strict choreography?

BOHM Yes, as if the score were evolving according to Schroedinger's equation, as if there were rules by which the dance itself is constantly changing. That gives you a fairly good intuitive picture of what the meaning of quantum mechanics is. We can say that the basic properties of matter—which determine chemistry, super-conductivity, DNA, life—come from this. They don't come from the mechanics; they come from this. There would be no chemistry and no molecules were it not for this property.

SHELDRAKE Why is it that if this implication of quantum mechanics is so clear it is not taken more seriously by chemists and biologists?

BOHM The reason has to do with the history of physics. DeBroglie proposed something like this in the beginning of 1927 at the Solvay

Congress but most of the physicists were against it because many of them were positivists and they didn't like this model; it had too many pictures in it that were unverifiable. Second, he didn't answer some important objections that Pauli made about the many-body problem. He wasn't in a position to answer it. Third, Einstein didn't like it—but that was for a different reason, because it was non-local. Since neither side liked it, nobody took it up. DeBroglie lost interest and gave it up.

WEBER   That's a good example of what Thomas Kuhn claims [in *The Structure of Scientific Revolutions*]: that scientific paradigms are accepted or rejected according to the interests and beliefs prevailing among scientists at a given time.

BOHM   Yes, and the result was the current physical interpretation, for which Bohr is the clearest proponent, that quantum mechanics deals with nothing but phenomena. It cannot discuss what is; it gives only statistical rules for connecting phenomena. That has become the accepted paradigm. People have forgotten where it even came from. Like the tribal legends, they don't even know they have them.

WEBER   Are you saying that this automatic response of physicists is analogous to the instant response to the shadow?

BOHM   Yes. I'm saying all paradigms work that way. That once they are picked up by consensus—in the same way you pick up your cues in the dark—you respond instantly to that situation according to conditioning.

WEBER   Even paradigms on a very high and subtle level?

BOHM   It then operates on a very subtle level.

SHELDRAKE   This would also apply to entire cultures, wouldn't it? Because one's entire culture gives one a whole set of values, meanings, and responses most of which are completely automatic.

WEBER   From your point of view, Rupert, this would then build up forms in the morphogenetic field and strengthen these automatic responses and feed back into that very behavior in the explicate domain.

SHELDRAKE   Yes, that's what I've been suggesting. There are two separate issues here. The first is the nature of fields in relation to meaning: how fields are the interface between matter and meaning. Fields organize what we call matter, or rather energy. And they organize it in accordance with what we can recognize as meaning. I don't know if David would see it that way.

Second, there is the question of how these fields come to be the way they are. Although a field of meaning—as David made extremely clear—is one that depends more on the form than on intensity, there are situations in the natural world where different fields of meaning conflict. This happens in biology when you hybridize two species which each have different behavior patterns and instinctive behavior. If there are two formative fields operating on the same system, there is a kind of conflict between them. They could be competing for control of the material bringing it the two different meanings. We have visual analogues for this like necker cubes, and so on, where the same soma can take on two different significances. It can flicker between the two. You either see it one way or you see it in the other.

BOHM   You can have a tremendous number of ways of seeing the same situation, yet there is something invariant that builds up the concept of the object.

WEBER   One thing is not clear: Do you two agree on what a field is? Rupert says it's the interface between matter and meaning.

BOHM   Yes, meaning is the bridge between the mental and the physical sides. The wave function is a kind of mental side of the electron, the information content determining its nature. But quantum mechanics is a very limited way of looking at this whole thing. There might be a super quantum field, a super quantum potential, which organizes the quantum field.

WEBER   But you will have an infinite regress: You could have many of these potentials, each organizing the sublevel—shading off into what?

BOHM   The unknown. We have to say that all meaning is always in a context. There is no meaning which is absolutely complete in itself. There is always the question of content and context: a given content of meaning always depends on its context, you never can define it exactly. The context is another content which depends on a context.

WEBER   The context and the meaning *for whom?*

BOHM   The one who understands meaning is part of the context.

WEBER   Now we are talking about human beings. In the human world it is natural to refer to meaning, information, interpretation, and context. Isn't it is much harder to know what it might mean to talk about context or meaning from the electron's point of view?

BOHM   That's what I've just been discussing. The wave function gives the information-content and the activity is the meaning of that. The electron is doing much the same as what we are doing when we react to a situation. I'm suggesting that if you are going to understand anything as strange as quantum mechanics you have to be ready to consider some strange ideas. Otherwise you can only calculate.

WEBER   Somebody might say you're anthropomorphizing matter in the way the ancients did.

BOHM   I don't know if anybody can help that. The mechanical view also anthropomorphizes. The idea of force comes from your personal experiences of pushing things around. Then you extend that and say it's universal.

WEBER   Does this trouble you, Rupert, that Dave seems to be attributing to the electron a kind of consciousness analogous to our own?

BOHM   Not awareness, but a kind of meaning.

SHELDRAKE   I think it makes total sense.

WEBER   Not a meaning for us, but a meaning for itself.

BOHM   When you say that the DNA has meaning, for whom does it have meaning?

WEBER   That's the question. For itself, or for us?

SHELDRAKE   Richard Dawkins thinks it is for itself. It is a self-referential "selfish gene" in relation to its own survival.

WEBER   One might get around this by saying that's a reflexive feedback system. It's life! But what sense would it make to say that the electron behaves like something that's alive? You are making it sound as if it's alive in a minimal way.

BOHM   Maybe it is! What sense would it make to say it's not? The electron must behave in all sorts of strange ways, like being a wave and a particle at the same time and jumping from one state to another without passing in between—and doing all sorts of things that cannot be understood but only be calculated. If you don't want to say it's alive I suggest that you should say that the electron is a total mystery and all you can do is to compute statistically how it will reveal itself phenomenally in certain kinds of measurements.

WEBER   Somebody could bring up a counter-argument: that in order for us to escape the frustrating epistemological dilemma of not knowing whether it is a wave or a particle, we impute a human model to it because it simplifies our understanding.

BOHM   That's exactly what the mechanist has done!

WEBER   How?

BOHM   By the idea of the mechanical system and forces, which is a human model of pushing things around. Mechanism began with people pushing things around.

WEBER   From the outside. But you're arguing that the electron is pushing itself around from the inside, for a reason.

BOHM   Well, why shouldn't it? Human beings used to think everything moves itself, then gradually we built up a paradigm which said that doesn't happen.

WEBER   Seventeenth-century mechanism, the clockwork universe!

SHELDRAKE   What could be more anthropomorphic in human modelling than to say that everything's a machine? Machines are entirely and specifically human creations. It is based on a particular kind of human activity.

BOHM   In fact it is based on projecting into matter the sort of things that you do with your body.

WEBER   Perhaps we trust that and feel it's more respectable because while we admit that we create and program the machine, we can step away from it. Then it's as if nature itself behaves neutrally through the machine, and we forget that we are its author.

SHELDRAKE   In the traditional model just as we are the author of the machine, so the universe is a machine created by God.

WEBER   In Descartes and in Newton.

SHELDRAKE   The traditional mechanistic model was a thoroughgoing and consistent application of the machine analogy. A machine is meaningless apart from the maker and designer of the machine.

WEBER   But then you are saying that the mechanistic model is anthropomorphic in the extreme.

BOHM   Obviously!

WEBER   This has never been brought out.

SHELDRAKE   It is extremely clear that it must be so. In fact, one of the main arguments in early nineteenth-century natural theology was the argument from design, which says that the natural world of living animals and plants shows extraordinary adaptation to their circumstances and environment. If we regard them as machines— and the theologians didn't quarrel with the idea of calling them machines—this presupposes a designer. This was the argument that Darwin tried to overcome by saying that you don't need a designer, it can all happen by chance through natural selection. Darwinian theory attempts to explain the problem of design— which was the principal problem Darwin was grappling with—in terms of random chance and physical laws. The fact of the matter is that the machine analogy is entirely anthropomorphic.

WEBER   Fascinating!

BOHM   In any case, why shouldn't it be anthropomorphic? If you think man is a manifestation of the cosmos, man may well find models of the cosmos in himself.

WEBER   That's the hermetic dictum again.

SHELDRAKE   If the electron and the atom are not alive, then how come the living organism is made of electrons and atoms? That leads straight to vitalism. A denial of life or anything remotely like life in non-living systems raises the question of how we get life in living systems.

WEBER   That seems to be the mystery. From what we've said, therefore, you choose your anthropomorphic models no matter what you do. You cannot escape them. It's the Kantian dilemma, slightly shifted.

BOHM   Why is it a dilemma?

WEBER   Science supposedly wants objectivity, wants to leave its own values and subjective views at the doorstep. Now we're saying that's impossible.

BOHM   You may get objectivity but the model doesn't come from the object, it comes from the creative action of the mind.

WEBER   Why don't scientists admit this?

BOHM   The model of the object doesn't come around and say: "My model is x, please use this model."

WEBER   We said that the electron has a kind of consciousness. How does that shed light on the idea of its field-like context?

BOHM   In quantum mechanics we have fields of information in the wave function, and perhaps super quantum fields which organize the quantum field itself. These fields are not in space-time but they are in this multi-dimensional space, at least mathematically speaking. Space and time are also anthropomorphic concepts. They are meanings. If you say this super wave function is itself not organizing space and time as we know it, then you have a field of a different nature. But the space-time meanings and the super wave function field may contact each other and all relevant meanings might be in contact.

WEBER   This is similar to Rupert's thesis that meanings vibrate as certain frequencies, tune in on each other, pass on the information, store it, and replay it in the morphogenetic field.

BOHM   There might be contact at this level, but the particles executing their dances take their cue from their own wave function. But you see, the higher level could affect the particles at lower levels.

WEBER   This dance of meaning in many dimensions is your idea of the meaning-field?

BOHM   It's some kind of field, isn't it, because it is not located anywhere and it doesn't manifest itself locally.

WEBER   It transcends the finite entities in it and explains them.

BOHM   Yes. To come back to the quantum field again, the information field, you could almost say the electrons are the difference between participation and interaction. If there's a common view of meaning, the electrons are participating in a common activity or common dance, whereas the mechanical view is that they are just interacting, pushing at each other. Even interaction is a meaning— being a particle is a meaning. Being mechanical is a meaning. It is impossible for anything not to be a meaning. It is true that meaning could be actually grasped in that way.

WEBER   This sounds very much like Spinoza, for whom everything can be looked at either as a system of extension, matter, or as a system of consciousness, which we are calling meaning; and that these are not two realities but two expressions of *one* underlying reality. They don't refer to two realities as they do in Descartes or in any other dualist; they refer to one reality which can be conceived in these two ways. As to this field of meaning, for Dave the field is primary; it is the organizer of what takes place in it.

BOHM   You might say there is an energy which is relatively un-formed and the field organizes that and this ultimately gives rise to the particles.

WEBER   How does Rupert view this?

SHELDRAKE   The field builds up the entities. What I am saying is similar to what David is saying. The field organizes the energy. The field and the energy can't really be separated. You can't have energy in a completely free-floating form. Both are important. The energy gives a kind of actuality or activity to something. The field gives it its organization. The two are related.

WEBER   Would you both agree as to how the organizing field gets built up?

BOHM   We are looking at different things. From the side of physics, you look at certain things primarily with the evidence available. You could say that the chemical molecule now has a field, namely the Schroedinger field, which organizes it and therefore there is not such a sharp distinction between the field and the particle. The organizing field is present everywhere and I'm proposing that there may be super-organizing fields which organize the wave function and that might shade over into all sorts of other fields, so that we are looking at two different areas in which this organization is taking place.

WEBER   As a philosopher I want to say, "Take it a step further back: How did it get there?" What's the real cause? It is not biology, it is not physics. What is it? Pure thought?

BOHM   At present physics or the study of cosmology is raising questions of the origin of the universe in which within the first few fractions of a second of the universe a tremendous evolution took place in which there were originally neither particles nor space nor time nor anything else as we know it. Then somehow it all developed. People take it for granted that during this whole process the laws of quantum mechanics were the same, though everything else changes. They *assume* that, even though quantum mechanics is supposed to refer to nothing but the results of measurements, although measurements would have been impossible without anything to measure.

SHELDRAKE   So, as to whether natural laws are eternally given or whether they are gradually built up—how do you see that?

BOHM   I think, in view of the implicate order, that the notion of formative fields gradually becoming necessary is what is called for. Even modern physics is pointing to that idea by saying there was a time prior to the Big Bang before any of these units like molecules, quarks, atoms, even existed. So if you said there were certain fixed and everlasting laws of the molecules and atoms, then what would you say if you traced it back to the time before the atoms and molecules existed? Physics can say nothing about that. It can say only that there was a formation of these particles at a certain stage. So there would have to be an actual development in which the necessity in a certain field grew more and more fixed. You can even see that happening as you cool down a substance that liquefies; at first you get little clumps of liquid which are transient, and then they get bigger and more determinate. Now physicists explain all this by saying that the laws of the molecules are eternal; molecules are merely consequences of those laws, or derived from those laws. But if you follow that back and ask, Where were molecules? Well, they were originally protons and electrons, which were originally quarks, which were originally sub-quarks. And it goes right back to a stage where none of the units we know even existed, so the whole schema sort of fades out. It's then open to you to say that, in general, fields of necessity are not eternal; they are constantly forming and developing.

SHELDRAKE   I think that the current conventional and scientific picture hasn't really faced up to this at all. You see, science started with a sort of neo-Platonic, neo-Pythagorean notion—the idea of timeless laws—which has been taken for granted in science for a very long time. I think that when the evolutionary theory in biology came in, it triggered the beginning of change. We then had an evolutionary view of reality regarding animals and plants, but it was still considered that there was a timeless background of the physical world, the molecular and atomic world. Now we've gone to the cosmology of the Big Bang, which is fairly widely accepted. So now we've got the idea of the entire universe as being a radically evolutionary universe. And this, I think, provokes a crisis, and should provoke a crisis. The idea of timeless laws that have always been there, somehow pervading space and time, ceases to have much meaning when you have an actual historical Big Bang, because you then obviously have the problem: Where were the laws before the Big Bang?

BOHM   You could carry this back to a point at which present quantum mechanics was just coming into being, that is, the entire formative structure of quantum mechanics may have emerged from some other state of affairs and so on, as a field of meaning.

WEBER   The "and so on" is the most exciting part. What does it mean?

BOHM   The very nature of meaning is such that it is always in a context. Any attempt to think about something abstracts the content which is then in the background or context. That is part of the limitation of thought. Thought does not explicitly grasp the whole but it grasps some aspect, something is abstracted out of it and then it takes the rest into account as the context. Therefore, it is not possible for thought to perceive and capture it all. This is even true in mathematics, according to Goedel. There are always presuppositions in your mathematical reasoning.

WEBER   Is there a meaning field before time and space began, before quantum mechanics ever arrived upon the scene? A pure manifestation of the meaning field?

BOHM   It seems that you are not going to get it by looking outwardly because every outward investigation is an abstracted content in a context.

WEBER   Then let's not look outward. Should we look inward?

BOHM   That's really our most immediate experience with meaning. If you want to understand meaning at that level of depth, you have to go into where you most directly experience it.

WEBER   Into inward consciousness, self-awareness?

BOHM   That level of depth, yes.

SHELDRAKE   If soma and significance are the way that all of these fields work, and if the "universe" as a whole is the soma—what's its significance? The meaning of the universe can't lie within the matter of the universe. This leads naturally to the whole question of the nature of God, the nature of consciousness or ultimate mind, the nature of meaning itself.

BOHM   That is, the question of the purpose of all this activity.

WEBER   If the physical universe is the *soma*, as in Spinoza—nature's or God's body—then the non-soma or meaning is the cosmic mind or nature's thought. Meaning is therefore a part of *all* the levels of being. Rupert brings in the notion of meaning, mind, or God, at this highest level we can articulate. Since all meaning is purposive and active, that adds up to a claim that everything is a partner in the evolution of the universe—at all the levels from the sub-atomic, biological, historical, and social domains, to something beyond that we only can dimly conjecture about. Is that too sweeping a generalization?

BOHM   That is the participatory universe.

WEBER   It is participatory, but physicists like John Wheeler mean it in the very restricted sense that the observer is somehow always part of the readout.

BOHM   But I'm saying that everything is the observer and everything is the observed.

WEBER   Let's pursue that.

BOHM   The electron, in so far as it responds to a meaning in its environment, is observing the environment. It is doing exactly what human beings are doing. The word "observe" means to gather, to pay attention.

WEBER   So the electron is observing us?

BOHM   It is gathering information about us, about the whole universe. It is gathering-*in* the universe and responding accordingly. Therefore it is observing, if you take that in its literal sense.

WEBER   The electron does it in its way, biological systems do it in their way. Certainly it is clearest in the social, psychological and political domain. There it is self-evident. Does it work at more subtle levels, such as in field–consciousness? If meaning is active, the meaning is the consciousness. Consciousness is essentially meaning, whether we are aware of the meaning or not.

BOHM   If you removed all meaning, where would the consciousness be? All that you are conscious of is meaning.

WEBER   To an amoeba which gets poked and stimulated, what is the meaning, Rupert?

SHELDRAKE   I'd use the word "mental" where David uses "consciousness." If in the word "consciousness" you include unconscious and non-aware behavior, then for an amoeba being prodded or coming into an acidic environment, the meaning is the "unfavorable environment." The amoeba moves away from that.

WEBER   It will respond and even learn, and we are using that as one criterion of meaning, even at the level of the amoeba.

BOHM   In some way the electron is doing that, too. There is no sharp break. Meaning is not only what consciousness is all about, it is also the whole activity of consciousness; meaning immediately acts in some way. So if you take the whole content and its activity, what else is there left of consciousness except meaning?

WEBER   You are saying that is its most fundamental characteristic.

BOHM   Its essence is meaning.

SHELDRAKE   And meaning's essence is action.

BOHM   Meaning is action.

WEBER   Is there ever anything at all without meaning? We've answered over and over that there cannot be.

SHELDRAKE   There may be things without meaning in a particular context for particular people or things.

WEBER   Then that's their meaning: that they lack meaning and they presuppose that they should have it, at least according to Heidegger and Sartre.

BOHM   To say "it is mechanical" is a meaning. To say "there is not much to it" is a meaning. Whatever you say about it is a meaning. If you are aware of it at all, it means something.

SHELDRAKE   There is a lot that you are not aware of.

BOHM   Well, then you don't know. Whatever you are conscious of or aware of is a meaning. Every action is a meaning. Every action which comes from that is a part of the meaning. Correct meaning for us would be where *our* meaning would be coherent with the meaning of a thing for itself.

SHELDRAKE But we have our own meanings. The wheat plant, for example, has a certain meaning for itself, like many grasses, but it has a considerable meaning for us since it is the basis for our agriculture.

BOHM The two have to be coherent to be correct; they do not have to be the same.

SHELDRAKE Coherent, yes. If we got the wrong idea about wheat plants, we wouldn't grow them very successfully.

BOHM Wheat would have a certain meaning for us, to eat it and do all sorts of things with it. But if we said rocks have that particular meaning for us, it wouldn't work out.

WEBER Could we say that the closer we get to the way the meaning of the universe is for itself, the more correct we will be about the meaning of it?

BOHM That's true with some proviso, because we are part of the universe and our meaning is part of the universe. Every time we create a new meaning, it's like several molecules coming together to form a larger meaning. They all move together and dance within that larger one. Therefore, if we create a new meaning of the universe in ourselves, we are involved in that movement and that whole movement has to be coherent, not merely a coherent reflection of that thing outside inside us.

WEBER That is not clear.

BOHM Suppose, as an example, we apply meaning to society. Karl Marx says society means to me a place where there are classes and where people are exploiting each other and where they should stop that. By creating that meaning Marx has already effected a change in society which he has spread to other people. In other words, the meaning is part of the very thing he is talking about either coherently or incoherently. Hitler was hoping his would be coherent. Other people say it wasn't.

WEBER The problem is: "Are we back to the correspondence theory of truth?" Are there coherent meanings which are in phase with the objects of the meaning, that are closer to some primary meaning than others? Is Marx closer than Plato or Christianity to the way things are?

BOHM The difficulty is that the meaning helps to create the very thing that is meant. Therefore, you can only ask, "Does the whole thing work without conflict, without breaking up?"

WEBER If that is the criterion, you have a coherence theory of truth which is Spinoza, and not Plato. It asks "Does the whole thing work as a unity?" not "Does it reflect some ideal truth?"

BOHM The reflection is secondary. The meaning that you have

about the radio set is a reflection of its actual structure because that is fairly mechanical and it doesn't respond to your meaning. But what you mean about other people and communicate cannot be separated. It becomes part of them and part of you.

WEBER   So the meaning field applies to both matter and consciousness and literally organizes everything.

BOHM   We have to add that in physics we have not been in a position to pay a lot of attention to how the general meaning field has evolved. In biology, as Rupert is suggesting, we can discuss the evolution of this formative field in the ways he is talking about. In physics the nearest we have got to it is by thinking about the origin of the universe. At present, it is rather early to try to discuss that question in physics.

WEBER   Why are things organized via meaning? Is it a hopeless question to ask what the meaning of meaning is?

BOHM   You can ask it, but it is the same as Goedel's theory. There will always have to be presuppositions in your answer. You can merely say: Can we ask this at a deeper level and understand more broadly?

SHELDRAKE   It seems to me that there will always be differences of opinion on this. There have been for 2,500 years and more. You will always have people who say that any meaning we attribute to the universe is simply a projection of our own minds and the only thing we can know is our way of seeing things. Now that view really says that reality is essentially mysterious and we can only know certain aspects of it. The idea that we can ever know reality itself is an illusion.

WEBER   Kant!

SHELDRAKE   Then there will be people who say our world is full of meanings, that it is a kind of messy and provisional reflection of a much more ideal world of mathematical formulae.

WEBER   Plato!

SHELDRAKE   In that interpretation the imperfections of our world are due to the darkness or intractability of the material world which imperfectly reflects that rational world. The third view is most fully developed in the ancient world by Aristotle. It's the doctrine of hylomorphism: with form and matter as two sides of the same thing. Since his interpretation of the meaning is teleological in terms of things having purposes or goals, the meaning of both sides gives coherence to a thing and also defines a unity of its different aspects related to its goal. My own view is in the Aristotelian tradition. In any case, there is a coherent tradition of looking at the world which is similar to what we are talking about.

WEBER   We could also map this on to eastern ideas where consciousness, or a meaning field, is primary and precipitates itself as matter.

The Brahman–Atman identity thesis in Hinduism is quite similar to what we've been discussing. From one point of view it is self-awareness and meaning, from another it's the manifested universe. The idea is found in a variety of cultural maps: Aristotelian, Spinozistic, Hindu, and also Buddhist. Of course the question that is unanswerable is "What is the point of the development of the thing?" We are partners in evolution, we change being by changing meaning. "Why?"

BOHM What kind of answer do you want? It is a part of our nature to find a coherent meaning because we are meaning. An incoherent meaning means that we are in some way unhealthy. Our being will not be right. Just simply the aim to be whole inspires the search for a coherent meaning. We are not in a good position now to understand your question deeply because there isn't much of a coherent meaning in society. People have more or less come to take it for granted that there isn't one. They can hardly even imagine what it would be like to have one. That's a temporary state of affairs, I hope. If there were a generally coherent meaning which was true in the sense that I've explained, and not self-deceptive, you would appreciate its value without question in the same way you appreciate being healthy. You don't ask "Why should I be healthy?"

WEBER You are talking about wholeness there. The other possible answer that has sometimes been given—in Hegel, for example—is that our meaning lights up the implicit meaning of the whole cosmos for itself. In that sense we are partners, information centers that register and encode and influence what's happening. So it is not just our health but the health of the whole that's involved.

BOHM But meaning is such that if there is unhealthiness in one part of meaning, the whole thing is unhealthy because we are all in each others' contexts.

WEBER So we are talking about it from the individual, the field, and the super-field level.

BOHM Yes.

WEBER Is the Grand Unified Theory that physicists are looking for similar to your super-organizing field?

BOHM Implicitly, yes.

In love there's never a pure identity because love involves two and yet the two become one. That's the great mystery.

FR. BEDE GRIFFITHS

When sensation, attachment, and possession are *not*, then love and compassion come into being.

KRISHNAMURTI

I think that to have a life entirely free from suffering would also mean a life free from compassion, because compassion is the last suffering of an Arhat, of an accomplished one.

LAMA GOVINDA

HIS HOLINESS, THE DALAI LAMA

7

Compassion as a field of emptiness

HIS HOLINESS, THE DALAI LAMA OF TIBET

> Some day, after we have mastered the winds, the waves, the
> tides and gravity, we shall harness ... the energies of love.
> Then, for the second time in the history of the world, man
> will have discovered fire.
>
> TEILHARD DE CHARDIN

OF all the figures in this book, this was surely the one with the
fabled background. The man I had come to interview had
prominent cheek-bones and wide-set, intelligent dark eyes framed by
glasses. His head was clean-shaven, and he wore the traditional bur-
gundy saffron-bordered monk's robe of the Gelugpa order with which
he is formally associated (although he is in fact the head of all Tibetan
Buddhists). Then in his mid-forties, the Dalai Lama conveyed a vitality
and strength that recalled the mountain-stock of his ancestors. He spoke
excellent English and was at home in western ways, tinkering with the
tape-recorder when its performance seemed doubtful.

His Holiness, the Fourteenth Dalai Lama, was born Tenzin Gyatso
in 1935 in Taktser, a small village in north-eastern Tibet, to a peasant
family. At the age of two, he was found by a delegation that had
travelled all over Tibet in search of a successor to the recently deceased
Thirteenth Dalai Lama, a delegation that for a variety of reasons had
zeroed in on this obscure child. After passing the standard tests in
accordance with Tibetan tradition, Tenzin Gyatso was proclaimed as
the reincarnation of his predecessor, and at the age of five became the
spiritual and temporal leader of the Tibetan people.

Like a large proportion of Tibetan males, the child was educated in
Buddhist philosophy and religion, and received the doctorate in Buddhist philosophy (Geshe Lharampa Degree) when he was twenty-five
years old. To this end, he had to pass a series of rigorous examinations
at three famous monastic universities—Drepung, Sera, and Ganden—
and be tested by some two dozen scholars and logicians, an ordeal he
is said to have passed with honors. He assumed his residence at the
Potala in Lhasa, and his official duties as the Dalai Lama of Tibet, in

1950 at the age of sixteen. Exiled in 1959 by the Chinese military occupation, he fled with many fellow Tibetans across the Himalayas to northern India. Dharamsala has since then been the seat of the Tibetan government-in-exile, and the home of the numerous Tibetan refugees whose cause he takes up in his appearances throughout the world. He has met with most world leaders, the Pope, and even with the Communist Chinese leadership in an effort to improve the lot of Tibetans, and to plead for world peace.

Tibetan Buddhists believe that a Dalai Lama, whose title means "ocean of wisdom," chooses to be reborn out of compassion for the suffering of others, which he strives to relieve. In his autobiography, *My Land and My People*, the Fourteenth Dalai Lama explains that his humble peasant origins allowed him to empathize especially with the Tibetan poor.

The Dalai Lama has been honored by universities and governments all over the world, and is much in demand at conferences here and abroad. Our interview was preceded by talks at the University of Wisconsin and followed by a seminar at Harvard. Like Lama Govinda and Fr. Bede, the Dalai Lama seems to translate many of his ideas into his life. A calm and restful man, he interspersed his remarks with frequent bouts of laughter, like so many Tibetans I have met. When I saw him a few years earlier at the Newark Art Museum, he had attributed the easy laughter and joy among Tibetans, which westerners repeatedly wanted explained, to Buddhist ideas about life. In Chapter 9 Fr. Bede will pick up on this, citing the *Dhammapada* of Buddha, "In joy we live."

The interview took place on a fresh July morning in 1981 at Olcott, the tree-lined estate of the Theosophical Society in America in Wheaton, Illinois. On the day before, the Dalai Lama had given several talks to capacity audiences that converged on this small mid-western American city. During the evening talk he had pleaded for universal tolerance and compassion before about eight hundred and fifty people who ranged from interested laymen to scholars from the nearby University of Chicago and other local colleges.

With him were a number of other monks, his staff from the Office of Tibet in New York, and Dr. Jeffrey Hopkins, a Buddhist scholar from the University of Virginia, who acted as the Dalai Lama's translator when a particularly subtle metaphysical issue was under discussion. The relationship between these two was easy and so attuned that the conversation could lapse from English to Tibetan and back to English without notice. I saw the Dalai Lama's same gift for communication with very large audiences three years later at Amherst College, where he led a five-day conference on "outer and inner science." Although in this dialogue the Dalai Lama's interest in physics does not come up, it is strongly expressed in Chapter 13, where he discusses the subject with David Bohm.

In the present dialogue, the Dalai Lama focuses on one of the most fundamental and difficult of all Buddhist concepts: the void or "emptiness" (*sunya*). It denotes the unconditioned ground of being (akin to the source-ground of David Bohm's super-implicate order in Chapter 2) about which we can only speak in symbols. For humans it is experienced as a state of undifferentiated unity beyond subject-object distinctions and beyond space and time. Buddhists consider this the highest state of spiritual consciousness, in which ultimate reality is directly apprehended. Buddha termed it a state that is "unborn, unmade, uncreated," beyond human language and thought, and in this it appears close to what Kant termed "the noumenon." It is from this level of wholeness that true compassion derives. Compassion—the central ethical value of Buddhism—is therefore no mere emotion but rather a force that lies embedded in reality itself.

In this dialogue, the Dalai Lama also clarifies the idea of *karma*, the Buddhist theory of action and reaction, or universal causation. Like Lama Govinda in Chapter 3, he emphasizes its strong link to the intent, rather than the outcome, of our actions. In an earlier exchange, the Dalai Lama told me he felt no hatred towards the Chinese who invaded his land, dispossessed its people, and even singled out the monastics for torture and murder. He saw the tragedy, he said, as a challenge and opportunity to practice compassion. In Buddhism, he explained, "the kind of love we advocate is love you can have even for someone who has done you harm."[12] This sense of directness and compassion were the dominant impressions I took with me of the man who has said, "My religion is very simple—my religion is kindness."[13]

WEBER   Can we talk about compassion? What makes compassion, the unconditional love that you speak about, possible? Can the mere intention or the will to be compassionate bring it about?

THE DALAI LAMA   Both these factors are involved. First you should have the will, and then use constant effort and certain reasons for thinking in this way. In general, the main point is that through our own experience we can come to realize the value of kindness. If someone shows us a kind attitude, we appreciate it very much. Similarly, according to our own experience, if I show a kind attitude to others, they will definitely appreciate it. In our practical affairs, on an international level, on an individual family level, we want peace, harmony, and both are based on kindness and reason. This applies to people in general, whether they are believers or non-believers. It is the way to cultivate kindness.

For believers there may be more reasons and more techniques, more ways to train oneself in this. If someone accepts the God-theory, the theory of a creator, then all mankind are truly brothers

and sisters of one Father. Even to our common sense, a family
where two brothers or sisters fight, everybody regards that—fighting brothers and sisters—as something bad. So you see, since all
men and women are the children of one Creator, there is no other
way than harmony and remaining brothers in the true sense. Once
you accept God as the ultimate reality or ultimate power, then it
is clear that it is our duty to follow according to the wishes of
God. Since God created mankind, if we serve mankind we serve
a part of God. God we cannot touch, we cannot see. Just to pray
may not be sufficient. Love for God, transformed into action, is
the service of mankind.

Now some other believers (say Buddhists or Jainists) do not
accept a Creator. They believe in self-creation. We accept the
theory of rebirth, the theory of cause and effect, the karma created
by our own mind. We want happiness. The result, the state of
happiness, comes from good causes or virtue. If you want happiness, you must create the cause of happiness. Also, our distant and
long future depends on our present life. The present life is at
maximum a hundred years, maybe. Compared with the infinite
future, a hundred years is very short. So you see, if all your energy
and all your thinking is concentrated on wealth, on material things
(all that wealth belongs to this life), there is a maximum benefit
for one hundred years. Beyond that there's nothing. When you
leave this planet, this body, you cannot take one single penny. All
money, or whatever valuables, you cannot take. The only thing
which will follow you is your *merit*. [*Merit* in Buddhism is the
good karma, resulting from selfless actions, that accumulates over
our lifetime, or lifetimes.] So, in order to create a good future in
this infinite future, you must utilize the present life to its maximum
usefulness. That is making merit. The best way to accumulate
merit is through serving others. The best safeguard of merit is
control of anger. Anger destroys. Anger will destroy a great amount
of merit. Thinking along these lines—thinking, thinking, thinking—creates more confidence, more conviction, and it enables you
to carry out these actions through your own convictions.

WEBER   I can understand that if we were really kind to one another,
even in ordinary daily life, we would change the world. But that
can be partly the result of our decision and reasoning about the
world, a kind of super-politeness. Doesn't the kind of compassion
you speak of require a deeper thing, something like a direct harmony with one's Buddha-nature?

THE DALAI LAMA   I don't think so. When I speak, at the beginning
there are definitely some Buddhist ideas influencing my mind. But
the moment when I express myself, I am not thinking as a Buddhist but just as a human being.

WEBER   No matter what we call it, it is rare. You spoke of love even for one's enemies.

THE DALAI LAMA   Right.

WEBER   That's very difficult for most people. My question is: For the few for whom that is possible, what is it that makes it possible?

THE DALAI LAMA   If we analyze events properly, enemies are not permanent. In Chinese eyes, in the early years the United States was enemy number one. But now, you have become friends. So that is looking for the beneficial point of view. If in adopting a hostile attitude you were to get more benefit, then it is worthwhile to adopt a hostile attitude. If you think you get more benefit if you adopt a more friendly attitude, then you should adopt a friendly attitude. Therefore, for the politicians, even the Chinese Communists themselves or the Russians, or anybody, the attitude does not come about just unintentionally. There may be some exceptions, but generally, through reason, through weighing things, there is a change of attitude. If we adopt a hostile attitude toward someone and create hatred, if you think in deeper or wider perspectives about that, the end result definitely will be negative. By understanding that factor, we can conclude that a hostile attitude is not good. It is far better to adopt a friendly attitude. This is true even though the person from a certain perspective and from his side has a wrong attitude, and you might therefore conclude that in these particular circumstances you need a harsh attitude, a hostile attitude. But on second thought, if you think in long-term interests, you realize that kindness is much better, and that despite his attitude I must show a friendly attitude. That is what I feel.

WEBER   You're saying that it isn't just surface politeness, but people discover for themselves—even politicians—that from a wider view a friendly attitude works much better. They discover that things work better through cooperation than through conflict.

THE DALAI LAMA   Yes.

WEBER   That is why they adopt a kinder attitude. Not necessarily because they have had a mystical insight into the unity of life, is that right?

THE DALAI LAMA   That's right. Despite their ill-feeling, the circumstances compel them to adopt a more friendly attitude. Not a spiritual reason or "Buddha-nature" feeling or something like that. Just that they have calculated the bigger benefit. Not thinking of a future life, not thinking of God, not thinking of the Buddha, but just as a human being and from the viewpoint of a human being. The circumstance itself is telling us: Don't make more anger. You need kindness and harmony. This is what I feel, so I am approaching it on that level and in that way.

WEBER   But if that is their motive, do they still derive karmic merit, since they used kindness as a tool only and in a calculating way?

THE DALAI LAMA   Let us see. There are actions done without intention, and there are those intentionally already planned, but not yet implemented. There are also actions that are intentionally done, and then there are actions that are none of these. So you see, from the spiritual viewpoint you have done a good thing, but it was not motivated by religious-mindedness (*bodhicitta*).

The case we were discussing belongs to the category where you have done a good thing, although not intentionally. So the part which you have done, and from which something good results, at least is not bad. [Laughter.] It is good.

WEBER   It's clearly better for the world, but is it better for the individual who calculates?

THE DALAI LAMA   If the world gets peace, he also gets peace. Even if he is a non-believer, he gets some good thing out of it.

WEBER   It's deeply moving for people to listen to you talk about love and compassion toward enemies. I can understand that if, let us say, an enemy is now in jail, you shouldn't want retaliation or revenge. But it's more difficult to know how love and compassion would work toward an enemy who is still in power and still continues to harm others. How can one love those kinds of people?

THE DALAI LAMA   For a believer in God, all the reasons mentioned earlier apply. Or you can realize that his act also somehow is against God's will, and from that viewpoint you can have even more compassion for somebody who is committing sins.

WEBER   While he's actually doing it?

THE DALAI LAMA   Right. Now as Buddhists, we are not only considering this life but future lives. From that viewpoint, that person is accumulating bad karma. In the future, he will face the consequences. Realizing that, you will grow more compassionate toward him. All that depends on how clearly you yourself realize the implications of bad action. If you have greater realization, then you have more anxiety about his behavior.

WEBER   What about the question whether you need to take steps to stop his behavior?

THE DALAI LAMA   Speaking theoretically, under rare and special circumstances violence may be permissible. That is brought out in one of Buddha's own stories, preserved in a poem. There was a captain of a ship that was carrying five hundred merchants and out of the five hundred, one person was planning to kill the four hundred and ninety-nine merchants in order to get their belongings, their wealth. The captain was one of the previous incarnations of Buddha; in a previous life he was a Bodhisattva but had not yet become a Buddha. He warned that you should not carry on such activities. Despite his several warnings, that fellow did not listen, did not stop his plan, but carried it further. Then the captain decided that, in order to save four hundred and ninety-nine persons' lives as well as to prevent the sin of four hundred and ninety-nine killings which would be committed by one person, he would act. In order to save the man from that, he sacrificed for him a sin of his own, namely the killing of one man. With this motivation and under those circumstances, he killed that person.

Now you see, theoretically, this is absolutely right. The man, if he had been allowed to kill, would have committed a sin in killing four hundred and ninety-nine persons, and later he would have faced the bad results. Killing him just shortened his present life, nothing more. Compared to the bigger consequences of his intended act, that suffering is much lighter. The captain did not have a selfish motive such as "I do not want to commit a killing," which in this rare case would have been a selfish motive. So he did it.

Thus, under certain circumstances in order to stop the others' bad activity, and if it is purely motivated, violence is permissible. Therefore, in order to stop the others' behavior, you may need strong action, a forceful reaction. But you should not lose your ultimate compassion and compassionate thoughts. Here, you see, there are two types of motivation: one that is causal and one that occurs at the time of the actual action. The immediate motivation and the distant motivation. The distant or causal motivation is the compassion and love. The immediate motivation is some kind of anger. That anger itself, no doubt, is bad; but in order to take strong action for that immediate motivation, some anger is sometimes required. That is the main reason those wrathful deities appear.

WEBER   In the *Tibetan Book of the Dead?*

THE DALAI LAMA   Right, right.

WEBER   What the story brings out, then, is that it would have been more selfish of him *not* to kill in order to keep himself pure, and to allow the other man to heap the karma of the death of four hundred and ninety-nine people on himself. In those circumstances, the motivation was selfless, for the captain knew that the karmic consequences to himself would still be *a* killing. Despite that, he felt that it would be all right in that circumstance.

THE DALAI LAMA   That's right.

WEBER   So you are really saying that the motivation, and not the act, matters most. The motive changes the meaning of the act, is that right?

THE DALAI LAMA   Right, quite right. We believe that the method is not so important. The main concentration should go toward the motivation and result. Again, a good act and a bad act are not independent; it will depend on circumstances. With regard to virtue and non-virtue, there are acts that are virtuous or non-virtuous by way of their being, and there is virtue and non-virtue by way of motivation; and then by way of association. So you see, the act itself we cannot identify as good or bad in an absolute way. Killing is generally bad; yet, under these circumstances, killing is good. Again, it involves the theory of emptiness.

WEBER   Can you say something about emptiness? Westerners think emptiness is the same as nothingness.

THE DALAI LAMA   [Laughter] That is a misunderstanding. Emptiness is a simple word. Roughly speaking it is something like this: Things are dependent on each other. Therefore their nature is not basically independent. Independent and dependent are contradictory to each other. There is no third possibility. So since things are dependent on each other, there is no such thing in nature as "independent." That means selflessness and emptiness.

WEBER   That step is not clear: Emptiness, but why selflessness?

THE DALAI LAMA   "Empty" means self-less, without self, non-inherent existence, absence of any inherent existence. It is like zero; if you look, zero itself is nothing. But yet it is something. Without a zero we cannot make ten or a hundred. Similarly, with emptiness: It is emptiness, and at the same time it is the basis of *everything*. We can investigate. When we investigate, we cannot find any *thing*. We will just find emptiness. As to their nature, things do not exist in accordance with how they appear. Since there is something, an object, therefore we can investigate, for it means there is something deeper. But its own nature is empty of inherent existence.

WEBER   Is emptiness related to universal consciousness or universal compassion?

THE DALAI LAMA   That's different. Universal compassion is the moral and ethical side. It is a conventional aspect as opposed to the ultimate aspect. It is a subjective aspect, from the point of view of the appearance of the object that is empty. Emptiness is the nature of the object. Because of emptiness, it appears and disappears. The living being is born and disappears, suffering comes and goes, happiness comes and goes. All these things, all these changes, appearing and disappearing, are possible because of emptiness, because of the nature of the non-self existence. If suffering, suffering as well as bliss, were independent, then it could not change. If it would not depend on interdependent causes or factors, then it would not change. Because there is this reality of emptiness, it is possible for the changes and transformation of the objects that are empty to take place. The very change and transformation of the objects themselves is an indication, a sign of the reality of emptiness. It is from the point of view of the objects that have the quality of emptiness, that you get compassion.

WEBER   In deep meditation, it is possible to experience that emptiness.

THE DALAI LAMA   Of course. Without meditation, without deep meditation, you cannot be absorbed in emptiness (*sunya*). You cannot understand it. It will be mere words. Just understanding by way of verbal images is not sufficient. The next step is to think, think, think, to make a conviction of it. Once you have attained a wisdom that has arisen from reflection, then you can meditate one-pointedly on what you have understood. Then your mind not only concentrates fully on the object, but your mind also gradually becomes subtler and subtler. Ultimately, when all five sense organs have stopped [their business] and when your sixth [i.e. a more superficial layer of] consciousness also becomes subtler and subtler, then the ultimate, the innermost subtle mind becomes active in some sort of union with emptiness. That is the real depth-experience of emptiness. [Buddhism teaches that we have six senses: the consciousness of sight, hearing, smell, taste, touch, and mental consciousness or "mind-consciousness"; the latter refers to the ordinary, daily mind that registers, relates, combines, and stores sense-impressions. This is not the highest stage of mind or consciousness.]

WEBER   First one has to be immersed in it, there has to be a real experience, then the mind reflecting on it gets to subtler and subtler dimensions of itself: it is this combination of experience and reflection?

THE DALAI LAMA   Yes, the mind becomes more subtle and it gets easier to experience complete absorption, to become more and more absorbed in the reality of emptiness.

WEBER   Is it difficult without a teacher, especially in the west?

THE DALAI LAMA   It is difficult to experience. It needs many preparations and a long time to practice. In special cases, with some exceptional person, it may be a question of years. In a few years, you have this deeper experience, but generally speaking we count aeons (*kalpas*). So there's no hurry. [Laughter]

Mathematics has been remarkably unsuccessful in dealing with biology and biological forms.

RUPERT SHELDRAKE

We are beginning to have a mathematical theory about irreversible processes which exist objectively.

ILYA PRIGOGINE

Somewhere behind these molecules there is something still more subtle which we call mathematics, which rules all that.

DAVID BOHM

8

Mathematics: the scientist's mystic crystal

DAVID BOHM

The whole universe is one mathematical and harmonic
expression, made up of finite representations of the infinite.

F. L. KUNZ

I N this dialogue, David Bohm goes further in drawing parallels between science and mysticism than he did in 1979, when we discussed
this subject in London, further in fact than at any time since I have
known him. In that discussion ("The Mystic and the Physicist: Is a
Dialogue between them Possible?"), he stressed the separation of these
two figures as much as he did the commonalities, but in the present
dialogue Bohm links the drive behind science and mysticism more and
more closely. What absorbs him here is the meaning of mathematics,
which Bohm considers closer to a spiritual than a material reality. Why
should mathematics—an invisible, non-physical sort of thing—be the
powerful governor of matter, which is physical and visible? Bohm sides
with Poincaré and Einstein, that mathematics may be a mystery. A
central part of this dialogue deals with the mystery of creativity.
Whether this expresses itself in the insight of the mystic or the mathematician interests Bohm less than the process itself. The mathematician,
like the mystic, believes that his sudden flash of insight originates
beyond himself. Bohm's emphasis on sudden creative insights—reorganizing previous structures—invites comparison with Ilya Prigogine's
theory of dissipative structures in Chapter 10.

This dialogue took place in April of 1985 at my home in Princeton,
where the Bohms were staying for several days. Returning to Princeton
after twenty-five years was an emotional experience for Bohm and the
climax, he said, of a three-week lecture tour through the United States
that took him to Notre Dame University, the University of Texas at
Austin (at the invitation of John Archibald Wheeler, with whom he also
held discussions), Ramapo College, and Rutgers University, as well as
a talk at the UN, on the applications of the implicate order to world
peace.

Before I describe the reception of these lectures by academicians, I should perhaps say something about the growing "David Bohm movement" here and abroad. In the past five years, he has become something of a guru or near-cult figure to large numbers of people who see in his work a bridge between the scientific and the spiritual paths. He is asked to speak at almost every national and international conference dealing with these themes, and whole gatherings have recently been built around his ideas. At these conferences, he is lionized by people ranging from fellow physicists to graduate students to scores of young people from a variety of backgrounds, whose imagination he has somehow caught. Since Bohm is such a low-key figure, shy except when he talks—with animated passion—about his theories, this unsought adulation surprises him.

A more complex and sometimes ambivalent reaction characterizes his reception in academia. Bohm is respected in his profession, where his books on quantum mechanics and relativity made his reputation. The Bohm–Aharonov effect, mentioned in Chapter 2, testifies to his expertise in physics. But many of his peers are bewildered by Bohm's recent turn towards philosophy, perturbed by his interest in consciousness and the prominence it plays in his writings. I saw both of these reactions surface in a fascinating contrast during Bohm's lectures at Rutgers and Princeton. At Rutgers, Bohm presented his implicate order in laymen's language, using the "imaginative models" he feels are crucial to our understanding of physics (as he makes clear in Chapter 2). The audience, which ranged from physicists to humanists, was divided in its response. Many people felt they were in the presence, as they later said, of a deep and creative mind and were captivated by the meaningful picture of our universe which Bohm unfolded. Others, mainly scientists, were bewildered and worried that he was turning physics towards mysticism. They did not dispute the data but rather his interpretations of it. They were, naturally, uncomfortable with Bohm's attacks on physics' undue preoccupation with equations to the detriment of imaginative models—by now a familiar argument to the readers of this book.

Bohm's lectures before the Mathematical Physics Colloquium at Princeton the next day was a marked contrast to the one at Rutgers. Before a packed audience of mathematicians and physicists, Bohm explained his causal interpretation of quantum mechanics and his theory of hidden variables almost entirely through equations, covering blackboard after blackboard with them. His talk was received enthusiastically, stretching to several hours of technical exchanges and questions. Not once did anyone accuse Bohm of mysticism. I later asked him if his presentation at Princeton (which was too technical for me to follow) covered the same territory as the one at Rutgers the night before, and Bohm assured me that it did. The philosophical meaning of each talk was basically the same.

Something similar happened the next night at the small dinner party for Bohm to which I had invited my colleagues in mathematics, physics, and philosophy of physics. My colleagues were at first guarded before the sweep of Bohm's ideas, and resisted the crucial role in physics which Bohm assigns to consciousness. As the evening wore on, Bohm shifted from philosophical language into equations. The effect of this shift was dramatic. Suddenly, there was genuine rapport amongst the other scientists and Bohm, as pieces of paper covered with equations were passed back and forth along my dinner table. When later that evening Bohm reverted to his "imaginative models" I was amused to find everyone acting as if they understood what he meant.

WEBER   Do you see any relationship between science and mysticism?

BOHM   It depends on how you define them. If science is defined primarily as a method of measurement and experiment, there is not much of a relationship. But science may be broader.

WEBER   What is your definition of science?

BOHM   To try to understand reality or nature as a whole. In this definition it begins to overlap with the area the mystics are interested in.

WEBER   What is the area of overlap?

BOHM   It is the question about the nature of reality. The inquiry into matter can lead us to ask whether there is something beyond matter, or whether matter is so subtle that it is beyond matter as we ordinarily know it.

WEBER   If we explore matter as far as it can be explored, would we find within matter something that lies beyond matter?

BOHM   Yes, matter in its ordinary sense. The extreme religious view is the absolute transcendence beyond the sphere of matter. At the other extreme we have the ordinary mundane view, and then there might be something in between. Some people have said that the implicate order is a world in between the transcendent and the mundane.

WEBER   Do you feel that it is a world in between or that it is itself a whole range of those worlds?

BOHM   Ultimately you can't put the transcendent into thought, so anything that you would define would have to be somewhere in between. There is a world immensely more subtle than the ordinary mundane world, and if you believe in something transcendent, it will enable you to understand how that slowly filters down to the mundane. One alternative is to say that the transcendent—God for instance—directly created the machinery of the universe and occasionally repairs it. That was the view developed at the time of Newton, which was due to an alliance between theology and science, which both thought would serve their purpose. Theology wanted to throw out things like alchemy and Rosicrucianism and witchcraft in order to emphasize the utter transcendence of God. Newton was both scientist and theologian.

WEBER   Of course we are discussing mysticism rather than theology, and there is a big difference between these.

BOHM   But Newton was a theologian and a mystic. He was interested in alchemy and he was also a scientist. In many ways he was a combination, perhaps a contradictory combination, of all these. In earlier times, until the late seventeenth century, mysticism, theology and science were actually quite interwoven. They gradually drew apart, as evolution and such theories developed.

WEBER   This seems true especially in the nineteenth century, where mechanism became entrenched and the earlier spiritual, Pythagorean roots of science were cut off.

BOHM   That still survives in the way mathematical physicists think of the essence of the world as a mathematical formalism.

WEBER   But they've severed it from its inner meaning which Pythagoras insisted on, namely that all this is a divine display.

BOHM   Many of them may have, but for example Sir James Jeans said: "God is a mathematician." In other words, some of the people who first came out with quantum theory probably did have that in mind: Eddington, Jeans, Schroedinger, even Heisenberg. I was told by von Weizsäcker that Heisenberg in his later years was known as "the Buddha," because he had a rather eastern view of things and his face began to adopt a Buddha-like expression.

WEBER   One really wonders why so many of the great physicists in this century seemed to have a mystical outlook. We should of course define mysticism: can we call it a sense of the unity of things?

BOHM   Yes. Mysticism is the sense of a direct contact with the ultimate reality in its unity.

WEBER   The physicist seeks direct contact with the ultimate nature of things. Does he have this unity?

BOHM   He hopes for this unity, obviously. Physicists are talking about the Grand Unified Theory in which everything would come together, the whole cosmos understood in one equation. This shows that the hope for unity is behind the essence of modern science.

WEBER   I have always felt that. In fact, we can see it in the search for understanding from the pre-Socratics down. They were looking for the unity behind multiplicity, from Thales on: one substance rather than millions of variables.

BOHM   Yes. One principle, one substance. One side seeks the unity in matter, the other claims that the unity of the world is basically spiritual and that matter has been created out of nothing from spirit, from intelligence.

WEBER   The modern physicist is more like the materialist.

BOHM   Basically, except for this tremendous emphasis on mathematics, which is like saying that God is a mathematician. If you emphasize mathematics as much as scientists now do, without any physical picture of matter, you are tacitly saying that the essence of the world is something abstract and almost spiritual, if you really think about it.

WEBER   Mathematics is pure thought.

BOHM   That's right. You won't find it anywhere in matter.

WEBER   You are saying that even today's physicists who might be least inclined towards anything spiritual are practically forced to assume that it is beyond the material.

BOHM   Tacitly, anyway. Physicists may not accept this, but they are attributing qualities to matter that are beyond those usually considered to be material. They are more like spiritual qualities in so far as we say there is this mathematical order which prevails, which has no picture in material terms that we can correlate with it.

WEBER   Is it an aesthetic principle or something deeper still that makes them hold out for one rather than for three or four ultimate laws? Is it a spiritual drive, without their realizing it?

BOHM   It probably is a universal human drive, the same one which drives people to mysticism or to religion or art.

WEBER   You're saying that this underlying drive, which even the materialistically oriented physicist possesses, cannot be explained in terms of prediction and control.

BOHM   They would find it rather boring to say: "We do nothing but predict and control." If you talk to any of them, Penrose or Hawking, for example, I doubt if they would be satisfied with that.

WEBER   But neither would they be happy if we called them unconsciously mystical.

BOHM   No, they would regard that as absurd. But that may be an overlay of language. People in science may be forced to adopt a hard-boiled language to meet their hard-boiled colleagues.

WEBER   To be respectable within the peer group.

BOHM   Yes, and gradually they come to believe it themselves.

WEBER   So you feel that behind their empirical pursuit of physics they are searching for this underlying unity.

BOHM   Otherwise, why should they be interested at all? Take Stephen Hawking, who is hardly able to do anything due to his illness, yet he is driven to understand what lies behind things. He doesn't merely want to predict and control nature. Why does he drive himself like that?

WEBER   He would probably say "I want to understand."

BOHM   Yes, but you might understand things in terms of plurality: why the drive for unity?

WEBER   He might say "It's a sign that we're getting closer to the way things work." He would use a rational justification, not a spiritual one.

BOHM   He might say that. But I think he and others have an aesthetic appreciation of the unity.

WEBER   Feynman said that those who don't understand mathematics don't realize the beauty in the universe. Beauty keeps coming up, together with order and simplicity and other Pythagorean and Platonic categories.

BOHM   Order and simplicity and unity, and something behind all that which we can't describe.

WEBER   Do the great minds working in physics sense something of that?

BOHM   Yes.

WEBER   When you say: "They talk like Bohr but they think like Einstein," is that what you mean?

BOHM   No. That refers to a much simpler point. Bohr proposed the idea of the entirely ambiguous nature of our thought about reality, while Einstein, along with Boltzmann, insisted that our concepts abstracted from ordinary experience should be unambiguous, that is, have meaning. Most physicists think like Einstein; Bohr is much too subtle for them to be moved by what he says.

WEBER   Subtle in a good way?

BOHM   It's both good and bad. He has some good points, some on which I think he is wrong.

WEBER   Both the scientist and the mystic see in matter as you are using the word, something that is both immanent and transcendent.

BOHM   The mystic sees in matter an immanent principle of unity, and this is implicitly what the scientist is also doing. There are some who would go beyond matter, to the transcendent. They tend to devalue matter in favor of the transcendent principle.

WEBER   In a sense mystics do that, but in another sense they do the opposite. They see within matter the signature of this divine principle, so that they *exalt* matter rather than devalue it.

BOHM   Yes. They would say that the real meaning of matter is that it mediates the transcendent.

WEBER   Or that it displays it.

BOHM   In the same sense that thought mediates between the direct immediate *now* and past experience. So matter in some ways is a bit like thought.

WEBER   It's a window on things, a delimited version of the whole which can only give hints of the whole.

BOHM   Yes. The materialist says, "On the contrary, matter is the basic substance of reality and mind is a structure or form on that."

WEBER   How would you refute that?

BOHM   You can't refute any of these views ultimately, you can merely discuss them. Maybe none of them is true. They are all just ways of looking at reality. We may have to transcend them all.

WEBER   Of course, the mystic can never really prove his claims.

BOHM   Neither can the materialist prove his point.

WEBER   That is harder to understand.

BOHM   He can't prove that there is nothing but matter, he can merely say that he doesn't see any reason why you suppose there is more.

WEBER   But the burden of proof is on the person who claims that there is something more, at least that is what most philosophers say. The common analogy is that if you insist that there are little green people on the moon, it's up to you to give evidence for it. It's not up to someone else to say: "It might be possible because nothing rules it out."

BOHM   Yes, but that shifts the question to: "What do you accept as evidence?" If you close off the evidence by assuming that the non-material could only come from matter, then you are stuck. The materialist says, "I see from the evidence that I can explain everything materially, therefore tacitly I don't accept mental experience as evidence." In that case, where are we going to find the evidence? I can say that I experience very subtle things which go beyond matter. Suppose I happen to feel that way, suppose I am a mystic or an artist. The materialist says to me, "No! We can show that every experience has a physical cause and we believe that this will ultimately be all explained by matter. Therefore I rule your explanation out."

WEBER   What would you answer?

BOHM   I would say that you haven't proved it and I feel you haven't established a case. A lot of things which people believed turned out to be untrue. In the nineteenth century they thought everything would be explained in nineteenth-century mechanistic terms and now most of that is untrue. Since twentieth-century science is also limited, we cannot assume that all our expectations about twentieth-century science are going to be fulfilled.

WEBER   They would say that they're on the right track because of Occam's Razor, the Principle of Parsimony.

BOHM   The nineteenth century would have said the same: "We have cut out everything except matter, as Occam's Razor demands. Our ideas of matter are such and such." But they were wrong about matter itself. Matter was found to be far more subtle than was supposed, both for quantum mechanics and relativity.

WEBER   Does "subtle" imply spiritual?

BOHM   It moves in that direction. The subtle is that which is intangible invisible, real. When we discussed this with [Robert Wein-gard] a philosopher of physics yesterday, I asked him whether he believes that mathematics is a property of matter. He didn't seem to answer.

WEBER   He said it is in the universe itself.

BOHM   But does it follow from the properties of matter? If you say: "Matter is first," mathematics must then be a feature of matter. But why should mathematics, which is a feature of matter, rule the whole thing? We don't experience mathematics as a feature of matter. It's just how we think about it. We may say that it de-scribes matter and that's how things work up to a point, but that doesn't entail that matter is mathematics. We could say, with Jeans, since God is a mathematician, he put mathematical form into matter. But unless you suppose matter to have a mind, I don't quite understand how matter could be mathematical.

WEBER   Is it a flaw in consistency of those who argue for materialism in the crude sense?

BOHM   They're leaving themselves and their mathematics out of the discussion and tacitly treating it as pure spirit. They're not point-ing to anywhere in matter where mathematics is supposed to come from. They might argue, finally, that the whole mechanism will produce mathematics, but that's a supposition. It's merely a way of thinking, because you do not actually find mathematics in ob-jects. Mathematics is the only way of experiencing objects; it is their meaning for us.

WEBER   The non-Platonists in mathematics say that it's just an ordering device in the human mind, it's not out there at all.

BOHM   All right, let's agree with that. But according to modern physics, the only thing that we know about matter are these equa-tions. If you manipulate these equations, then for some mysterious reason you will come out with results which are correct. They have no picture of what the mathematics means. The only thing known is the mathematics. So they are really saying that mathematics is truth about matter.

WEBER   This objection is different from your first one. In the first one you say it's tacitly spiritual but they don't perceive or admit that it has to do with spirit.

BOHM   If you say that it's only man doing it, that's not very different from saying that the spiritual is a property of matter in the form of man. But if you had some picture of matter existing indepen-dently of mathematics and you're just simply describing it mathe-matically, that would be a more consistent view. But people have no such picture. There's nothing but the mathematics.

WEBER   Then they're back in this trap that this is *our* ordering of nature and it is not necessarily the way the universe is.

BOHM   What their view entails is that all that we know is invented by us, in which case we don't know the universe. It could all be mentalist, physicalist, or anything.

WEBER   The other view moves them implicitly closer to the spiritual interpretation.

BOHM   People like Heisenberg took the view, which he regarded as Platonic, that mathematics is the essence of reality. He felt that mathematical order has an objective being in matter and is its essential being. But mathematical order is something which seems very, very subtle and abstract and very close to what is usually meant by spirit. Spirit has always been thought of as something very subtle, something that at times we call intelligence. Later, scientists say: "No, that's just a lot of molecules computing things," but then somewhere behind these molecules there is something still more subtle which we call mathematics, which rules all that.

WEBER   Your question is: How did it get there, what is its status, what does it mean?

BOHM   Yes. Especially: What does it mean?

WEBER   Do you personally feel that God geometrizes?

BOHM   No, that's just a figure of speech. I don't know why mathematics is so important. In this era we happen to have developed it a great deal. In another period it might turn out some other way.

WEBER   Is it the cosmic mind expressing itself rationally?

BOHM   It may well be.

WEBER   The mystic who looks at matter says that within everything there is an order, that the universe is contained within every particle of matter, and that the whole thing has an intrinsic and powerful meaning. If a scientist looked deeply enough into matter, would he come up with that?

BOHM   I don't know; but those who work in particle physics or cosmology are attributing some direct meaning to the mathematics. They start with the equations and then work out the imaginative scenarios which are the interpretation of the equations. But the equations are the source of everything.

WEBER   What is the status of the equations?

BOHM   I don't know, except that they happen to work at this period of time.

WEBER   A rational mystic like Plato, with a high esteem for mathematics, claims in *Republic* VI that mathematics is just the third level and that the fourth or highest level is beyond all languages, including the language of mathematics. He faults mathematics for still making use of unproven axioms and unproven presuppositions. Therefore it's still one level beneath the ultimate approach to reality, which is the direct apprehension of it.

BOHM   And yet many mathematicians of the highest rank, Goedel and others, take a somewhat mystical attitude toward the source of their perception in mathematics. They don't know what the source of their mathematics is, they call it "mysterious." Poincaré called it mysterious, as did Einstein.

WEBER   Did they call mathematics as such mysterious or their particular mathematical insight?

BOHM   Their new mathematical insights. Einstein said that the whole universe is basically mysterious, ultimate reality is mysterious, which is close to what the mystic says.

WEBER   Yes.

BOHM   Einstein must have felt that he had a direct perception of this mystery, otherwise why would he have said this?

WEBER   That could account for the high proportion of physicists working at the frontiers, who along with mystery keep stressing ideas like wholeness, awesomeness—especially in cosmology—the sense of unity behind things, beauty and symmetry. It's as if they're getting a glimpse, through their own work, of something larger.

BOHM   Yes. I think that many physicists feel that they are glimpsing something which is a bit beyond—some kind of truth.

WEBER   Their challenge is to put that "something else" which they sense into accessible language.

BOHM   Yes. The language is mathematical formulae.

WEBER   Which is highly stylized and formalized and pure. You've compared it to a musical score. Behind it there lies this music of the universe.

BOHM   Yes. This is the way Plato might have talked.

WEBER   Plato and Pythagoras. When a musician reads the score he perceives this "something else." For a physicist, looking at the mathematics is like reading the music of the universe.

BOHM   Yes, and then he works out scenarios.

WEBER   The mystic does it without any language at all. He claims that he hears the music without any score at all. Anything can trigger it, he doesn't need a formalized language to catalyze his awareness of this background behind things.

BOHM   That's what he claims.

WEBER   Let's talk about methodology. The physicist seems to turn outwards and the mystic inwards: is that a cliché or is it correct?

BOHM   The mathematician is turning within as well as outwards. Physics emphasizes proof by the outward experiment, trying to abstract from the outward experience. Einstein and Boltzmann and other physicists thought that the ideas come from perception as a whole rather than from limited areas, and possibly that may be a major source of mathematics.

WEBER   That isn't clear.

BOHM   Many mathematical notions are highly affected by the general perception of the world.

WEBER   I've written that meditation is to the mystic what mathematics is to the physicist. Do you agree?

BOHM   Perhaps so, yes, it's hard to say. The mathematician has to go through a certain operation in order to define and to discipline his thought. Would the mystic look at meditation in that way?

WEBER   Yes. Meditation involves focusing the mind and setting aside things that would interfere with depth perception. The mystic goes as deeply as possible into consciousness, the physicist into matter. Can we say that?

BOHM   Yes. But of the pure mathematician, we have to ask: What is he going into? In some ways he is going into one of the aspects of consciousness. Although it may be inspired by the experience of matter, nevertheless once it has entered consciousness he is trying to find something that goes on in consciousness which has an order of its own.

WEBER   Does the mathematician create or invent mathematics?

BOHM   People have argued about that. Much of it is clearly invented, but he may have a creative perception of some new relationship. If you take Newton, for example, when he saw the apple falling, he suddenly grasped that the moon was also falling, and thus came up with the idea of universal gravitation. That was an immediate perception of a relationship, which was blocked before. Archimedes, similarly, had a perception as he was getting into the bath that the volume of water displaced is independent of the shape of the object. It was such a tremendously passionate moment that he shouted "Eureka!" For Newton it also must have been like that. These sudden direct perceptions require a very intense and unusual passion.

WEBER   A high energy?

BOHM   Yes. And creativity emerges at that point.

WEBER   Through this high energy.

BOHM   Yes.

WEBER   That may be the common denominator between the mystic and the scientist. It's as if at that moment the veil of nature is parted for them.

BOHM   The veil of the mind is parted. The mind is caught in things that it takes for granted. The ordinary low-energy mind just goes through things over and over and takes its old assumptions for granted, but this high-energy dissolves the veil so that the mind can function on a new level.

WEBER   That's beautiful. I'd like to come back to the view of matter for both the mystic and the physicist. You claim that if the physicist understood matter correctly, he would not see himself as a "materialist" in the usual sense of the word.

BOHM   Yes.

WEBER   But that is what the mystic has been saying for thousands of years.

BOHM   The question is whether matter is rather crude and mechanical or whether it gets more and more subtle and becomes indistinguishable from what people have called mind. You have written that in idealism the form is primary. One suggestion is that the form enters into an energy which gives rise to a determinate activity and eventually to a determinate structure of matter. If you look at it in that way, which modern physics tends to approach, you could say that this distinction between idealism and materialism is gradually eroded. I'll extend Gregory Bateson's definition of information to say that it's a difference of form that makes a difference of content and meaning. The form is carried out as meaning and energy. If you read a printed page, which is a form, the meaning gives rise to an energy from which you act. Therefore we could say that the distinction of materialism and idealism is eroded, it gradually dissolves.

WEBER   It would also redefine "materialism." If a person were really a materialist, he'd be involved in the spiritual.

BOHM   Yes. It redefines "idealism" too.

WEBER   It anchors it in the plane of physical manifestation.

BOHM   Yes. This would suggest that mind is never absent from any aspect of matter, however simple. It would be a very rudimentary form of mind for the electron, our mind is on another level, and perhaps there's a greater mind on yet another level, and so on.

WEBER   Unlike some people who question the validity of mapping physics onto the mysticism of the ancient wisdom traditions, you do not question it, if it is properly done.

BOHM   What kind of mapping?

WEBER   For example, what Capra tried in *The Tao of Physics*. Ken Wilber, in *Quantum Questions*, criticizes this approach and all similar attempts as invalid. By implication, your own work is open to the same attack.

BOHM   Part of this ancient alliance between science and theology at the time of Newton was to make matter as "materialistic" as possible, as we said earlier, to emphasize the transcendence of God. There is sort of a trace of that in Wilber.

WEBER   Wilber says that matter is at the lowest level of the hierarchical universe which he identifies with the great Chain of Being. The upper levels contain the lower levels but not vice versa. People who try to ignore that, Wilber argues, are guilty of a kind of reductionism.

BOHM In the view I'm presenting nothing is being reduced. Pure idealism would reduce matter to an aspect of mind. Hegel was an example of that. Pure materialism attempts to reduce mind to an aspect of matter, and of course that's what we see in a great deal of modern science. My view does not attempt to reduce one to the other any more than one would reduce form to content.

WEBER Spinoza says for every aspect of matter there is a concomitant aspect of consciousness, and vice versa. Do you accept that?

BOHM They're interwoven. They're correlative categories of reality, always woven together just as form and content are woven together. Every content is a form and every form is at the same time a content. Another way of saying that is that everything material is also mental and everything mental is also material, but there are many more infinitely subtle levels of matter than we are aware of.

WEBER Or that we ever could be aware of?

BOHM Yes. We could think of the mystic as coming in contact with tremendous depths of the subtlety of matter or of mind, whatever we want to call it.

WEBER A depth where the distinction no longer applies?

BOHM Yes. Rather than use the word "contact," we can say the mystic enters into it.

WEBER Plato says "to behold the form and enter into union with it."

BOHM Yes. If you don't distinguish mind and matter then it becomes conceivable that you can enter into it. If you believe that matter is purely material, then how are you going to enter into it? Or if you think of it as purely mental then we have to think of it as some far away thing and some mysterious leap is required. But what if one supposes that actually it's not far away at all.

WEBER The *Upanishads* calls it "nearer than the nearest."

BOHM Yes. But then we have to maintain that this distinction is like form and content and that ordinary thought makes too much of it; it makes it too rigid and sharp.

WEBER Let's use your vocabulary. How do you "enter into" it?

BOHM The mystic wants to do it. The pure mathematician thinks tacitly that he is doing it, that he's entering into a source of truth.

WEBER Is it pure thought contemplating pure thought?

BOHM Yes, but he feels that there is a source of truth behind that. Many mathematicians feel that it's a perception of truth beyond what can be expressed.

WEBER And that in understanding the mathematics they're in touch with the thing behind it.

BOHM Yes.

WEBER How the mystic does it is of course hard to explain. But we've been discussing subtle matter, and it makes one think of

Meister Eckhart, perhaps the greatest mystic the west has produced. He said, "To find nature herself, all her forms must be
shattered."

BOHM   Well, any form which appears in nature is relatively exterior.
The question is, what underlies it?

WEBER   Isn't that what the mystic is after? He tries to get to the
most universal level possible and to strip away delimitation and
particularity.

BOHM   Yes. To get to something more and more general within
consciousness, less and less restricted, leading to the universal.

WEBER   That does sound like what Meister Eckhart must have meant
by finding "nature herself." In this book I've raised the question:
"Is the search for unity in science itself a spiritual path?" and I
have answered in the positive. What is your view?

BOHM   In the current practice of science that isn't necessarily true.
But probably its ultimate aim is to find unity, as we were saying
earlier.

WEBER   Does that lead to the charge of anthropomorphism and
ultimately to scepticism about our knowledge?

BOHM   You can overcome that problem only if you accept the premise that in some sense man is a microcosm of the universe; therefore what man is, is a clue to the universe. We are enfolded in the
universe.

WEBER   That is the missing link, the step that's needed?

BOHM   Yes. All our experience is a clue to reality because we are of
reality.

WEBER   It always seems to come back to the hermetic principle.

BOHM   Yes. If one doesn't postulate that, then what remains totally
unexplained is why mathematics should have anything to do with
reality. Wigner, for example, says it's an utter mystery why mathematics works. And without that postulate, we would have to ask:
Why should the manipulation of symbols have anything to do with
the way reality works?

WEBER   Kant's problem was: We cannot see things as they really are
because we impart our structures to experience, so we bar the way
to the noumenon with our own inner categories.

BOHM   But my view is to say, "I am the noumenon," so there is a
way out of Kant's trap. At least, I am *of* the noumenon.

WEBER   Or I can come into harmony with it, become commensurate
with it, which Kant of course denies.

BOHM   Yes. I am participating in the noumenon.

WEBER   And therefore this is not an alien reality but my own reality.

BOHM   Yes, which is what Hegel said, too. If you don't say that,
then there's absolutely no explanation; everything is quite arbitrary, including the fact that mathematics works. Wigner and even

Einstein said that the greatest mystery about the universe is that it is comprehensible.

WEBER   Steven Weinberg also says this. One of his papers ends up on the note that the most astonishing thing would be if it turns out that everything we *think* to be true about the universe in fact *is* true.

BOHM   If we enfold the universe and are participating in it, and if the universe participates in us, then there is some basis for saying that what we think can be relevant.

WEBER   So it's another approach to the question of mysticism. The mystic enters his own inner being because he feels that the universe is embedded in it.

BOHM   Yes. Fundamentally, this is the only way of understanding why science and mathematics should ever work.

When we come to light, we are coming to the fundamental activity in which existence has its ground.... Light is the potential of everything.

DAVID BOHM

That's why I value Dionysius the Areopagite so much. He speaks of the divine darkness. ... That's where you meet God.

FR. BEDE GRIFFITHS

This ocean of energy could be thought of as an ocean of light.

DAVID BOHM

In a Hindu temple, the inner sanctuary is always dark.... When you come to the inner sanctuary you come to the ... inner center of your own being, and you encounter God in the darkness.

FR. BEDE GRIFFITHS

All of our consciousness ... arises in dependence on this mind of clear light.

THE DALAI LAMA

FATHER BEDE GRIFFITHS

9

Sacred simplicity:
the style of the sage

FATHER BEDE GRIFFITHS

> There are two wings that raise a man above earthly things—
> simplicity and purity. Simplicity reaches out after God:
> purity discovers and enjoys Him.
>
> THOMAS A KEMPIS

FR. Griffiths sits cross-legged on the floor of the little veranda of his hut at Shantivanam, part western monastery, part eastern ashram and—in response to my prodding—recounts its history and his own. There are a number of similarities between Fr. Bede and Lama Govinda: both expatriates in Asia for decades, both scholars and monks, both intent on reconciling east and west, science and mysticism, both proclaiming the underlying unity of all religions and yet completely committed to expressing a particular one in their lives: Roman Catholicism for one, Tibetan Buddhism for the other. Both are sage-like in appearance and style. Both illustrate the principle that the sage's "work" and "research" and "product" are his life itself.

Fr. Bede Griffiths was born in 1906 into a middle-class English family. He graduated from Oxford, where he became a close friend of C. S. Lewis and other literary figures. Increasingly disillusioned with industrial England, he became a Roman Catholic and entered a Benedictine monastery, spending his life in study and prayer. Drawn to Indian philosophy and religion, he went to India in 1955. He has lived there ever since. A scholar in comparative religion and Christian theology, Fr. Bede also seems to have managed a rare integration of body, mind, and spirit. Tall and lean, almost gaunt, his muscular frame reflects the years of hard toil under the Indian sun, his ascetic face dominated by high cheek-bones, deep-set blue-grey eyes, and a brilliant smile. He is ecumenical and an internationalist, as his views in the dialogue make clear. Though a devout Christian, Fr. Bede wears the saffron *kavi* habit of the Hindu holy man and goes mostly barefoot. Even after thirty years in India, his accent is pure English, which makes for an interesting incongruity.

Saccidananda Ashram, Shantivanam lies a few miles west of the city

of Tiruchirapalli in south India, along the banks of the sacred river
Cauvery, "the Ganges of south India." "Shantivanam"—"abode of
peace"—is a contemplative hermitage that revolves around both Christian and Hindu ideas. We sit on the floor, Indian style. Everything
about him, everything about his hut, everything about the ashram
conveys the message of simplicity. It is a value central to Fr. Bede's
life and to the ashram which he has headed for seventeen years.
"Doing without" has been a leitmotif since his student days at Oxford.
Security, he says, has been the ruin of the religious life and of many
monasteries.

Shantivanam is in the heart of rural India, its customs little changed
by the centuries. Fr. Bede feels strongly that the members of the community must live as the local Indians live and this, together with his
commitment to primordial Christianity, dictates their lifestyle of extreme simplicity. The ashram is almost self-supporting. It raises rice in
its own rice-paddy, coconuts, vegetables, fruit and milk, and is helped
by contributions from visitors on meditation retreats who want to pay
for their stay. The ashram charges nothing, so there is no fixed income.
Fr. Bede says that they live from month to month, sometimes from
week to week, and adds that "this is the way it should be."

To an outsider it seems austere, but to the long-term inhabitant of
the ashram and of India it is sufficient, a slow-paced life whose dominant theme is freedom from endless artificial needs. There is a palpable
sense of unhurriedness and calm about Fr. Bede and the life of the
ashram, as if time were irrelevant. A day at Shantivanam begins, like
days all over India, at dawn. There are prayers in the small chapel,
preceded for some by meditation at sunrise on the banks of the Cauvery
river. The vegetarian meals are eaten Indian style, without utensils, on
the floor of a simple dining hall, and though ample they are simple to
the point of austerity. The community gathers four times each day
amidst incense and candles to meditate and chant Hindu, Buddhist, and
Christian prayers, with both Indian and western participants, following
the universalist vision of Fr. Monchanin.

There is a modest library of books, on all the religious traditions and
on philosophy and theology. The library also holds Fr. Bede's own
works which include *The Golden String*, an autobiography of his spiritual search; *Return to the Center*, thoughts on the unification of religion;
Christ in India, essays towards a Hindu-Christian dialogue; *The Marriage of East and West*, on comparative religion and philosophy, and his
latest, *The Cosmic Revelation*, on the *Vedas*. Fr. Bede participates at
conferences on science and mysticism with people like Capra and of
course Sheldrake, to whom he seems especially close. Though anchored
in this remote spot which he obviously loves, Fr. Bede is learned and
sophisticated, in touch with the intellectual currents of the modern
world.

To accommodate the visitors who pour in from all over the world, there are tiny rooms, akin to monkish cells. The social life of the ashram centers around the courtyard, where people chat over mid-morning and afternoon tea, surrounded by tall palmyra trees and flowers, cows and bullocks wandering nearby, unsegregated from the life of the humans, as is the custom not only in rural but also in urban India.

The dialogue was taped over several days in January 1983. I came away with a sense of a man who is rooted: in nature as a whole, in the earth of India, in his Christian faith. I am told that the local villagers consider him a *sannyasin*, a holy man, and that description sums him up for me as well. A *sannyasin* not in theory but in daily life, living his voluntary poverty and minimal consumption whatever the inconveniences. I have encountered such simplicity as a philosophy, but only rarely have I seen it embodied.

But to Fr. Bede it is natural, so much a part of himself that he denies doing anything special or saintly. It is this simplicity about simplicity itself—not all the fuss of the people who inveterately talk or write books about it—that startles, attracts, and inspires.

What fascinates me in this dialogue is Fr. Bede's discussion on light. You may recall that in Chapter 2, David Bohm and I ponder why light is the classical symbol for the mystic's experience. The Dalai Lama, in Chapter 13, also supports this view. Fr. Bede, however, expresses a different, quite unusual view as you will see, referring instead to "the divine darkness" as the deepest metaphor for the religious experience.

Fr. Bede's penetrating observations about Krishnamurti in some way evoke those of Lama Govinda in Chapter 3.

WEBER   Your lifestyle is part of your teaching, Father Bede, and is very inspiring to those of us who are caught in a complexity and multiplicity that we equate with necessities. You live here in rural India under rather austere conditions. It is something that most of us couldn't do, and to an outside observer it seems to require renunciation and sacrifice, although these may be the wrong words. What makes this possible?

GRIFFITHS   I wouldn't emphasize the renunciation and sacrifice, to be quite honest. India has been much more like a revelation to me, and I find living in this simplicity more enjoyable than I do living in the west with all its complications. I've come to it gradually. When I first came to India as a Benedictine monk we set up a small ashram in what I thought was a very simple style. Though we had tables and chairs and spoons and forks and beds, and wore European clothing and shoes, I thought it was a good and very simple model. But after a few months I realized that scarcely anybody in the neighboring village had any of these things. So I began to see Indian culture as something quite different. Gradually we got into the habit of following the customs of an Indian ash-ram—going barefoot, sleeping on the floor, praying and eating sitting on the floor, and with our hands. These happened gradually and have become simply natural to me after a time. So I don't honestly feel it's a sacrifice.

There is a second aspect to this; in order to be spiritually free one must not be attached to anything. One may use things but one must not be attached to them. To live in a very simple life-style is one of the best means of learning this detachment. In India, partly because of the climate, one is able to live in almost incredible simplicity, and I have found that this is a wonderful way to attain to inner freedom and joy. This has taught me that the elaborate system of material conveniences built up in the west is not neces-sary for the real enjoyment of life. Many people find after a short stay in the ashram that one no longer feels the need of innumerable things which before one considered necessary.

WEBER   What does a spiritual seeker really need and what have you, as a *sannyasin*, found here in this peaceful place?

GRIFFITHS   I think if you live in peaceful surroundings related to the natural world it gives you a balance and a harmony in your life, and in your whole relation to people and to God. That is why I'm opposed to urban civilization. I think small towns—Athens, Flor-ence, Rome—these are meaningful; but vast conglomerations like New York and London are not human. We should emphasize decentralization and more human communities. To create a com-munity which is living in harmony with its natural environment is fundamental. With regard to human relationships, it is best to have a comparatively small face-to-face community, where people know one another. So these are the conditions I feel are necessary for the growth of humanity and for the experience of the reality of the spirit of God in one's life. It's the ecological environment and the human environment; to have a loving community is required. Then you are open to the divine and you can experience it day by day, hour by hour in your life.

WEBER   Does it have to do with being close to nature?

GRIFFITHS   Living close to nature is very important. For me the great discovery in India is the discovery of the sacred. In India everything is sacred: the earth is sacred; food, water, and taking a bath are all sacred, a building is sacred. Here one is still living in the old "sacral" universe, which means everything to me. I had glimpses of that in Wordsworth and the Romantic poets. But in India I found it alive in the villages and among the people. I really feel now that I've discovered what I was quite blindly seeking when I was a young man of twenty in England.

WEBER   At Oxford. *The Golden String* tells the story of your rejecting hyper-intellectualism, and the whole industrial environment, the "uglification" of former beauty. The churches struck you as still beautiful, coming from an era when beauty was organic. You reacted by forming a kind of commune with your friends.

GRIFFITHS   In Gloucestershire, in 1930. It was an adventure in the dark. But really I can see now I was trying to shape a kind of life there which I'm now able to live here.

WEBER   "Here in India everything is sacred." Why is that *not* so with us?

GRIFFITHS   That is the great change which has taken place just in the last 500 years. From the earliest times men and women all over the world lived in this sacred universe, whether it was the Australian Aborigines, the American Indians, the tribal people of Africa; they all sensed a sacred living universe of which humans are a part. And this divine power, whatever name it is given, penetrates through the earth, the water, the air, and through your own being. You belong to this sacred universe. But in the sixteenth century this sacred universe began to be destroyed, and the idea was viewed as superstitious. It was a deliberate effort to get away from the sacred, to rationalize everything. Only now, in the last 50 years, are we recovering the sense of the sacred.

WEBER   But you feel in India there's been an unbroken tradition of the sacred.

GRIFFITHS   Yes, but it is being broken today with a gathering force. Western culture is invading India at every level, right into the villages. Even since I've been here, people's values have been changing. The younger generation have the values of the west, while the older generation keep the traditional values. But it's a losing battle.

WEBER   In the west, ironically, there is a reverse movement. Some of the younger generation are turning eastward, or looking to the American Indian or the ecology movement, the back-to-nature movement. They are aware of the tragedy in losing those values, and fighting it.

GRIFFITHS   That is a paradox. The young Indian is looking west: engineering, medicine, every form of industrialism. With that come all the cultural values of the west. But in our ashram we are invaded by young people from the west who are looking for what the east can give them.

WEBER   Do you think it's a bit Hegelian—thesis, antithesis, and synthesis?

GRIFFITHS   I honestly feel a synthesis will come. It will take time and there may be a great sphere of conflict, but I do believe—as I tried to put in my book, *The Marriage of East and West*—that a profound cultural change is taking place. The west is really

discovering the east and the east the west. There will eventually
be a union of the *profound* values of each.

WEBER   Have we identified those deep values from which this union
will come?

GRIFFITHS   I attended a conference in Bombay last February [1982]
on the meeting of western science with eastern thought. I felt then,
and I feel now, that western science has really gone very deep, and
the *philosophical* implications of this whole scientific movement are
now being brought out. David Bohm's idea of the implicate order
is a philosophical idea of profound importance. So the west is
probing deeply in that way. In the east, there has been a revival
of Hinduism from the time of Ram Mohan Roy at the beginning
of the nineteenth century, then through Ramakrishna, Vivekan-
anda, Rabindranath Tagore, Sri Aurobindo, and Ramana Maharshi. Hinduism experienced a renaissance. A great deal is superficial, but a genuine penetration into the deep meaning of Hindu
culture is also emerging. Perhaps I should also add our founder,
Father Monchanin, a French priest who began this ashram in
1950. We owe everything to him: he said he felt that the need was
to go to the *source* of Hinduism and Christianity before they developed into systems and theologies. At that source the meeting
can take place.

WEBER   I'm wondering what you feel about the idea that in all religious movements one can discern two strata: the exoteric and the
esoteric. The esoteric is close to the source and here all religions
are unified; the exoteric contains the more peripheral and separa-
tive elements. The claim is that the religious vision is *one* and is
unified somewhere, say in Bohm's implicate order—several steps
before it gets expressed within various cultures. At that level it's
whole and hasn't been translated yet into this or that symbol
system.

GRIFFITHS   That would be my view; that there is an original truth,
the "divine mystery" I call it, and that as soon as it begins to be
expressed, even in a Buddha or a Jesus, it is already coming into
the temporal world and distortions are already on the way. So each
tradition enshrines this eternal truth but each explicates it in a
particular way with historic, cultural, and linguistic limitations. What
we have to do today is discern this inner truth within each tradition.

I agree with Clement of Alexandria who maintained that the true
gnosis was *in* the Church. People don't realize how profound was
this mystical understanding in the Church, in Clement of Alexandria, in Origen, in the whole Alexandrian school; then in St.
Gregory of Nyssa, who was a great Platonist, and finally in the
most interesting person, Dionysius the Pseudo-Areopagite, who
was supposed to be a Syrian monk in the sixth century, and who

really incorporated all the esoteric wisdom of Platonism into Christianity. There were also the Fathers and the schoolmen, like St. Thomas Aquinas; Dionysius was an authority for him. So the whole of this genuine gnosticism was taken up into the orthodox tradition, but around the fourteenth century orthodox tradition began to harden, and a great many distortions arose. But up to the thirteenth century the orthodox tradition had this profound *esoteric* wisdom.

WEBER   Was it experiential for them?

GRIFFITHS   Yes. It comes out in the Byzantine icon, for instance, or in the cathedrals, like Chartres, and in Dante. Gnosticism and kindred movements preserve certain aspects, but to me the main esoteric tradition was preserved in the Church, and it's only after the fourteenth century that it began to be lost. By the nineteenth century only fragments remained, and now again we're beginning to recover some of this.

WEBER   Will that tradition be able to flourish within the Church?

GRIFFITHS   Yes, things have changed tremendously since the Vatican Council. It opened the doors and windows. We're really open to all these traditions now. It's slow, many people resist them, some say it's of the devil, but I think the central movement is to be open to truth wherever it's found. The synthesis of the "new science" with oriental mysticism, for example, can bring about a renewed and deepened Christian orthodoxy.

WEBER   Why is it necessary to bring science into it?

GRIFFITHS   The problem is that the Church in the Middle Ages built its theology on Platonism and Aristotelianism, which of course are very profound and created a wonderful system. But that system is no longer valid—Aristotle's physics went out a long time ago—and the whole system, though it still has profound insights in it, is no longer adequate. We're now being challenged to create a theology which would use the findings of modern science and eastern mysticism which, as you know, coincide so much, and to evolve from that a new theology which would be much more adequate.

WEBER   You're saying that if the vitality of Christianity is going to persist and even to gather more momentum, it cannot be grounded in a world view that won't hold up scientifically. It's going to have to ally itself with contemporary science: with quantum physics, with Einstein's physics, with Bohm's sort of synthesis, and build on that as a background. But the uniquely Christian view will have its own dynamic message within that?

GRIFFITHS   Yes. I think there will be great resistance to such new ideas within the Church, but as with science, it is almost inevitable. The old view simply cannot hold water any longer, so the new ideas will gradually penetrate, and we shall have a merging of a new world vision which will also be a new theology. It's a very exciting future.

WEBER   Are we moving towards the spiritualization of physics?

GRIFFITHS   We had a visit from a very interesting astronomer, Kim Malville from Colorado, who brought this out more than anyone I've ever known. He really feels that the universe—he calls it, in Mircea Eliade's phrase, a "hierophany"—is a manifestation of the sacred. Science itself is rediscovering the sacred and awesome reality of the universe. We're getting back to the old idea of the microcosm and the macrocosm—that the cosmos is reflecting itself in us, this vision that was lost in the Renaissance, when the split took place between the human person as an observer, separated from a material universe outside himself.

WEBER   So this coming together of science with the spiritual was overdue.

GRIFFITHS   It's a very great event and we are just seeing the beginning of it. It's a change in the whole cultural environment.

WEBER   How does one translate it into how we live and interact with people?

GRIFFITHS   I start from meditation. To me meditation is the way in which you get beyond your senses, then beyond your mind, and then begin to experience something of this transcendent reality. As that experience grows, it begins to affect your whole attitude to other people and to the world around you. The purpose of an ashram is to create a center where these values can be lived. What people find today, especially so many of the people who come here, is that in the west, particularly in the towns, the pressure of life is so great and the whole system is organized in such a way that it's extremely difficult to live out this vision. Therefore I think we need to create the centers I spoke of. In that context, the reality of this transcendent mystery begins to manifest again and we begin to experience it.

WEBER   We were saying that everything is sacred. Does that have one kind of meaning in a Christian context and another one in a Platonic or eastern context, more symbolic in one, more pantheistic in the other?

GRIFFITHS   That's an important question. The sense of the sacred does often lead to a kind of pantheism. I think Christians have been rather on their guard against it for that reason. I believe that, though there is pantheism of some kind in India, the ancient tradition of the *Vedas*, the *Upanishads*, the *Bhagavad-Gita*, is not pantheistic. It's a vision of the totally immanent and the totally transcendent. That is the reality of the sacred—that the one divine mystery is manifested in the earth, in the water, and that is a profoundly Christian idea, the biblical idea that man is an image of God. But the other side, that the universe itself is sacred and mirrors God, is much less common in the west.

WEBER   The idea of *ahimsa* therefore seems countermanded by God's giving everybody dominion. [*Ahimsa* is the Sanskrit word for "reverence for life."]

GRIFFITHS   Dominion over the earth—that was a very unfortunate phrase.

WEBER   If God had said to "tend," as you tend your flocks, that would have been different, but "dominion" became exploitation with a license. You're saying immanent and transcendent: everything is saturated with the divine, but the divine itself is inexhaustible.

GRIFFITHS   Yes. It is in the world but also beyond manifestation.

WEBER   In the *Gita*, there's a wonderful phrase where Krishna tells Arjuna, "With one atom of myself I sustain the universe." And he's just talked about being brighter than a thousand suns, so that gives one a glimpse into the enormity of it; just one atom will do, and there are infinitely many left over. Isn't that a good example of God as immanent and transcendent?

GRIFFITHS   It's very good. This total transcendence is clear in the *Gita*. Krishna says: "I am the taste and the water"—he's everything. The paradoxical phrase used by the great Tamil mystic Manikkar Vasaggar was: "You are all that is and you are nothing that is." All and nothing: *Neti, neti:* not this, not that [the *Upanishads*].

WEBER   Father Bede, what is your unique vision of Christianity?

GRIFFITHS   In the biblical tradition, which is Semitic, the transcendence of God is emphasized above all, and the immanence comparatively little. Again man is master of the universe; and the sense that the earth is his mother, that he depends on it, is resisted. The idea was considered to belong to the surrounding peoples with their nature gods, so it was rejected. All kinds of sacredness of the earth, the moon, the stars, and the sun were lost. But if the biblical view is complemented with the oriental view, then you get a deeper understanding. In other words, God is not only the transcendent deity of the Old Testament, but he is also the immanent deity of the whole Hindu tradition. So it really is two world views which are fundamentally complementary. I think the Christian churches today have to discover that oriental world view. They've never done it. Only now are we really encountering Hinduism, Buddhism, Taoism, Confucianism, the whole oriental culture, and that I feel is the work of the next thousand years.

WEBER   Aside from people like yourself and the late Thomas Merton, is this movement much in evidence?

GRIFFITHS   It's rather embryonic at present. But I've traveled quite
a lot recently in Europe and America, and I've been amazed to
find a ferment is going on. It hasn't surfaced to a great extent in
many places, but the movement is there.

WEBER   I sent you Bishop Hunthousen's eloquent speech on "Faith
and Disarmament," exhorting us to "take up the cross" and even
to lose our lives in resisting nuclear armaments. He is an inspiring
man.

GRIFFITHS   Yes. You see, that sort of thing wouldn't have been
thought of some time ago.

WEBER   You radiate a sense of such simple joy in things. What do
you draw on for this?

GRIFFITHS   Well, I would credit a lot to India. So many people who
come here feel this sense of the sacred, this sense of cosmic unity,
of cosmic mystery. For me it started with Wordsworth and Shelley.
I got a sort of ecstasy in that as a boy. In India this is universal,
this sense that you are living in the midst of this cosmic mystery,
and all the art of India, the dance, the temples, the ritual, the way
people even walk and dress and so on, it's all got this character in
it. The other aspect is this sense of liberation, this experience of
God, when you begin to be liberated from your own mind and all
its limitations, and discover this *ananda*, this bliss which enfolds
the universe.

WEBER   Is a necessary precondition for that, that one lets go of the
self?

GRIFFITHS   That's *the* secret.

WEBER   You said, "It isn't sacrifice to me, it's joy." But if you hadn't
learned to let go of the self you couldn't have experienced that.

GRIFFITHS   That is the whole thing. Sacrifice always brings in a
rather negative sense: killing, destroying. But this is a letting go
which sets you free. It's beautiful in the *Dhammapada* of the
Buddha, "In joy we live."

WEBER   In giving something up, one is filled with something.

GRIFFITHS   Yes. But you do give yourself up.

WEBER   You said: It's a daily thing. In Madras, at this small seminar
we had with Krishnamurti, he said, to everyone's consternation,
that when you meet another person in the same way, at the same
level, with the same intensity, then you really hear the person, and
that is love. There's nothing between you, no barrier. He says it
is love, and it is also meditation. Some people said, "I've had that
experience, I know what it's like," to which Krishnamurti replied:
"But what happened afterwards? Why aren't you transformed?"
People said, "It leaks off after a while. Sometimes I can do it and
sometimes I cannot." Then Krishnamurti made a categorical statement: If it ever is *not* there once it has been there, that means it

was never there at all, and you were self-deluded. That caused great consternation. It's either this or that or nothing—no gradualism, no change, no evolution. I had difficulty accepting that, as did others. Do you have any comments on that outlook?

GRIFFITHS   I think that's a weakness of Krishnamurti's doctrine, and that it's due to his very unusual experience. He was brought up in the Theosophical Society. The whole thing was built around him, and he realized he had to get out of it. He made a total break, and therefore for him the spiritual life has been something solitary, a marvelous experience that he's had himself. It's totally fulfilling, and all the steps to it have been abolished. But the normal person has to have these steps. That's why I think ritual has a place, *bhakti* and devotional singing have a place, prayer has a place, and community has a place. All these are *ways* towards something. It's a little like the Zen distinction between sudden enlightenment and gradual enlightenment; and I firmly believe in the gradual. In fact many, many people have a very obscure but very real awareness of this transcendent mystery without being able to put a name to it. It may be very obscure, and it may disappear at times, but it's always there and it can always be renewed. It's only very rarely that you reach the state when you live totally in it.

WEBER   You are actually saying the opposite of what Krishnamurti said. You are saying once you have it, you can never completely lose it. You've had a glimpse of something that isn't in time.

GRIFFITHS   It is not in time.

WEBER   How can what is not in time ever be completely lost in time?

GRIFFITHS   I believe every human being is in some way open to this transcendent mystery, and often through some very little thing—being kind to people, having a love of nature, of beauty—without quite realizing it, they make contact with this transcendent mystery.

WEBER   When you see an entity in nature, this coconut tree for instance: is it God, or is it an expression of God, or is that the wrong question?

GRIFFITHS   Ah, that's a very difficult question. In the east, in Hinduism especially, they say it is God. But for a Christian that is very difficult, and I would always prefer to say that God is *in* the tree, and the tree is in God, but the tree is not God, and that to me makes a lot of difference. Because God is *neti neti*, not things. He's beyond things.

WEBER   He is not an object of perception, what Kierkegaard called "the green parrot with the red beak." That's paganism for him.

GRIFFITHS   Yes. I think we have to interpret the eastern texts, the *Upanishads* and so on, cautiously, because they often use language in which they will say "All this world is Brahman," which sounds pantheistic, but then later they correct it by saying "Brahman is not this." So it is very often a matter of language, and if you take the pantheistic expressions and give them a metaphysical value, you can misinterpret them. We should always interpret them in the light of the other expressions as well. I don't believe that Hinduism as such is pantheistic.

WEBER   You do not?

GRIFFITHS   Not at all.

WEBER   And Buddhism?

GRIFFITHS   Nor Buddhism.

WEBER   Which doesn't have a God at all in our sense.

GRIFFITHS   Now that raises a very interesting question. We use a word like "God" and think it's got some definite meaning, but actually the word "God" has an infinity of meanings, and none of them is adequate. A word like that is pointing to something which is beyond words and beyond things. Therefore the Buddha didn't want to name it because once you begin to name God you get an idol and then you idolize that concept.

WEBER   And you've limited it. When you use the word "God," Father Bede, it's your own careful meaning of that word. It isn't really the conventional term.

GRIFFITHS   St. Thomas Aquinas said very explicitly that God cannot be named. The nearest, he says, you can come to a name is "Being." He is, "I *am*," similar to the *Katha Upanishad*, which says: "How can we speak of Him except by saying He *is?*" So Aquinas says God cannot be named. Dionysius has a whole treatise on the divine names, and then says you've got to go beyond all these names into the darkness to get to God. But of course Eckhart makes the distinction between God and Godhead, and that perhaps clarifies it.

WEBER   When he says, "There is nothing so much in all the universe like God as silence," he implies that all words falsify, but in silence nothing stands out. You haven't favored any point of view or any word, and therefore you haven't broken it up.

GRIFFITHS   Yes, that is like Bohm's implicate order again, and it goes back to the One. That's why we always have to live in these two worlds: on the one hand, in a world of multiplicity, relating ourselves to people and to things; on the other hand, at every moment we should also go beyond that world and realize that it's the One who is present in this person, this thing, in my action.

WEBER   If we integrated these dimensions, we would bring sacredness into our daily acts and treat one another differently.

GRIFFITHS   That is the point. It changes your attitude.

WEBER   How can we learn to do that?

GRIFFITHS Meditation is the secret. If you experience this reality in yourself, it begins to spread through everything.

WEBER Is there a danger that meditation will be self-aggrandizement or self-serving?

GRIFFITHS There is a great danger of that. The greatest danger is to seek an experience of God, which means you're seeking God's reflection in yourself—in your feelings and your thoughts. You think you've found God but God's evaded you. You've got to go beyond yourself each time. That is where many people living a practical life, who are very unselfish, very dedicated, probably experience God deeply without knowing it or seeking to do so. Most people get glimpses.

WEBER Is one earmark of it a sense of unity with others and compassion towards them?

GRIFFITHS Yes. The full sense, of course, is a total unity. Karl Rahner, the great German theologian, whom I admire more than anyone else, once said that if you really love somebody totally and unselfishly, you are encountering God in that person. Rahner has a real mystical insight behind his theology, and that to me gives it extraordinary value.

WEBER There is a whole school of aspiring mystics and meditators who feel theology kills—puts the heavy hand over the mystical experience. But you feel it needn't happen.

GRIFFITHS It needn't happen. St. Thomas Aquinas himself wrote this terribly logical, rational *Summa Theologica*, and at the end of his life he said, "Everything I've written seems to me like empty straw compared to what I've seen." Then his followers take up the system, repeat the whole rationalization and conception, and lose this understanding. That's why you have to go behind the theological terms to the source of mystical experience that they're supposed to be serving.

WEBER Some people discern the emergence of a planetary culture. Can you describe your vision of the marriage of east and west?

GRIFFITHS There are several components. First, science has changed its whole understanding of the universe—as a field of energy and not simply as a materialistic, mechanistic model. This opens physics, biology, and psychology to the spiritual dimension of reality. It also opens western science and philosophy to oriental mysticism and philosophy. I am interested in how science and mysticism relate to Christianity as a religion. My understanding is that Christianity began in the east in Palestine and has always moved westward. So its whole culture, its theology, its organization, its way of life has developed as a western organization. To a Hindu today, Christianity is a foreign religion, a western religion. What I see is how the Christian faith—the pure Christian faith, coming down from Jesus—can be expressed and lived in the oriental tradition, and also supported by the modern western scientific understanding. The convergence of those three is what I'm interested in.

WEBER   Those are the elements that can be married. Is there something that cannot be married?

GRIFFITHS   At the deepest level I don't find anything incompatible. The deeper you go into Hinduism or Buddhism, the more you see how there's a fundamental unity with Christianity. On the surface there are many differences and contradictions, and even below the surface there are still problems. But the deeper you go, the more you converge on this One. That is my vision of the future: that in each religion, as you go deeper into it, you converge on the original Source. We come forth from the One and we're returning to the One. But you can't mix on the surface. Syncretism is mixing on the surface—you take something of Buddhism, Hinduism, Christianity and you mix them. What we call Ecumenism is going beneath the surface to the convergence in the One, the Source. That is the real whole.

WEBER   Does that also apply to prayer and meditation in their depth?

GRIFFITHS   Yes. Again it's a question of orientation. Prayer, especially in the Christian and Semitic tradition, is addressed to God above, and man feeling himself a sinner on earth, opening himself to God the Father in Heaven, receiving grace coming down from above. It's always got a dualistic edge. Typically Christian prayer is either standing or kneeling—you're always relating yourself to something beyond. In the east, meditation is the normal form of relating—you're sitting and you realize God within. These are opposites, in a way, but to me they are complementary. Of course, in the Hindu tradition we have *bhakti* and *jnana*. *Bhakti* is relating to God in love and devotion, and there's always an element of duality in it. On the other hand you have *jnana*, knowledge, contemplation, where you simply realize your unity. Many Hindus would say that ultimately *bhakti* and *jnana* coincide. Again, on a certain level they're opposed, but on the deepest level they converge.

WEBER   An apparent difference is that in the Judeo–Christian framework prayer concerns sin, therefore the ethical dimension. Meditation concerns *avidya*, ignorance and its overcoming, therefore the epistemological dimension. There isn't anything to ask of the outside. One simply aims to clear away *avidya*, i.e., not seeing things as they really are.

GRIFFITHS   That's an important difference. For the oriental, what we call sin is ignorance. Relation to God and to the infinite is conceived of in terms of consciousness, a lower form of consciousness evolving into a higher form. But in the Judeo–Christian tradition,

the relation to God is conceived of in terms of sin and righteous-
ness; it's a moral tradition. Often, in practice, they tend to be
opposed, but I think one can interpret sin and ignorance as interrelated. Sin is in the will, ignorance is in the mind and consciousness, so the two are interdependent. I would agree with the Semitic
view that the fundamental difference—what separates us from
God—is in the will.

This leads to another point: in the Hindu tradition God is *sat-
chit-ananda*, being-knowledge-bliss, a state of pure consciousness,
giving this ultimate bliss. But in Christianity, it's not simply a
state of consciousness. It's a communion of *love*. The doctrine of
the Trinity is fascinating from that point of view: God is being,
and also wisdom and knowledge, but that Being is expressing itself
in its word and communicating in love. So the Godhead itself is
communion, personal relationship. To me that is a particularly
Christian insight. It reveals being as essentially relational. I was
struck by a remark of Suzuki that the Void of Mahayana Buddhism
is not merely static but dynamic. There is, he said, an urge to
differentiation in the Void and at the same time a need to remain
always in itself. Creation, the manifestation of the One in the
many, is the result of this urge to differentiation. This could be
applied to the doctrine of the Trinity.

WEBER   Is Christian love parallel to *ahimsa* in Hinduism and to
compassion (*karuna*) in Buddhism?

GRIFFITHS   They're parallel in many ways, but the compassion of the
Buddha and the *ahimsa*, and perhaps even more *prema* or love, in
the Hindu tradition, are very closely akin to Christian charity. But
each has its own distinctive character. In both the Hindu and
Buddhist traditions the person disappears in the ultimate but in
the Christian tradition the ultimate reality is personal or interper-
sonal, so that for us the highest state is a communion of persons
in love.

WEBER   Could you go into that, Father Bede?

GRIFFITHS   In knowledge we receive the forms of things into ourselves: we look out and see the trees, the earth, the sky, and receive
these forms into us. We commune with things in knowledge, in
consciousness. But in love we go out of ourselves, we surrender
ourselves to another, each gives himself to the other but you don't
lose yourself in the other, you find yourself. That is the mystery of
communion in God and with God—the Father and the Son become a total unity and are yet distinct, and that is true of man
and God as well. We are one, and yet we are distinct. There is
never total loss of self. In consciousness there is a pure identity, but
in love there's never pure identity because love involves two, and
yet the two become one. That's the great mystery. It's a paradox.

WEBER   The Indian metaphor of the ocean and the droplet that re-merges with the ocean is not the correct one for Christianity then?

GRIFFITHS   It's not adequate, no. You can say the drop merges in the ocean, but you can also say the ocean is present in the drop. In the new science, the whole is in the part and the part is in the whole, and that is very important. In the ultimate state the individual is totally there, totally realized, but also in total communion with all the rest. There is the illustration, often used, of mirrors. There is one light and each mirror reflects the one light and reflects all the other mirrors. So it's diversified and yet it is all one.

WEBER   Leibniz says that all the monads mirror each other and God has pre-harmonized them. What is probably difficult for the east is to understand the Incarnation from this perspective. In the east it seems to be cyclical and almost like an *office* that is occupied by many great enlightened beings (*avatars*) in different epochs. In the west it seems to be a unique climax in history.

GRIFFITHS   I think that is the distinction between cyclic and linear time. The oriental view is cyclic so an *avatar* comes again and again, but the Hebrew and Christian view is linear, time is moving towards an end. We speak of an eschatology. Therefore in the Hindu tradition, Ramakrishna and others come and others succeed, and nothing is final. But in the Christian tradition the whole creation and humanity are moving to an end, and Jesus comes at the end to bring all things to a head. It's a convergence of everything at that point in time and space, when time and space are transcended, a culmination. Then at the resurrection, time and space are taken up into the infinity—what T. S. Eliot called the "point of intersection of the timeless with time."

WEBER   Did Buddha, when he realized divinity under the Bodhi tree, also touch that intersection?

GRIFFITHS   Yes. I think there are many stages by which the infinite is manifesting in time, in fact the whole creation is a manifestation of the eternal in time. But there are many degrees—at first, in the physical universe, the power of God is manifest but life is not present. Then life comes into the universe. Then in ordinary human consciousness—this consciousness of God, the *chit*, is being manifested, but it's hidden in most people. In the great seers—a Buddha or the *rishis* [sages] you get a certain transparency. For a Christian, I think Jesus would be the point at which the total transparency is realized in that human being, and the divinity could give itself totally to the human. It's the meeting point.

WEBER   What is the role of the mystic in the Christian view?

GRIFFITHS   Christian mysticism begins in the New Testament, first of all with Jesus. Jesus had a unique experience of God that he expressed in the word "*abba*." They all say now that this word "*abba*," Father, was a word of wonderful intimacy, and He knew himself in relation to God as Son to the Father in a unique way. No one knows the Son but the Father. No one knows the Father but the Son. He had this unique relationship of oneness with the Father—unity in relationship. That was a mystical experience. The Spirit is the self-communication of God. The Son is the revelation, the Spirit is the communication, and at Pentecost the Spirit comes on the disciples and *they* participate *now* in this mystical experience. In the early Church there was a very strong sense that this mystical divine experience was being transmitted through the Bishops. But as an organization develops and gets further from the source, it becomes increasingly a more human reality. Though the mystical tradition always continued within the Church—you can point to holy men right up to the present day—the organization, the dogmatic formulas and the sacramental system tend to cover it. They were meant to reveal it, but they tended to cover it. But I feel now it's opening up again. Certainly, it's the mystical tradition which is the very life of the Church. Without that, it has no meaning at all.

WEBER   Are you saying that these features could reveal, but people take them as ends, whereas they are guideposts: they require our insight and self-transformation?

GRIFFITHS   Exactly. You see, what actually happened was the Fathers had this tremendous experience of Christ. They tried to find words to express it, some formula. We need some conceptual form to focus the reality for us. The descendents take over the formula and lose what it's intended to express. And so it gets hardened into dogma. One has to relive it, and that is difficult.

WEBER   In fact it raises another question about an assumption underlying eastern philosophy. From a Christian perspective, *can we become God?*

GRIFFITHS   It's to some extent a matter of language. After all, St. Atherasius, who was the greatest doctor of the divinity of Christ, said God became man that man might become God. But it really depends on how you understand that. Karl Rahner has a very interesting understanding of this. He says that in every human being there is the capacity for self-transcendence. Beyond our body, beyond the normal faculties of the soul, we are open to the transcendent reality. That *capacity* is in us at all times, and it can grow and become total, so it is possible for the human being to give himself *totally* to God. Rahner says that in Jesus a human being was found in whom this capacity for self-transcendence was totally realized so that he could become God. He could realize himself in a total unity with God, and God could give Himself totally to him. Each one of us can transcend ourselves and experience oneness with God. But it's not really *becoming* God [as in Indian *Advaita*], because God is always beyond. The human being is always limited, and though we can transcend ourselves and receive this gift of divine life, it's never total in us. As St. Thomas Aquinas says, we are not comprehensive: we don't comprehend God. Though we are one with Him and experience His love, He always remains beyond, at the same time.

WEBER   The fact that Christ was a being who could do that raises the question—who was he? Was he a man who was very spiritually evolved and who could therefore *learn* to do this, or was he of another order of being from ourselves from the very beginning?

GRIFFITHS   I think we have to say, in the strict Christian tradition, Jesus was a man. He belonged to this humanity, and he had the body of a Jew and the psyche of a Jew, and he belonged to his time. In that sense he is totally human and he shares the whole human reality, including suffering and death. In him as in all, there is the capacity for self-transcendence. But in him, as I understand it, that capacity was unlimited. In the depth of the spirit, he was open to the *total* reality of God, so that St. Paul says, "In him dwelt the fullness of the Godhead bodily." He is totally one with God and totally one with humanity. The rest of us have varying degrees of openness to the divine. We all participate according to our capacity in the divine life, divine *satchitananda*, but there is always a limit to it.

WEBER   Why was there this extraordinary openness and capacity for self-transcendence *precisely in Jesus*? Could this have happened before, or did it happen before, say five centuries earlier, with Buddha? Can it happen again other than in the eschatological dimension? Can it ever happen again as an historical event?

GRIFFITHS   In the Christian understanding we would say, no. It was a particular historic revelation, it came to a definite historic end and finality in Jesus, and the total reality is realized there; but that is not denying that the divine mystery is revealing itself in all different religions, in all different human experiences. But they are all related to this final eschatological event.

WEBER   I was at a small seminar with Krishnamurti and a group of scholars in Ojai, California a few years ago, and as often happens at these conferences there is great excitement but also frustration. At the end of each day a question kept coming up that is relevant here. It was phrased as follows—and I would ask it also of the historical Jesus—was this a *man* who had learned to swim consummately, or was it a *fish*? If it's a fish, it's another order of species, and there is little hope for us. If it was a man, then potentially it can be learned by anyone. That's the crucial question.

GRIFFITHS   Definitely I think it is a man. To me one of the great
weaknesses in modern Christianity is that really almost from the
time of the Council of Nicea in the fourth century, Jesus has
moved over from the human to the divine. They've never actually
denied the human reality, but it is so much emphasized that he is
God, that he is presented more as a God appearing on earth than
as a man. But the man standing before God—the epistle to the
Hebrews brings this out so clearly—offered loud cries and tears to
Him who was able to save him, and he was saved by his Godly
fear. So he is standing as a man before God. Thus it is definite
that he belongs with us. Yet at the same time he is the point where
we go beyond and become one with God.

WEBER   Potentially, could any Christian mystic or any deeply devoted spiritual human being do this again?

GRIFFITHS   I think in a sense that's the whole point. The epistle to
the Hebrews calls him the pioneer of our faith. He is the one who
has gone beyond. He has opened the way, and now it is open to
everybody, really, to enter in and to participate in his experience
of God—become sons in the Son, to participate in the Holy Spirit.
I'm hoping, if I am spared long enough, to write another book on
the subject, to try to show how Jesus—I would like to put it in
Hindu terms—*is a man* who *realized God* in this unique way. For
it is a unique way.

WEBER   Would that be accepted by the orthodox Church?

GRIFFITHS   I think it could be put in a way which is acceptable. The
tendency now is to emphasize that Jesus had to grow, he had to
learn Aramaic, he had to study the Bible gradually to discover his
calling, probably at the baptism he underwent a kind of initiatory
experience, he still had to face the question of suffering and death.
Only gradually did he realize that he was called to undergo this,
and only at the Resurrection does he pass beyond human limitations and become totally identified with the work; but all the time
he is moving toward that fulfillment.

WEBER   In *The Marriage of East and West*, you point out that Christianity cannot grow as a religion today unless it abandons its purely
western cultural set, with its emphasis on the rational-masculine.
You say that faith is a function of the intuitive-feminine aspect of
ourselves. Might it not be said that the east wants knowledge
rather than faith?

GRIFFITHS   No, faith is simply a preliminary stage for knowledge,
knowledge in the deep sense of *jnana*. In fact, faith in the strict
tradition is an illumination of the mind. It's an opening of the
mind to the transcendent reality, but like a seed it's just an opening, a beginning, and faith has to grow into experience. Perhaps
one of the great differences in the Christian tradition since the

Middle Ages is that we've tended to concentrate on intellectual knowledge, theology—faith becoming theology—but not on faith becoming experience.

WEBER   Faith in your sense is not synonymous with belief.

GRIFFITHS   No, we make that distinction now.

WEBER   Faith is the movement towards a living experience, which requires one to change, not to just endorse an article of belief.

GRIFFITHS   Exactly. Belief doesn't save you at all. St. Thomas again makes an interesting distinction between *fides informes* and *fides formata*. *Fides informes* is what we would call belief. You believe in God, in Christ, in the Church, but it doesn't change you at all. It is not moved by love and not by a transforming power. It's helpful as far as it goes; but it is extremely limited. But his *fides formata*, "faith working by love," is a transforming faith which opens you to the divine. That is terribly meaningful because there are millions and millions of Christians who believe, but they have got very little real faith.

WEBER   One is *about* the reality, and the other is moving towards experiencing it.

GRIFFITHS   Yes, exactly.

WEBER   Like all mystics. Father Bede, you emphasize our direct experience of the divine. From Plato on down, with his symbol of the sun as the supreme reality, light has been the privileged metaphor. Is it also so for you?

GRIFFITHS   No. That's why I value Dionysius the Areopagite so much. He speaks of the divine darkness: You must go beyond all your imagery, beyond your thoughts, into the divine darkness. That's where you meet God.

WEBER   In darkness, not "divine light"?

GRIFFITHS   No, darkness.

WEBER   That is unique, isn't it?

GRIFFITHS   Yes.

WEBER   Because the religious metaphor . . .

GRIFFITHS   Is always "light."

WEBER   What were his influences?

GRIFFITHS   Well, it comes from St. Gregory of Nyssa, who saw the journey of Israel through the desert culminating in Moses going up to meet God in the darkness, in the cloud on Mount Sinai; so the culmination of the spiritual journey through the desert, ascending the mountain, was in the cloud and in the darkness. He was hidden with God.

WEBER   One could also connect it to those dimensions of ourselves that are dark, not lit up, since we rarely explore them. We do not know them.

GRIFFITHS   And really the journey towards God is a journey into the unconscious. There you encounter many demons and other things, but eventually God is hidden in the depths of the unconscious.

WEBER   Perhaps the darkness is the ground, like *arupa*, formlessness, in Indian philosophy, and by the time we see it through light, it's the visible manifested expression of the divine *rupa*, the formed. But what makes it all possible cannot be seen.

GRIFFITHS   Yes, surely. You know, in a Hindu temple the inner sanctuary is always dark. You go through the courts of the temple, which are filled with light, the figures of the gods, but when you come to the inner sanctuary you come to the heart, the inner center of your own being, and you encounter God in the darkness. God without form.

You could say that creativity is fundamental in the implicate order, and what we really have to explain are the processes that are *not* creative.

DAVID BOHM

To my mind [Bohm's] enfolding and unfolding is exactly as conservative as his point of view on hidden variables. It always comes back to something which is there and then is developed.... Time is creation. The future is just not *there*.

ILYA PRIGOGINE

If you had absolute creativity—absolute novelty with no past—then nothing would ever exist because it would all vanish at the very moment of creation.

DAVID BOHM

We can't explain creativity, so we prefer to say that creativity is not creativity at all, but merely the expression of something "archetypal" that already exists in latent form. That denies creativity.

RUPERT SHELDRAKE

ILYA PRIGOGINE

10

The reenchantment of nature

ILYA PRIGOGINE

> If our senses were fine enough, we would perceive the slumbering cliff as a dancing chaos.
>
> NIETZSCHE

IT was like being drawn into a vortex, the image of nature's flow that Ilya Prigogine so delights in. My first impression was one of sheer dynamic energy compressed into a man, a metaphor that seems well-suited to Prigogine, whose work revolves around the most dynamic of nature's aspects—time. His efforts, after twenty years of benign neglect by the scientific community, brought him in 1977 the Nobel Prize in chemistry, and fame as "the poet of thermodynamics."

New York City, host to the 1984 American Association for the Advancement of Science, had provided a flawless June day. Prigogine had flown in from Brussels only the night before to attend and address the gathering. Though he admitted to jet-lag, I saw no signs of it. As Prigogine described "man's dialogue with nature" in his room towering above the New York maelstrom, he seemed in perpetual motion, like one of his dissipative structures. He took calls (requests for lectures are booked as much as a year ahead), saw to the coffee that was brought up, and punctuated his conversation with motion—all without slackening his pace.

Prigogine is a muscular man with a powerful stocky frame that supports a leonine head. His lively brown eyes and sudden smiles lend him a youthful charm and appeal that belie his sixty-eight years. This vitality is enhanced by a powerful personality that settles over his listeners, and a vibrant voice that spins out his views with an unrelieved intensity. Because of this tumultuous energy, Prigogine was the most demanding of my partners in dialogue, and yet one of the most spellbinding.

Ilya Prigogine was born in Moscow in 1917, at the dawn of the Russian Revolution, and raised in Belgium. Educated in the classics, history, and philosophy, and seriously schooled in classical music, he became an accomplished pianist. But his chief focus was chemistry, which he studied at the Free University of Brussels, receiving his Ph.D. there in 1941.

He had concentrated in thermodynamics, the interface between physics and chemistry which deals with the relationship between mechanical energy and heat. From the beginning, his main interest lay in the concept of time: its structure, its meaning, and its neglect by classical physics. This was to turn into his life-long preoccupation with the dynamic processes in nature, encompassing such diverse areas as cosmology, particle physics, and biology. His Nobel Prize in chemistry was awarded mainly for Prigogine's theory of dissipative structures, which built a bridge between living and non-living systems. But his prize citation also acknowledged the wide implications of his work for other areas. In the Nobel Committee's words, "Prigogine has fundamentally transformed and revised the science of irreversible thermodynamics. He has given it new relevance and created theories to bridge the gap that exists between the biological and social scientific fields of inquiry."

Prigogine's theories are set forth in two difficult recent books, one rather technical, *From Being to Becoming: Time and Complexity in the Physical Sciences* (1980), followed in 1984 by *Order Out of Chaos: Man's New Dialogue with Nature* (which he co-authored with chemist and philosopher Isabelle Stengers). In *Order Out of Chaos*, Prigogine argues for the unity of man and nature. By contrast with the mechanistic world-view, this unity manifests itself as a "new dialogue" which brings back the "reenchantment" with nature that man has lost through a mechanistic conception of her. He seeks, in particular, to explain process—change and becoming.

The second law of thermodynamics states that the available energy in the universe is inevitably running down, moving from maximum order to an ultimate disorder in which all available energy will have been spent. This principle of entropy, first introduced by Clausius in 1865, decrees that certain processes cannot be reversed. As Boltzmann first pointed out in describing our evolution toward equilibrium (a state in which no further energy exchanges can take place), entropy is related to probability; entropy grows because probability grows. This is related to the arrow of time (a phrase coined by Eddington) which holds that it is extremely unlikely for events to go backward.

The arrow of time is a key concept for understanding Prigogine's work. An organism is born, develops to maturity, and dies—it has a history. The arrow of time, which can be disregarded in subatomic particles, cannot be disregarded in living organisms. Still, Prigogine's work teaches that living systems can to some degree escape entropy through their capacity for self-organization; in them a higher order not predicted by entropy can emerge out of the dead end of chaos. Prigogine insists that order emerges because of entropy, not in spite of it.

Living systems are open systems, far-from-equilibrium or near-equilibrium complexes of organization which Prigogine calls "dissipative structures." These are states that reflect their interaction with the environment with which the dissipative structures are constantly trading energy, maintaining themselves through an endless dynamic flow. An important factor is contributed by fluctuations or perturbations, sudden shifts that allow for novelty to emerge even when entropy would rule it out.

A single fluctuation adding its strength to other fluctuations may become powerful enough to reorganize the whole system into a new pattern. The points at which this happens are "bifurcation points," at which deterministic description breaks down and the system follows one of several possible forks in the road.

These random or "stochastic" (i.e. not predictable) processes demonstrate, says Prigogine, that open systems—and hence most of our universe—are not mechanistic but random. Prigogine uses the idea of randomness quite differently from the way other scientists do. For Jacques Monod (*Chance and Necessity*), for example, randomness entails a world governed by blind chance which points to a universe that in human terms is meaningless, akin to the "absurd" world of existentialist philosophy, with which Monod buttresses his arguments.

But for Prigogine randomness is a synonym for non-determinism, spontaneity, and novelty—in a word, for creativity. The Prigogine universe is akin to a living organism precisely because it has room for random behavior, allowing dissipative structures—anything from a chemical solution to clouds to the brain to a human being—to recreate themselves into unforseeable patterns. These novel patterns are often triggered by small variables or perturbations whose presence can pull the entire system away from one kind of behavior toward a new and unexpected one, thereby defying both a mechanistic interpretation of entropy and a conventional reading of the arrow of time.

Dissipative structures thus introduce constant creativity into nature. As a result, matter is no longer seen as something static—inert molecules that are governed solely by pushes and pulls—but as something active and alive. Except for systems at equilibrium (a rock or the rust of a sheet of metal) in which no further exchanges take place, near-equilibrium or far-from-equilibrium systems are constantly attuned to their environments. In these open systems, matter is not the isolated, solitary, and solipsistic affair described by mechanistic science—Prigogine has called such particles "hypnons," sleeping their way through interactions—but instead it is responsive, relational, and self-modifying in response to the activities of other matter. In these far from equilibrium systems, the smallest change may "destabilize" the system—a synonym for creativity in Prigogine's vocabulary—and this brings about an outcome not predicted by the logic of linear equations.

The mathematics of Prigogine's schema is represented by non-linear equations in which multiple factors act on one another simultaneously, and by "phase-space," in which the system is represented by a single point in 6-n dimensional space. Phase-space allows for the dynamic representation of the evolution of a system by means of a trajectory, so that each region can contain an infinite number of represented points.

Prigogine complains that classical science has forgotten nature's interiority. Within each particle of being there is a history—time, change, interactions with other particles—that has caused *irreversible* changes, i.e., the qualitative aspects of experince that are embedded in the arrow of time, in evolution, and in history. Physics, especially particle physics —the present stronghold of reversibility, for physicists treat particle-interactions as if they can be run forwards or backwards in time—tends to disregard this qualitative aspect. He hopes to show that even sub-atomic particles are subject to his law of dissipative structures, just as macro-processes are, and hence that all matter in the universe is characterized by responsiveness, creativity and—in that sense—by dialogue.

Just as Prigogine's theories seem to reach out into multiple directions, incapable of parochial confinement, so does his life, which extends over two continents and into multiple commitments. Based in Brussels with his family, he directs the Solvay International Institute of Physics and Chemistry and teaches at the Free University of Brussels. He also shuttles back and forth to Austin for part of each year. There, at the Ilya Prigogine Center for Statistical Mechanics and Thermodynamics of the University of Texas, Prigogine pursues his research surrounded by a large and supportive team of co-workers. His wide range of interests is, of course, parallel to his theories. These can be applied to an astonishing number of fields from physics, chemistry and biology to the study of droplets in a waterfall, and other dynamic flow patterns that form the basis of a growing sub-speciality in science known as "chaos," for which Prigogine's work is an important foundation.

Still the Renaissance man with multidimensional interests, Prigogine continues his involvement with art, especially primitive art, of which he is both a connoisseur and collector. He relates it, not surprisingly, to his theory of becoming. "Artistic activity," he says, "breaks the temporal symmetry of the object."[14] His latest book ends with an appeal: "We can no longer accept the old *a priori* distinctions between scientific and ethical values.... Today we know that time is a construction and therefore carries an ethical responsibility.... As a result, individual activity is not doomed to insignificance."[15]

WEBER In your most recent book in English, *Order out of Chaos*, you argue for the unity of man and nature, rather than their opposition. Would you spell that out further?

PRIGOGINE In the beginning of the book we point out that the

Newtonian classical view of the world is that it's a kind of auto-maton described by deterministic and time-reversible laws. This contrasts greatly with the view we have of our inner world, which is neither deterministic nor time-reversible. The direction of time is a basic experience of man.

Today we are going through a reconceptualization of physics which brings the picture of the inner and outer world closer to-gether. In 1900, physicists were pretty much unanimous that the basic processes in nature are deterministic and reversible. Today, a growing minority takes the opposite point of view, that some of the basic laws are irreversible and stochastic [i.e. probabilistic]. This requires a more complex vision of the physical world, but also one which does not put man and nature in such opposition.

WEBER   In the book you talk about seventeenth-century models of a deterministic universe, "hard determinism," in which man's place is meaningless. But aren't there other interpretations of that seventeenth-century model? For example Kepler, Galileo, and Newton did not draw reductionist conclusions from determinism; on the contrary, they felt that through it they glimpsed God's eternal order and beautiful mind. They found meaning there—unlike Monod and Sartre.

PRIGOGINE   That is true, but let's see what is behind that. Classical science was born in a culture dominated by the alliance between man—situated midway between the divine and the natural order—and god, the rational and intelligible legislator, the sovereign ar-chitect we have conceived in our own image. But it is clear that this classical view of reason may lead to some form of alienation. We are closer now to Kierkegaard or Monod, who say man's place in the universe is what he makes of it.

The classical notion of time as an abstraction was leading to the concealment of time and therefore to a basic difficulty in under-standing *our* time in a world of time. At the moment we are seeing a revival of time as an empirical fact: Time appears in elementary particles, in cosmology, in non-equilibrium structures: more and more time-oriented or irreversible processes are found throughout the universe. This brings men closer to nature because it shows us that our human orientation in time is a very general feature. But there is a deeper problem: Once you find irreversible processes in nature, like the ones described by the second law of thermo-dynamics, you have to decide how to view them. You can take the classical view that irreversibility is only an approximation of the dynamical time-reversible laws. Or you can take the opposite view.

WEBER   Reverse it.

PRIGOGINE   Reverse the whole situation.

WEBER   So you say that irreversible processes may be primary. What the seventeenth century thought was the privileged model—time-reversible processes—are the special cases.

PRIGOGINE Exactly. Now instead of saying irreversibility is an approximation and secondary law, it can be considered as a *basic* law. In order to do that we need a lot of new physics and new mathematics and at the end of my book I give some ideas about how it will probably go, but there is still a lot to be developed. Some of it has indeed been developed after the publication of our book.

WEBER The notions of time and evolution—creativity, you say in your book—are built inside everything, and that is what classical and quantum physics ignore.

PRIGOGINE Right. We can now formulate, or at least think about creativity in matter. Those are the two cornerstones out of which the new concepts can now arise. However, let us be a little careful. Creativity has a psychological connotation and therefore it is not directly applicable to, say, elementary particles. Still, we see today life deeply rooted in non-life, and this is because of the progress in two fields, non-equilibrium physics and non-linear dynamics.

WEBER What would you say to somebody who took the view of Kant and the eastern mystics that the time-generated creativity you're talking about is in the phenomenal world and due to our partial and limited perspective?

PRIGOGINE Give time the status of an *a priori* tool of the human mind, Kant completely avoided the problem. His solution was to introduce a basic duality. This is an extreme solution, which we can begin to overcome through the inner progress of science.

WEBER It still brings up the question: Can we *trust* what we know?

PRIGOGINE There may be a road to truth which has nothing to do with experience. But I have nothing to say about that. It's not my domain and therefore I cannot address such questions. However, if we look at what is around us, we see that irreversible processes are essential ingredients in biological structures. If Kant were right, and irreversibility is just a category in the human mind, we would be responsible for our own existence. Our irreversible lives would be the outcome of our *a priori* category of time in our own mind. Now that is impossible.

WEBER Some people like Ken Wilber argue that all physics, by its own admission, is bound in Plato's cave and that there's another way of apprehending reality—through mysticism and direct intuition.

PRIGOGINE As I just mentioned, I have little to say about that. I personally feel that we come at present to the insight that we are embedded in the world as a whole. We begin to find a link without appealing to some kind of external, extraneous mysticism. How you interpret this link between man and nature is open to everybody. In classical physics you really had no choice. You either had to accept an alienating science, which men like Monod [in *Chance and Necessity*] expressed very clearly; or you had to go to an anti-scientific, metaphysical view, such as that of Whitehead or Bergson. Today things come closer together. Psychoanalysis emphasized that what is accessible to us is only a very small part of all the activity which is going on. There is a lot of *opacity* below the layer of transparency. Classical physics saw a transparent world. This transparent world was in complete opposition to our own opacity. However, once you discover time and fluctuations in which irreversibility plays such an important role, you come to a world which is much more opaque as compared to the classical physical world. You come to a closer relation between what we see outside and inside.

WEBER   But could one object that opacity in us is due to insufficient self-knowledge?

PRIGOGINE   Maybe; there is no mathematical theory of how the mind works. However, we know simple situations in which the outcome of each individual experience is undetermined in our present theoretical frame, while the outcome of repeated experiments can be predicted in the sense of probabilities. In those simple cases, we know therefore that the opacity I mentioned is not related to insufficient knowledge.

WEBER   Because of quantum mechanics?

PRIGOGINE   Not only because of quantum mechanics, though you are right to speak of it. Quantum mechanics in this perspective was only the first step and perhaps not the most important one. Quantum mechanics introduced this kind of opacity, through the wave-function, which measures a probability amplitude. In addition to quantum mechanics there is another type of randomness which comes from the instability of dynamical systems. When the system is unstable we can only speak about our knowledge in a finite region of phase-space. We have lost the possibility to speak of individual trajectories or individual space-time elements. Therefore, the transparency associated with an individual trajectory is lost.

WEBER   Your own work stresses interdependence and interconnection of the whole.

PRIGOGINE   That is very natural. By emphasizing interdependence, we may show that life and non-life are not opposed. That has to be so, because otherwise you would have on one side a mechanical world and on the other a biological world and then a human world, all separated by absolute barriers. If that were so, then you would need to make an appeal to some transcendental knowledge to go beyond the barriers. In my opinion that's not necessary.

WEBER   What is especially unique and appealing about your work is that you show that order can arise from disorder. Must order arise from disorder?

PRIGOGINE No. It depends on the type of non-linearity present in the system. That is very nice because not everything is living and not everything is dead. Also, generally speaking, both order and disorder are generated through irreversible processes. . . . The duality of order/disorder is the outcome of a single basic feature: irreversibility.

WEBER Can we talk about the Big Bang, this glamorous notion in physics? If the Big Bang is the source of everything, literally, and it is maximum order, doesn't that tilt toward order in the universe?

PRIGOGINE The question of the Big Bang and cosmological questions are, in my opinion, still at a preliminary stage. When you read most of the popular literature you get the impression that the Big Bang and the possible cyclic universe are already facts. But the only thing we know for sure is that our cosmic environment evolved from a hot dense state. Is this the starting point of our universe? Is the Big Bang describing the origin of our cosmological environment or of the universe as a whole? There are still many questions to be solved before we can come to a deeper understanding. The majority of theoretical physicists is working on the incorporation of quantum physics into general relativity, which gives the theoretical framework for the Big Bang. But there are other problems, such as the relation betweeen general relativity and entropy, and the validity of the entropy law related to the distinction between stable and unstable systems.

As I have recently shown, the second law is based on two features: first, it is applicable only to unstable dynamical systems; second, we have to take into account that for unstable dynamical systems, the concept of initial conditions is a very complex one. For such systems, starting from a finite region in phase-space, one can get diverging trajectories, often called "sensitivity to initial conditions." As a result of these two features—instability and finite information corresponding to a finite window on temporal evolution—we can prove the validity of the second law of thermodynamics, in which there is a basic time-dissymmetry, as future and past don't play the same role.

Today, we have to incorporate the second law of thermodynamics into general relativity. In a view in which the second law plays an essential role, the Big Bang would be less a starting point than a point of thermodynamical instability. Starting with this point, irreversibility leads to the creation of both order and disorder; more specifically, to the two components we find in the universe: photons and baryons. The latter are in a metastable state of decaying, and the photons are "waste products" which can no longer decay into other forms of matter.

WEBER   But doesn't that just push the problem further back?

PRIGOGINE   Then you ask me what is the meaning of the universe? That is not a question to which one may hope to give a simple answer. Perhaps, as an approximation, I would even dare to say that time precedes existence, just as irreversibility precedes—in the sense I just indicated—the creation of our universe.

WEBER   Yes, it's a big question. Let me ask you another. Can the laws of nature themselves undergo transition?

PRIGOGINE   The laws of nature may indeed depend on the state of nature. For example, my colleagues and I have recently worked out a formulation of the entropy law which would include the gravitational state of the universe. The entropy itself would then depend on the history of the universe. But we may imagine simpler examples. Can you speak of laws of biology if there is no life? Obviously not. In other words what we call laws or regularities, depend on their realization, on the bifurcation which the universe is following.

WEBER   This is like nominalism.

PRIGOGINE   No. I take it as an empirical statement. Laws of nature correspond to regularities and their validity and formulation contain a basic empirical element.

WEBER   But, still, the ever dissatisfied question of the non-nominalists then is: How does matter know how to act? There is no *entelechy* in it, there is no god directing it. What makes it do what it does?

PRIGOGINE   Once more, you are asking a very ambitious question. I am satisfied with a much more limited, but still important, aspect: the existence of this extraordinary jump between the way which we know matter is behaving at equilibrium and far-from-equilibrium. At equilibrium we know that each particle is surrounded by other particles, but they are very short range forces and each particle sees only its neighbors. We now know that in non-equilibrium conditions, long-range correlations may arise in macroscopic distances and times. Therefore we can say, by contrast, that matter at equilibrium is blind.

WEBER   This is the state of matter you refer to in *Order Out of Chaos* when you speak about "hypnons" or "sleepwalkers."

PRIGOGINE   Yes. When matter is in equilibrium, it is formed by disordered "hypnons". By contrast, when matter is disturbed by non-equilibrium conditions, long-range correlations may arise. It may appear undesirable to introduce such a neologism as "hypnons." This is in fact related to some technical problems which we have largely clarified since the publication of our book. We wanted indeed to emphasize that the basic element is no longer a point trajectory (or a wave function, in the case of quantum mechanics), else there would have been no irreversibility in the basic description. We now know what hypnons may be in classical mechanics. They are bundles of trajectories in unstable dynamical systems, which cannot be distinguished through subsequent observations. The hypnon is essentially a delocalized object with a broken time-symmetry.

WEBER Even if I try to keep my question modest, doesn't the way you speak of matter border on saying what David Bohm has said, that matter is "alive?" Or is that too anthropomorphic for you?

PRIGOGINE Not only is it too anthropomorphic, it's burying the question. What I want to emphasize is a different type of behavior: that equilibrium matter and non-equilibrium matter have different properties. Because of non-equilibrium you can go to states of complexification and cooperation. But in equilibrium conditions matter doesn't behave like that.

However, I cannot discuss in detail the relationship of what I am saying to what Bohm is saying because I have not understood him exactly. My feeling when I hear or read him is that his is a rather conservative view, in the sense that he very much emphasizes enfolding and unfolding. To my mind enfolding and unfolding is exactly as conservative as his point of view on hidden variables. It always comes back to something which is *there* and then is developed. The hidden variables are there and if we were not so stupid we could see them. In spite of his great originality, and of many things which I admire in Bohm's views, I still feel he is trying to come back to a classical transparency of nature.

WEBER I follow what you are saying. The factor that is conservative and not acceptable to you is that even if it's within the implicate order, it already pre-exists in some realm. Your view is that order is being made, created, literally *on the spot*.

PRIGOGINE Exactly. Time is creation. The future is just not *there*. We reach an idea of time different from the classical Aristotelian subdivision of past, present, and future along a straight line, with the present as a point separating the past and the future. The classical concept is very difficult to hold because the present would be only a point. But if the present is only a point, how can it really separate the past and the future? In a sense it is the past and the future which are there, not the present. Finally, you conclude with Leibniz: the world of instantaneous consciousness is also unconsciousness. But by including the second law of thermodynamics, we come to a concept of time in which the past is there, the present has a finite duration, and the future is not yet there. It's a concept of nature very similar to biological time.

Heidegger put the problem very clearly; in science there will be no temporal element in either being or becoming, because becoming is simply a display of what is already in the present. That is what I feel in Bohm's view also. The view which I defend is different. We come here to the frontiers of science. What is already established is the constructive role of irreversible forces. Here I go beyond that. I am saying that physics itself will become a physics of irreversible processes in which classical or quantum theory will appear as a simplification, valid for very simple systems, but no longer the prototype of physical knowledge, as it appears at present.

WEBER   You consider the creative universe primary, and anything else as an abstraction from that, almost an ossification of it.

PRIGOGINE   Yes. An ossification or a simplification.

WEBER   You have said that the world of physics and the activity of physicists cannot be divorced from the human world of daily life, from psychology, politics, and so on. Do you think that irreversibility has been looked down upon is because it reminds us of *our* death and our finitude?

PRIGOGINE   I am inclined to think science is deeply rooted in social history. Western science originated at a time of absolute monarchies. The idea was that the monarch, like God and like the scientist, has an eternal wisdom, and therefore truth has to be eternal, unchanging. The universe had to satisfy eternal laws. What could be the meaning of uncertainty in the spirit of God? What could be the meaning of uncertainty in the spirit of a scientist who is in a sense a representative of some superior knowledge? It was very fortunate that this attitude prevailed at first because it permitted us to study very simple systems. If we had immediately started to study very complex systems, perhaps modern science would never have arisen. We would have stayed in the period of Aristotle. Therefore, it is very difficult to know exactly why irreversibility has been neglected. However, it is quite remarkable that this interest in complex systems, in time, in new visions of transformations arises at a period of transition of human society.

WEBER   Now, in the twentieth century.

PRIGOGINE   Yes, at a moment where the density of population will require a new dialogue between man and nature. It is very interesting that now we are beginning to be able to understand much more complex systems: climatic systems, meteorological systems, geological history. We are beginning to decipher much more than we could before. This may lead to knowledge which is of great value for what I think is finally the aim of science: to improve the human condition.

WEBER   One of the loveliest phrases in your book is "the reenchantment of nature." In what way is the dynamic outlook on the universe which you are describing a reenchantment of nature?

PRIGOGINE   Because it reintroduces diversity and therefore the unexpected. Lévy-Bruhl and Durkheim said about forty years ago that nothing can really astonish western rational man because he knows that whatever he sees can be related to the fundamental laws of nature he has already discovered. It is precisely that which has been shattered, not only shattered in the domain of high energy physics, elementary particles—which have a very different structure from what we expected—or in cosmology, but shattered on our own level. The molecules around us, turbulence, chemical clocks, biological clocks, present the behavior of matter as very different from what was the classical view. There is a new interest in nature around us. That is a very important phenomenon because, after all, to do science is to be open to the world around us, including the human world. That is a kind of reenchantment, because you see new possibilities. It used to be that the only interesting fields were high energy physics and cosmology. But for a growing minority, perhaps already a majority, that is no longer true.

WEBER   I suppose the nonenchantment and even the disenchantment had to do with the fact that much of science was obsessed with prediction and control, not with understanding and the poetry of it all. You are stressing the opposite.

PRIGOGINE   Exactly. Once you know that everything is controlled and that everything can be predicted by a few general laws, what can be the interest of it? Only to unfold what is already there.

WEBER   I suppose Einstein would have said: To unify the whole thing, all the laws. The four laws currently known to physics: gravitation, electromagnetism, and the strong and weak nuclear forces.

PRIGOGINE   Many scientists today are fascinated by the "Grand Unified Theory." But we do not know at present how it could include the temporal dimension, which is so essential to the human experience. This unification would occur at very high energies, and the very first fraction of thousands of milliseconds of the existence of the universe. In other words that will not effect our life very much. The dream of eternity and of unification is a Newtonian dream. It is the dream of an infinite universe in which there is no structure and no place for men.

WEBER   The macroscopic until now has been *faute de mieux*, second best. But you claim that its value is intrinsic, it is not a stepchild.

PRIGOGINE   No, because in the conceptual structure of the new description the macroscopic has displayed features such as irreversibility, which are still to be formulated more precisely on a more basic level, such as general relativity or Grand Unified Theory.

WEBER   You speak about the symbols for science: the clock in the seventeenth century, and the thermal engine in the nineteenth century. What is our symbol? What represents the twentieth century? You hinted that it is like a work of art, the dance of Shiva. Why would art be the symbol for the science in our time?

PRIGOGINE   Art is essentially an expression of something very fundamental in nature. In art we see irreversibility and unpredictability. They are the characteristics which today we would like to ascribe to the universe as well as to a work of art.

WEBER   You are probably not sympathetic to the notion that the sculptor just frees the statue by chipping away what's already there, and thus reveals the real statue.

PRIGOGINE   No. My point of view is that in our very existence we have broken time symmetry, and this broken time symmetry is of course more intense in us than in any other object in the universe. As a result, I think sculpture has to be viewed as a transmission of this arrow of time to the stone. In other words, what we are doing first is to mark our presence, to give to the stone a date. Sculpture is a marker. You see that very well in prehistorical sculpture. The first manifestation of what will later become sculpture in a more pure form than tools—tools of course are also a form of art, especially in the later period—are the famous cusps. These are small holes which people a hundred thousand years ago made on rock. We don't know what these holes, or semiholes, mean. Are they habitats of the dead? Are they simply indications of the presence of men? There is certainly something which marks the passage of human existence on objects which have a longer lifetime. I see art in a temporal perspective. But these are very complex questions, and I don't want to sound too dogmatic about them.

WEBER   It's fascinating to try to relate that to what we were saying before. Could science now be symbolized by the dance of Shiva?

PRIGOGINE   Yes, eternity and time.

WEBER   Shiva is traditionally interpreted as the destroyer but it has been pointed out by Buddhist scholars like Lama Govinda that this interpretation is incorrect. Govinda suggests that Shiva should be called the transformer, the dynamic principle in cosmology. That would be more in line with what you are saying.

PRIGOGINE   Yes. I have heard from my Indian friends that Shiva has a musical instrument, a drum, in one hand and a flame in another. The flame is destruction and the drum is creation. The spirit combines both destruction and creation.

WEBER   When I read your work it evokes the birth, manifestation and death of everything from the smallest particle of matter to the galaxies to ourselves, as a kind of creative dance. In your framework, is death, our death, a perturbation in the system or the destruction of the system?

PRIGOGINE   I have nothing to say about that. I believe that we are living in a world which is not given to us. It is not like an open book which we can read and open at this chapter or that. We have hints, fragments. But to know how to make out of these a general picture would require a different type of knowledge, or at least a much more complete knowledge than we have. I would not necessarily say it requires a transcendental knowledge, but I certainly think we are only living in the prehistory of the understanding of our universe. Science is a very recent enterprise. From the point of view of *science*, to find an answer to your questions at this stage seems to me absolutely disproportionate. I believe, or at least I feel, that my view about our connection to time and irreversibility gives more meaning to human life by showing that we are embedded in something we see also in us.

WEBER   I understand. Coming back to man though, some people argue—for example the Buddhists and David Bohm—that human suffering and its problems are really due to the fact that we have not learned the very thing that other systems know how to do, namely to live dynamically: to arise, manifest, and let go every millisecond, so that no residue is left over. To live like that would be psychologically analogous to the nonequilibrium systems that you describe—dynamic and always reorganizing themselves.

PRIGOGINE   Part of our suffering and our dogmatic behavior comes from a misinterpretation of human rationality. Human rationality is of course an extremely important element which has given human life its unique flavor. But it can lead to some strange behavior. Kant was obsessed by human rationality and thought it had to follow the rationality of the planets. That is why he took his famous daily walk always at exactly the same time, in order to imitate the rationality of the planets. Samuel Beckett in one of his plays has a man coming in every few minutes on the scene, looking around and going away. That is supposed to be an allusion to human rationality. The idea of classical science with its determinism, implying the possibility of absolute knowledge, leads to intolerance and finally to violence. I think that the idea of limited rationality more correctly expresses our situation. Of course that is one of the reasons why stochastic descriptions in physics—in quantum mechanics or more recently the new time concept we discussed before—have often been violently attacked. Classical rationalism leads easily to some idea of a superman, a kind of James Bond who in every circumstance knows what to do. We have to live in and accept a pluralistic world, with a limited rationality. This doesn't mean failure.

I am very interested in insect societies. I was always very impressed by the fact that insects like ants are ecologically enormously successful. According to estimates today, there are millions of ants per human being. Therefore the total mass of ants is probably larger than the mass of human beings. And they can claim a much greater ecological success than even humanity in the twentieth century. This success is a very interesting success, because each ant has a very limited rationality. It is a rather stupid small animal, but very oriented to the outside world, obviously very observant of what is going on and able to amplify the impression it receives from the outside world by communicating it to the other members of the insect society. Therefore, a limited rationality doesn't necessarily mean a failure. I think that the overestimation of the power of human rationality may be one of the reasons for intolerance and for a mythological view of the world which is probably one of the reasons behind ideological struggles.

WEBER   You attribute the problem to rationality. Others might say it's the lack of it, dogmatic belief, and precisely not rationality that have created wars and intolerance.

PRIGOGINE   Yes. I have no disagreement with your statement. Call it "limited" or "renewed" rationality. In many cases it expresses a more subtle view of nature than the one related to eternal laws and absolute truth. I must say that this new view of rationality is not well received in France, the country of Descartes, as it may be assimilated to some kind of obscurantism, with which it has of course nothing to share.

WEBER   You are speaking of a self-critical rationality with the awareness of its limitation. That will create this openness.

PRIGOGINE   Yes.

WEBER   I think I can see why France might feel a bit uneasy with some of your theories because, emotionally, I share that uneasiness. If the universe is something that is creating itself as it goes along, it is as if you are pulling the rug out from under us. The picture generates a sense of insecurity as well as excitement. We don't know what the universe is going to do until it does it. There are no archetypes, no gods, no platonic ideas, no eternal laws, no immanence in anything, no implicate order. That seems bleak and austere.

PRIGOGINE   Yes, I can understand this type of reaction. Let me respond to this on two levels. First, I am not describing the universe as I would *like it* to be. I try to describe the evolution of science at the moment. To go back to the beginning of our discussion, why in the middle of this century have we discovered unstable elementary particles? Why have we discovered that the galaxies are moving away? that there is a microwave radiation? that there are chemical clocks? All this *changes* our view, and because of the impact of all this knowledge we cannot avoid the change in view. I am trying in a little more systematic way to express what the view may be and to situate my own work in relation to it. We do not choose the world in which we live.

The second level is to compare this view with other solutions. If we come up with the solution that the world is deterministic in the classical sense, what is our role in this world? It is to play a part which has been predicted but is unknown to us. This is even more difficult for me to accept: that without knowing it, we are a kind of lower machine. We are just following some master plan which has not been communicated to us; we are just conditioned to follow it. That seems to me even repulsive, if I may say so.

WEBBER   On the other hand, people like Pythagoras, Plato, and Bruno found the regularity less a determinism than an exaltation because the divine mind, as we said, was still in the picture. They didn't feel like puppets, they felt more like dancers dancing that cosmic dance themselves. The fact that they were in harmony with it was exalting, not depressing, to them.

Buddhist cosmology claims that some humans experience multi-dimensional consciousness where, by contrast to three-dimensional Cartesian consciousness, it's possible to convert time into space. If you stand back far enough, then instead of seeing time and the arrow of time with its flow, you perceive them simultaneously as conscious, present experience. Time is transformed into space. Do you have any comments on that?

PRIGOGINE   I agree with this description. In the Benard instability we see long-range correlations in the convective currents which arise in a heated thin layer of liquid. Here time is transformed into space. My colleague Serge Pahaut has recently recalled for me the splendid sentence in *Parsifal*: "Time here becomes space." Indeed, life and even the existence of the universe may be conceived of as the inscription of temporal irreversibility in space and matter, but this could be the subject of some other discussion. Time is something much more complex than the number you read on your watch. Of course, it has to keep track of the watch, but there is much more to it than that. In our recent work on dynamical systems, my colleague Misra and I have introduced the idea of internal time. This internal time cannot be completely independent of astronomical time because we are living in a single universe. Things have to be synchronized. Therefore the change of the average internal time has to be related to the time of the planets, to the time of the watch. However, the detailed way in which this internal time is going on may be unbelievably complicated. In fact, it may not only go forward but partly backward. And it may indeed contain the simultaneity you speak of more or less in qualitative way, a lot of possibilities. You could say that space is a realization, or related to one vision, of internal time. In other words, this internal time on the average progresses, but it can also recover elements which were in the past, and for that the best analogy is musical time. When you play a sonata, at some point you have repetition. However, this is not real repetition, because if it were real repetition it would be cyclic. It would be going again and again, and time cannot be cyclic because that would violate the idea of a single direction. However, it may bring in elements which existed already in the past.

WEBER The fact that the musical phrase is being played again changes the experience, because you've heard it before.

PRIGOGINE Exactly. You are completely right.

WEBER Even the fact that it's now the second or third time, though it's the same musical phrase, it's not the same.

PRIGOGINE Yes, it's not the same. Therefore internal time may be a freer time. By describing the internal, we also emphasize the autonomy of human beings.

WEBER My last question is a difficult one, straight out of Heidegger. In *Being and Time* he asks "Why is there anything, rather than nothing?"

PRIGOGINE Are you sure that this question is meaningful? Perhaps it is from the point of view of some Being external to the world, one which had to choose between creating or not creating this world. But from our point of view, I believe it is meaningless. However, there is a deep drive—which goes from Neanderthal to our century—to explore the surroundings in which we have been thrown. Let us hope that some improvement in the global condition of mankind will lead us further along this road.

If we were certain about the answer as to what happened in that first second ... we'd have solved all the problems and it would be rather dull.

STEPHEN HAWKING

If you said there were certain fixed and everlasting laws of the molecules and atoms, then what would you say if you traced it back to the time before the atoms and molecules existed?

DAVID BOHM

I certainly think we are only living in the prehistory of the understanding of our universe.

ILYA PRIGOGINE

But the puzzle is, what happened before time began?

DAVID BOHM

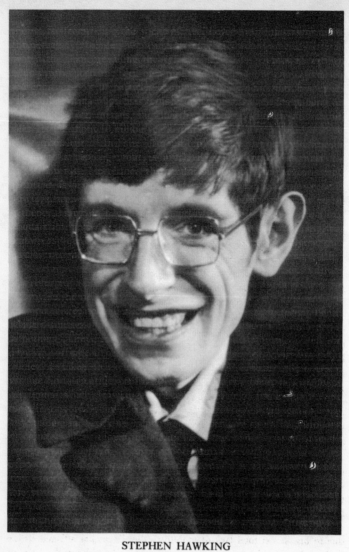

STEPHEN HAWKING

11

If there's an edge to the universe, there must be a God

STEPHEN HAWKING

The philosophic content of a science is only preserved if science is conscious of its limits.

HEISENBERG

HE lives in a minutely restricted space and at the same time in a space of staggering immensity, and in this he is worthy of both a Zen paradox and the paradoxes besetting quantum mechanics. I have resolved, while researching Stephen Hawking's background, not to allow his physical condition to dominate my portrait of him nor to have it dominate the reader's impressions of the man whom many consider the greatest mind in physics since Einstein. Firmed up by the many Hawking articles I have been reading in which his illness was the leitmotif, I renew this resolve on the train ride up to Cambridge. As I walk about the university town on a cool and pleasant mid-July afternoon in 1985, I try to capture something of the flavor of Cambridge, where Stephen Hawking has spent most of his professional life. It is a beautiful, quintessential academic town, built entirely around the needs of its scholars and students. Yet facing Stephen Hawking's person in his office later that afternoon, my resolve gives way before his physical reality. It is impossible to tune it out.

Hawking arrives rather late in his motorized wheelchair, maneuvering the controls that permit him to make the daily half-mile-long trek from his home to his office. Despite the many published reports of his condition that should have prepared me, I am still unprepared. This is less due to his almost total lack of mobility—the illness has affected all his limbs—than to his struggle for speech. Indeed, without the help of Colin Williams, his young "translator," there could have been no interview. Still, by the end of our time together my perception of Hawking has changed drastically.

Hawking appears, as he always does at his office, rather formally dressed: grey trousers, a sports-jacket, shirt and tie. He is slender and slight, his elongated face boyish, younger than his forty-three years; his limbs lie slack and inert against his wheelchair, vanquished by the

201

incurable and progressive motor neuron disease (amyotropic lateral scle-
rosis) that has afflicted his body since his early twenties. But if his body
has succumbed, his mind and head have defied this fate. Even his face,
though restricted in expression by the encroaching paralysis, has to
some degree escaped. It is a marvelous face: grey-blue eyes behind thick
granny-style glasses, a wide mouth that only occasionally on that day
breaks into a grin—all topped by a head of silky-fine brown hair, cut
Beatles-style with long bangs covering the forehead. My eyes are repeatedly drawn to his hands, which—though lying limp on his lap,
wrists crossed, unable any longer to obey his driving will—are slender,
sensitive, and beautiful.

Sitting behind his desk, Colin Williams at his side, Hawking listens
carefully not only to my questions but to the translations of his answers,
which Williams keeps up in a steady stream. On the few occasions when
he is dissatisfied, Hawking makes Williams reformulate his statements.
Williams, a twenty-five-year-old English physicist who has been Hawking's research assistant and translator for a year and a half, seems
completely devoted to him—during the tea break he sees to Hawking's
every need in a matter-of-fact, unsentimental way. The complete rapport between the two men is evident. Williams is clearly aware that he
is working with and for a man of rare gifts, and so attuned is he to his
mentor that he understands speech patterns which to an outsider are
unintelligible. The business of verbal exchange is laborious and taxes
everyone: Hawking, Williams, and the listener. Yet a coherent communication emerges at the end, and allows one to come away with the
assurance that, despite the obstacles, Hawking's views are being rendered accurately.

This I realize to be a matter of overriding importance, since it is
quickly borne in upon me that his voice is the last physical tool left to
Hawking for translating his will into action in the world. Colin
Williams, in our moments alone, concretizes Hawking's vulnerability in
this regard. During his many travels to conferences, he is treated with
utmost respect and deference by airline personnel and others aware of
his identity as a renowned physicist; but at times patronized by those
unfamiliar with him. Still, Hawking travels frequently and leads an
intensely active life, sparing himself nothing. Only a few days earlier he
has hosted a conference at Cambridge and on the day following our
interview he is to fly to Geneva for another gathering.

He begins our interview by saying: "I am not really at my best today
because of fatigue; I don't really know why," an assessment that Colin
Williams later confirms. Still, we speak steadily for an hour and a half,
not counting the tea break during which we repair to the common room
nearby frequented by a number of young physicists who seem to have
an easy and affable relationship with him.

During the considerable time during which I await Hawking's

arrival, I observe his office, trying to find some clue to his personality. Located in the Department of Applied Mathematics and Theoretical Physics on Silver Street, just off King's Parade—a rather nondescript building lacking the beauty of most of the Gothic architecture for which Cambridge is famous—Hawking's office is modest and sparsely furnished with a desk and a few chairs that are as nondescript as the building itself. What does draw the eye are three things: the blackboards, covered from end-to-end with equations (do they hold, one wonders, the secret of how the universe came to be?); a photograph of Einstein and an engraving of Newton on one wall; and the numerous photographs of his three beautiful and exuberant-looking children that line his bookshelves. These latter cover one entire wall, with books mostly on gravitation, quantum gravitation, the early universe, and other topics in cosmology.

I have been captivated by a large and finely lettered poster on the wall directly opposite Hawking's desk and in his line of vision, on which a long passage from Einstein appears exquisitely hand-lettered in script on parchment paper, reminiscent of medieval manuscripts. It is an oft-quoted passage in which Einstein expresses sentiments that border on a near-mystical awe before the universe. Seeing it takes me by surprise, for I have read that Hawking characterizes all attempts to interrelate science and mysticism as "pure rubbish." Since the Einstein poster comes up at some length in our interview, I will cite its contents even though Hawking—as the reader will see—rejects its message. What Einstein had written was this:

> The most beautiful emotion we can experience is the mystical. It is the power of all true art and science. He to whom this emotion is a stranger is as good as dead. To know that what is impenetrable to us really exists, manifesting itself as the highest wisdom and the most radiant beauty, which our dull faculties can comprehend only in their most primitive forms—this knowledge, this feeling, is at the center [of] true religiousness. In this sense, and in this sense only, I belong to the ranks of devoutly religious men. . . .
>
> A human being is part of the whole. . . . He experiences himself, his thoughts and feelings as something separated from the rest—a kind of optical delusion of his consciousness. This delusion is a kind of prison for us, restricting us to our personal desires and to affection for a few persons nearest us. Our task must be to free ourselves from this prison by widening our circle of compassion to embrace all living creatures, and the whole [of] nature in its beauty. Nobody is able to achieve this completely, but the striving for such achievement is, in itself, a part of the liberation and a foundation for inner security.[16]

After the interview, I gather more details about Hawking's professional life and background. If status at a university can be gauged by the support provided for a given faculty member, Cambridge obviously treasures Hawking. His staff revolves around him: not only Colin Williams, but also Laura Ward, his personal secretary with whom I have dealt frequently in preparation for my visit, who handles his mail and schedule and seems to devote her main time to his work. In response to my request, she provides me with the following biographical background on Hawking:

Stephen Hawking was born on 8th January 1942 in Oxford. His father was a Research Doctor specialising in tropical diseases and his mother was a former inspector of taxes. He was brought up in Highgate, N. London. He attended St. Albans School from 1952 to 1959, when he won a scholarship to University College, Oxford. He took a B.A. in Physics at Oxford in 1962 and then he went to Cambridge to do a Ph.D. on Gravity and Cosmology under Dr. D.W. Sciama. About this time he developed the first signs of A.L.S. or motor neuron disease. He married Jane Wilde in 1965 and was elected to a Research Fellowship at Gonville and Caius College in the same year. His first son Robert was born in 1967, followed by a daughter Lucy in 1970 and another son Timmy in 1979. Jane and he and the first two children spent the year 1974–1975 at Caltech. He was given a Personal Professorship at Cambridge in 1977, and was elected to the Lucasian Professorship in 1979 [i.e., the Chair held by Isaac Newton].

Hawking's list of honors and prizes is so long that here I must do with only a few extracts: Fellow of the Royal Society, Eddington Medal and Hughes Medal from the Royal Astronomical Society, Commander of the British Empire, elected to the American Academy of Arts and Sciences, Honorary Doctorates from Oxford, Princeton, the University of Chicago, Notre Dame, New York University and so forth. His list of publications is enormous: *The Large Scale Structure of Spacetime* (with G.F.R. Ellis), *General Relativity: An Einstein Centenary Survey* (ed. with W. Israel), *Superspace and Supergravity* (edited with M. Rocek), and *The Very Early Universe* (ed. with G.W. Gibbons and S.T.C. Siklos)—books all published by Cambridge University Press. In addition, there are over a hundred articles spanning two decades from 1965 to 1985, titles such as "Cosmological Event Horizons," "Spacetime Foam," "Euclidean Quantum Gravity," "The Limits of Space and Time," "The Cosmological Constant," "The Quantum State of the Universe," "Wave Function of the Universe," "The Unification of Physics," "The Edge of Spacetime," and "The Arrow of Time in Cosmology," to cite those that particularly appeal to my imagination. But there are over ninety others, and they have been appearing steadily every year right up to the present, an average of five papers or books per year—a feat even for someone with less besetting problems.

Since, as these excerpts from his bibliography reveal, Hawking is extremely prolific, a summary of his work will at best have to confine itself to a few basic ideas, the highlights of a body of work that has dealt with just about every major issue arising in physics and cosmology over the last twenty years. Three key theories provide at least a glimpse into Hawking's work. One, he is trying to unify general relativity with quantum mechanics. This entails reconciling the minute micro-world within the atom which has thus far eluded order and predictability, with the macro-world of large objects like stars and galaxies.

Second, and perhaps Hawking's chief interest at the moment, is a sub-specialty in astrophysics known as "the early universe," which concerns itself with the origin of the cosmos, in particular with the concept of time. Hawking's preoccupation (close to an intellectual obsession) is with the universe about 15 billion years ago, its first second. The burning issue is to learn what happened between the birth of the universe—the postulated Big Bang—and the first second in its expansion. Hawking has, in other words, pushed back the probable history of the universe to something on the order of 10^{-33} seconds of its being, but sees the need for pushing it back even further to 10^{-43} seconds, an extension of a factor of one billion times. Of this first infinitesimally small fraction of a second after the Big Bang, Stephen Hawking says that the answer to all the questions about the universe—and that includes life itself—lies here.

Hawking's speculation that the universe had a definite beginning in time bases itself on the validity of Einstein's theory of general relativity. The period of from three seconds after the Big Bang is no problem any more, he says, but about the first crucial second we do not know very much. This minute and elusive time frame obviously intrigues him the most. On the other hand Hawking hopes that there may not be a Big Bang, no "edge" to the universe that can be singled out and pointed to as the initial starting point (the singularity). His resistance derives from the fact that he believes an edge entails a God—at least a causal principle that functions like a definite starting point. This hypothesis, it is clear, Hawking intends to resist in favor of alternative ones as long as possible.

Hawking's third major area concerns black holes. To this field he has made such an important contribution that a postulated effect bears his name—Hawking radiation. Before Hawking's work, black holes (stars collapsed under their own gravitational weight) were thought of as invisible large masses of such intensely condensed matter that nothing can escape from their powerful gravitational field, not even light. When in 1973 Hawking proposed a new model for black holes, the world of astrophysics was stunned and at first incredulous. Hawking's calcula-

tions suggested that black holes, far from being the spent matter they
were supposed to be, might actually "explode," emitting streams of
particles. This proposal violated the then prevailing theory that black
holes cannot emit anything, and introduced the idea of a multitude of
small black holes, radiating a constant flow of particles (gamma rays).
This view was so startling that at first many physicists refused to accept
it, but Hawking painstakingly calculated the details, showing that there
could be many tiny black holes, lasting about 10 billion years, minuscule
in size (10^{-13} cm, or roughly equivalent to the size of a proton) yet
weighing a billion tons more than a proton, about as much as the
highest mountain on earth, Mt. Everest. He termed them mini-black
holes. Since the particles emitted as Hawking radiation—sub-atomic
particles—belong to the study of quantum mechanics and black holes—
macro-masses—to relativity theory, Hawking had taken a step towards
the hoped for unification of quantum mechanics and general relativity.
He aims towards a hybrid known as "quantizing gravitation," and if he
succeeds he will have moved closer to solving a problem that has defied
physicists up to this time.

In the interview Hawking's recurrent words are: rational, logical, and
coherent—concepts he feels provide the necessary basis for all science.
As for the *unity* which I have postulated to underlie the aims of both
science and mysticism, Hawking dismisses all metaphysical connotations
of the word and treats it as nothing more than a logical concept. This
matter-of-fact attitude in Hawking is indeed pervasive and it surfaces
at every turn. Still, I am somewhat taken aback by it. I feel awed by
Hawking's intellectual brilliance and scientific creativity and yet let
down by the philosophical limits which Hawking—by contrast to
Einstein, Heisenberg, Schroedinger, or Bohm—deliberately imposes
on his work. Something is missing in Hawking which these other
figures possess—a broader philosophical dimension that seeks to
explore the meaning and implications of their discoveries for human
beings. Perhaps it is the poetic dimension that sees in the equations something beyond the equations, which Hawking consciously
shuts out as irrelevant to the business of science. In that sense, I am
disappointed.

And yet I come away moved and inspired. It is by the man himself
as much as by his impressive achievements. All the way back on my
train ride to London I try to sort this out, until suddenly I realize
that if ever there was a living proof of the power of consciousness,
it is Stephen Hawking. It goes far beyond the fact that here is "the
perfect cerebral man"—as many write-ups portray him—freed by
his condition from all ordinary obligations, free only to think. That
interpretation suffers too much from Cartesian dualism. It depicts
Hawking as trapped inside a matter which is thought to localize and
confine him to the wheelchair, that tiny space which "he" inhabits. As

an interpretation, it seems inadequate to all but naive realism, the most commonplace, surface-level understanding—a level on which it is, of course, quite correct.

But in a deeper sense Hawking inhabits a space of staggering magnitude, for he seems not merely to "think" about the space and superspace of our universe. It is his basic reality, where his energy and prodigious intelligence are focused most of the time. In one of those paradoxes that completely violate common sense—on any non-dualistic or Spinozistic view—Hawking therefore *is* or *lives in* astronomical space, and does not merely engage it as an object of thought. If subtle matter is real, then Hawking's consciousness expands to converge on the vast distances over which he daily roves.

That to me provides the key to what his doctors, colleagues and interviewers all dwell on: that Hawking's very existence is a medical miracle. Defying the odds, he has lived decades beyond what the statistics allow for victims of ALS. Hawking's triumph has been attributed to his rare drive and will, and to the equally rare devotion of a remarkable wife determined at all costs that her husband live as normal a life as possible—two factors which no doubt must account largely for Hawking's endurance and creativity.

Yet I wonder, as I stare out the window and watch the Cambridge countryside hurtle by, about the role of this third factor, which everyone around him may well take for granted. In a sense more real than metaphorical, Hawking lives in the immensity of a space where magnitudes of 10^{25} are common, which his consciousness expands to explore, and where his genius is energized and comes alive. In that subtler sense, his environment is far less confined than that of most of the people who run about on two legs. Once I have dared to countenance this image—of a man confined but surely not handicapped—another one swiftly settles over me.

Does not Stephen Hawking's position symbolize the paradox of quantum mechanics itself—that the very small and confined aspect of being (the particle, the quark) contains immensity within itself? The tiny particle is *enormous* (10^{-33}) in its smallness, though to ordinary common sense it is minuscule and confined. Despite the fact that the paradoxes of quantum mechanics are rarely applied to the macro-world, it seems appropriate to invoke them to Hawking. Does he not embody the paradox of quantum mechanical matter itself, sharpening itself around the question of whether, in sum, he is a particle or a wave? Although such a question is officially forbidden in the macro-world of classical physics, the image of the beleaguered titan I have just left, slowly shifting himself in his wheelchair, rises up before me. A particle, without doubt, localized and confined. But what of the marvelous consciousness that has mastered spacetime as few of his living peers have? Surely a wave spread out unconfined, in control of its destiny, roaming the universe in search of an edge that he hopes is not there.

WEBER   Why are you so interested in the early universe?

HAWKING   I think everyone is interested in where they came from and how the universe arose.

WEBER   Since this is completely inferential and has to cross so much distance in time, can we trust our inferences?

HAWKING   Obviously, we can trust some things more than others, but I think we're reasonably confident that we know the history of the universe up to one second after the Big Bang. What happens before that is much more speculative. We have various ideas, but they might well be wrong. But I think that after one second, we're fairly confident that we know the theory.

WEBER   The part that I'm most interested in is precisely this one second.

HAWKING   I think that is the most interesting question. But if we were certain about the answer as to what happened in that first second, it would be much less interesting, because we'd really know everything then. We'd have solved all the problems and it would be rather dull.

WEBER   Would we have solved the problem as to how or where the raw material that gave rise to the Big Bang originated—the singularity?

HAWKING   We might decide that there wasn't any singularity. The point is that the raw material doesn't really have to come from anywhere. When you have strong gravitational fields, they can create matter.

WEBER   But that's assuming that there's already something, namely the strong gravitational field which is the source for the matter.

HAWKING   It may be that there aren't really any quantities which are constant in time in the universe. The quantity of matter is not constant, because matter can be created or destroyed. But we might say that the energy of the universe would be constant, because when you create matter, you need to use energy. And in a sense the energy of the universe is constant; it is a constant whose value is zero. The positive energy of the matter is exactly balanced by the negative energy of the gravitational field. So the universe can start off with zero energy and still create matter. Obviously, the universe starts off at a certain time. Now you can ask: what sets the universe off?

WEBER   Yes. After all, we think causally.

HAWKING   There doesn't really have to be any beginning to the universe. It might be that space and time together are like the surface of the earth, but with two more dimensions, with degrees of latitude playing the role of time. In that sense, you can say that the surface of the earth starts off at a single point at the north pole and as you move downwards in latitude, the circle gets bigger, and that corresponds to the universe expanding. When you get down to the equator, you reach a maximum size, and that corresponds to the universe reaching a maximum size.

WEBER   Why is it so important whether there is or is not an edge to space-time?

HAWKING   It obviously matters because if there is an edge, somebody has to decide what should happen at the edge. You would really have to invoke God.

WEBER   Why does that follow?

HAWKING   If you like, it would be a tautology. You could define God as the edge of the universe, as the agent who was responsible for setting all this into motion.

WEBER   You are invoking God because we need an explanatory principle for the edge.

HAWKING   Yes, if you want a complete theory, then we would have to know what happens at the edge. Otherwise, we cannot solve the equations.

WEBER   In the sense that you're using God, it's rather like a principle that's synonymous with the laws of the universe. It doesn't imply a moral being.

HAWKING   There would not be a connection with morality.

WEBER   You're using it as a logical and causal principle.

HAWKING   Yes.

WEBER   You said *if* there is an edge, then we'd have to invoke God. Do you think there is evidence for an edge?

HAWKING   At the moment, there's not much evidence either way. It seems that we can explain the present state of the universe on the assumption that there wasn't any edge.

WEBER   Is that preferable because of Occam's Razor?

HAWKING   Yes, it's obviously preferable, because it removes a great deal of the arbitrary element in the theory.

WEBER   You said earlier that if we knew the answers to these questions, it wouldn't be as interesting. But even supposing that we do understand: why will it lessen the mystery? It could as well deepen the mystery.

HAWKING   Whether you feel that there is a mystery is very much a matter of personal taste. We understand the laws of chemistry and most people do not feel there's any mystery in that.

WEBER   But on your wall here there is a sign quoting Einstein, saying that the most beautiful sentiment man can have is a sense of the mystery of things.

HAWKING   I completely disagree with that. It was sent to me by someone, and I just put it to one side. It seems the secretary found it and thought it would decorate the office.

WEBER   How long has it been hanging on your wall?

HAWKING   About a year. I rather object to it.

WEBER   Why?

HAWKING   Because it's mystical and I very much disapprove of mysticism.

WEBER   I've read your views on mysticism. Can I ask why you oppose it so much?

HAWKING   I think it's a cop-out. If you find theoretical physics and mathematics too hard, you turn to mysticism. I think people who have this idea about mysticism in physics are people who really can't understand the mathematics.

WEBER   You're drawing a contrast between using the mind and shedding it. I've read that you consider the current attempt in some quarters to relate physics to eastern philosophy as nonsense, and I'm interested in your reasons.

HAWKING   It comes back to my dislike of mysticism.

WEBER   The idea of a cop-out may apply to some people, but what about those who do understand the equations, people like Bohm and Capra, who are at home in theoretical physics and still try to draw a connection: How should one view them?

HAWKING   I'm not sure that they do understand the latest theories. I'm not sure that anyone does. The whole idea of a scientific theory is that it produces a definite logical model and definite predictions. But on the other hand, eastern mysticism clouds it with obscurity. It does not make any definite predictions.

WEBER   Even though its model of the universe is also one that is infinite, without beginning and end, and so on?

HAWKING   The trouble is that it is not a good theory in [Karl] Popper's sense, in that it does not make definite predictions which can be falsified.

WEBER   You've written on the unification of physics. Why is that so important: Why does it matter whether we have four basic laws or two or one?

HAWKING   It would not matter if we had four laws, as long as they were consistent with each other. The trouble is that the theories we have at the moment are not consistent.

WEBER   Does that limit our ability to predict and control, or does it limit our theoretical understanding?

HAWKING   It's not very important for practical purposes. We now know enough to predict more or less what will happen in most normal situations even though those theories are not consistent. But if we want to understand the deeper significance of the theory—to understand the origin of the universe—then we do need a consistent theory. That is what we are trying to find. In fact, consistency is really the main guiding principle.

WEBER   I understand. The question is, why should this be so?

HAWKING   Because the theories that we have so far differ in their predictions at very high energies—much higher energies than we can simulate.

WEBER   In that case whether we have one or several theories does have practical, not merely theoretical ramifications, doesn't it?

HAWKING   They all agree at the energies that we can simulate.

WEBER   What I'm really asking is: Is the demand for unity logical or is it non-logical? Is it aesthetic or is it something that is intrinsically required by science?

HAWKING   I think any reasonable scientific theory has to be consistent.

WEBER   Are you subtly sneaking in a spiritual or pantheistic principle in this emphasis on consistency or unity?

HAWKING   I think that's really a matter of definition. I would not be satisfied with a scientific theory which was not consistent with other theories.

WEBER   But isn't that because you've already postulated that there *is* consistency at the deepest level of nature?

HAWKING   That is what all scientists believe. It is the basis of all science. If we were not to believe that, we might as well give up.

WEBER   But isn't that quite a jump?

HAWKING   A jump from what? This is what we've always believed [that there is an underlying unity in nature]. If you believe that the universe can be understood by reason and logic, then you believe that there's a consistent theory.

WEBER   You're saying that this axiom of consistency is the driving principle of science.

HAWKING   Yes.

WEBER   Is the search for consistency or unity—even though it is not needed pragmatically—a spiritual demand of man's mind?

HAWKING   Most of theoretical physics is connected with an urge to *understand* the universe, rather than with any practical applications, because we already know enough to deduce practical applications.

WEBER   I've talked with David Bohm about these issues, and he says that people like Stephen Hawking and Roger Penrose obviously must be after something more than prediction and control or they wouldn't go through all this trouble. He says that in looking for the ultimate wave-function of the universe, you're searching for something beyond a purely physical principle. Is he right?

HAWKING   We're after something beyond practical application, but I wouldn't have said it was beyond physical principles.

WEBER   Can one make a philosophical model of those equations which explains what they *mean*?

HAWKING   They mean the same as any other model. There is no difference between our present theories and Newton's theory of gravitation except that our present theories are rather more complicated. They have a meaning in exactly the same sense.

WEBER   But in the seventeenth century the context was different. Kepler and Newton felt that they were looking at the logical, orderly, beautiful mind of God. Since we don't believe that any more, what are we looking at when we look at these equations?

HAWKING   We still believe that the universe should be logical and beautiful. We just dropped the word "God."

WEBER   Have we substituted anything for it?

HAWKING   No.

WEBER   The logic is built into matter and energy itself?

HAWKING   They seem to behave in ways that can be understood by reason and logic.

WEBER   Are the inherent limits in us that Kant or Heisenberg described no deterrent to our understanding the universe?

HAWKING   Obviously there are limits, but it's not clear that they will prevent us from understanding the universe in principle. They will certainly prevent us from understanding it in detail because we would have to know the position of every particle in the universe, and that's quite impossible.

WEBER   You've said that science wants consistency and unity in its laws, but the scientist himself seems to be left outside of the things he studies. Does he fit in, and how does he fit in?

HAWKING   He obviously has to be included.

WEBER   But he's the one who is looking at it, so he is always one step behind. Isn't it a regress?

HAWKING   No, not really. In the first place, because of a favorable physical and chemical composition on this planet, certain highly organized systems were able to develop. When these developed brains, they were able to analyze their surroundings. Some of the ways of analyzing their surroundings were more successful than others. Therefore we now have people who are quite good at analyzing their surroundings. But I don't think there is much survival advantage in discovering the ultimate theory of the universe, because it doesn't have any practical applications.

WEBER   Just purely aesthetic or logical pleasure?

HAWKING   You can't talk about logical and aesthetic pleasure. Those are not objective quantities. But if you were looking at the universe from the outside, you'd be able to see these creatures whose elaborate nervous systems correlated with their surroundings in a certain way which enabled them to survive. But it would be meaningless to talk about their aesthetic pleasure.

WEBER   If you solve the unified equation, is that not going to give you a sense of joy and aesthetic satisfaction?

HAWKING   That's looking at if from the human perspective, not from outside the system.

WEBER   Of course. We are the observer, it all goes through us, doesn't it? Everything you have said is said from the viewpoint of a human consciousness.

HAWKING   But if we were outside the system—if we were viewed from outside—we would appear just like ants.

WEBER   But if we were outside it, wouldn't we give a different description from the one we give now? Would it be the same universe?

HAWKING   In a way, it's really rather meaningless to talk about being outside.

WEBER   Because we are inside the system.... Since so much of your work is on time, I want to ask: Is time in us or is time "out there"?

HAWKING   I think that time and space and everything else are really in us. They're just mathematical models that we've made to describe the universe.

WEBER   Does the physicist study nature or his conception of nature? I'm thinking of Heisenberg's phrase [i.e., the physicist's concept of nature].

HAWKING   I don't think that that's a meaningful distinction. We're just studying our models.

WEBER   Yet you said time is in us.

HAWKING   That's part of our model.

WEBER   And time cannot be by-passed in science.

HAWKING   If it can, I certainly don't know about it.

WEBER   You've said that the early universe holds the answer to the ultimate question about the origin of everything, including life. Your work starts from the earliest known moment of the cosmos and its consequences; as you conceive your work, are you studying creativity in the universe working itself out, or are you studying what is implicit in that first set of conditions all along?

HAWKING   Are you asking about determinism?

WEBER   In a way. Prigogine, for example, resists any suggestion of pre-existent models or archetypes or eternal laws: anything but a creativity that works itself out, literally, as it goes along.

HAWKING   I don't think the first moment was really anything special, just as the north pole is not a special point of the earth's surface. It's just that we chose to measure latitude from the north pole.

WEBER   Is that analogous?

HAWKING   Yes, I think it is. We chose to measure time from the Big

Bang. But I think the Big Bang is a point of spacetime rather like any other point of spacetime.

WEBER   Before that the laws don't apply.

HAWKING   Asking what happens before the Big Bang is rather like asking what happens at the point one mile north of the north pole.

WEBER   Because that itself is our measure. I follow. For you, is the principle that underlies nature creativity?

HAWKING   I don't think that's a good word to use. I think the universe is completely self-contained. It doesn't have any beginning or end, it doesn't have any creation or destruction.

WEBER   Can its laws change?

HAWKING   No, because if they appear to change then that merely indicates that there's some other quantity which enters into the laws and which varies from point to point.

WEBER   You said earlier that, in so far as the possibility of an edge of the universe is concerned, it could go either way, and you correlated the edge with a God or some sort of God-like principle.

HAWKING   It's very difficult to prove that there isn't any edge, but if we could show that we can explain everything in the universe on the hypothesis that there is no edge, I think that would be a much more natural and economical theory.

Deep down the consciousness of mankind is one. This is a virtual certainty because even in the vacuum matter is one; and if we don't see this it's because we are blinding ourselves to it.

DAVID BOHM

Humanity has every reason to place the proclaimers of high moral standards and values above the discoverers of objective truth. What humanity owes to personalities like Buddha, Moses, and Jesus ranks for me higher than all the achievements of the enquiring and constructive mind.

ALBERT EINSTEIN

It is very interesting ... that in modern physics the more logical you are, the more wrong you are. This shows very clearly the limits of our logic.

LAMA GOVINDA

KRISHNAMURTI

12

Two people taking shelter in the rain

KRISHNAMURTI

Whence come I and whither go I? That is the great unfathomable question, the same for every one of us. Science has no answer to it.

PLANCK

IT was the third interview with Krishnamurti that I had done in the last decade, and it turned out to be the most interesting of the three. This was due in part to a most unexpected and indeed maddening turn of events that greeted me when I arrived at Krishnamurti's chalet in Rougemont, Switzerland, in a fine, drizzling rain in mid-July, 1985. It was, in fact, no interview at all because despite our agreement months earlier, Krishnamurti would not let me tape. Whether he was playing the Zen master or whether—as I suspect—there were other reasons, I cannot say.

It is well-nigh impossible to condense Krishnamurti's life into a short background article. An Indian philosopher-sage, he is known throughout the world through his lectures, books, and tapes. Now barely 90, he has been lecturing in the west for over fifty years, travelling widely, dividing his time mainly between England, India, California, and Switzerland. He has attracted enormous audiences world-wide, and influenced such writers as Aldous Huxley, Henry Miller, and many artists, among them the French sculptor Bourdelle, who has done a bust of him.

Readers may be familiar with the dramatic events that made Krishnamurti famous in the 1920s and 1930s. Born in 1895 into a poor south Indian family in Madras, there is a story that Krishnamurti—to all outward appearances an ordinary child—was walking on the beach as a boy of only fourteen when he was noticed by C. W. Leadbeater, a clairvoyant, who later said he was startled by the fact that the boy's aura—a most rare phenomenon—revealed a completely selfless human being. Raised and educated by Dr. Annie Besant of the Theosophical Society (and to some extent by Leadbeater), Krishnamurti was groomed for some years for a major spiritual role. He was to become a world-

217

wide teacher, around whom a large international organization formed itself. But in 1927, Krishnamurti dissolved this group, proclaiming that truth could not be organized and that organizations were inimical to spiritual life. He has insisted ever since that "truth is a pathless land" and has opposed all traditional teachings, religions, authorities, systems and writings. For the past sixty years, he has spent his time lecturing and holding discussions with people around the world. Under the auspices of various Krishnamurti Foundations in India, England, America, and Canada, he has established schools ranging from elementary to high schools.

Krishnamurti's fundamental teaching can be summarized in a few sentences: truth is within, and it can and must be discovered by each person alone. No book and no authority can help us to find it, but unrelenting, single-minded, constant awareness of who we are and how we operate will bring the truth to the surface. To do this, we must begin with observation and fact, not theory, fantasy, or preconceived images. To live in truth is to live in the moment, to be dynamically in step with it without gathering *in* the residue which he calls time— thought, memory, the past—and equates with falsehood. Living fully in the present fuses the observer and the observed, and in this lies a state "for which the whole world is seeking and longing," as Krishnamurti once referred to it. Although he is reluctant to name that state, at times he calls it love, beauty, order, the timeless—a state of being which he claims lies beyond death. Many of these ideas are discussed at length in Krishnamurti's books, most of which have been gathered from his taped talks. There are 21 books out by now: *The Urgency of Change*, *The Awakening of Intelligence*, *Freedom from the Known*, *Truth and Actuality*, *The Wholeness of Life*, and (with David Bohm) *The Ending of Time*, to cite some samples.

As I set out on that afternoon in July 1985 from Saanen towards Rougemont, where Krishnamurti is expecting me, I cannot foresee the complications that await me. For several days, hiking around the trails near Saanen and Gstaad, with their spectacular views of the Alps and the beautiful valleys of the Bernese Oberland, shimmering with flowers, I have been preparing for the encounter, thinking of ways in which I can engage Krishnamurti on the theme of nature and science, hoping for his willingness to focus on this topic. Hoping, but not expecting it, for I know from our earlier interviews that Krishnamurti cares nothing about prearranged scripts and that he, not I, will strike the direction on which we embark. Still, nothing in our past interactions has prepared me for the turn of events that is about to unfold.

All day a steady, gentle rain has been descending over the Saanen valley on this cool July day, enveloping the mountains in a mist so opaque that only the valley remains visible, adding an atmosphere of mystery to its already romantic scenery.

It is my first visit to Saanen, and already I have succumbed to its grand panoramas and peaceful atmosphere. In summer, of course, its major attraction are the Krishnamurti talks, held in a huge tent; they draw thousands of people from all over the world. Krishnamurti is a household word here; every bookshop prominently displays his books in German, French, English and other languages. Despite the fact that I have arrived after the (six-week-long) talks have concluded, on my walks I still meet people who have come here expressly for the Krishnamurti talks. As I set out from my hotel above Saanen for Krishnamurti's chalet in Rougemont, I find questions floating across my mind: "Krishnaji [an Indian term of respect], some people say that you are not interested in science and may even be against it—is that true?" "Are the scientist and the sage looking for the same thing in their different ways?" "How do you perceive nature?"

By the time I reach Rougemont a scant quarter of an hour later, these have receded into the background of my consciousness, which is now absorbed in registering the impressions of the chalet and its surroundings. Rougemont, far smaller and simpler than Saanen or nearby fashionable Gstaad, is if anything even more picturesque. It is really a small Alpine village in the midst of dairy-farming country which in winter turns into a ski resort, dominated by Videmanette, its 2200-meter peak. There is a tiny main street with shops, a village fountain and some tidy, wood-carved flower-bedecked houses scattered about the town, in the valley, and clinging to the mountainside. It is a village out of earlier centuries, rustic, earthy, simple, and beautiful.

Krishnamurti lives in a first-floor chalet apartment off the little main street. I am met by Mary Zimbalist, his long-time friend and companion who looks after him and through whom requests for interviews generally must go. Poised and courteous as she ushers me in, she chats with me on this as on other occasions, as we await Krishnamurti's arrival. But unlike other times in Ojai, California, where I taped Krishnamurti, I soon become aware that there is to be a problem today, for Mrs. Zimbalist is beginning to prepare me.

Despite the fact that I have long since had written permission from the Krishnamurti Foundation of England to include my 1978 interview in this book and to tape a new one, and that Mrs. Zimbalist herself has seen my table of contents and helped arrange for today's taping, she questions me closely about the entire project. Above all, she wants to know who the other figures in the book are to be. I explain, but she is not reassured, saying that Krishnamurti is not used to being in a book along with others—the issue that begins to emerge as the stumbling block. Although I try to marshal some persuasive arguments, she still looks dubious and suggests that I place all this before Krishnamurti.

Though I begin to have a foreboding, still, settled into a deep armchair, I install my recorder on the coffee-table, the fine directional mike poised near where I assume Krishnamurti is to sit, a chair very close to my own. When he enters the room, Krishnamurti is warm and hospitable, greeting me with outstretched hands.

He looks remarkably well. Although he has just passed his 90th birthday, his body is slim and straight. His face—once famous for its almost preternatural beauty (George Bernard Shaw called him "the most beautiful human being" he had ever seen)—shows age but it is compelling still and even beautiful, with its subtle planes, intelligent eyes, aristocratic nose, silky silver hair, and sculptured head. The hands, now reposing in his lap, are slender and smooth, and might belong to a man of forty. As always, Krishnamurti looks impeccable; today he is informally dressed: navy blue jeans, a navy sports shirt, and a tan wool cardigan sweater.

Settling himself in the chair close by, he returns to the theme Mary Zimbalist has pursued. "What is this book? Who else is in it? Why do you want to do it?" My attempts to answer are unsuccessful, for Krishnamurti cuts me off. It soon becomes clear to me that he is already resolved that there will be no interview. Seeing this suspicion on my crushed face, he tries to soften my disappointment, gently touching my hand from time to time as he explains his objections. He says that "It would have been difficult to put all this into a letter," and asks me to look at the matter from his point of view. Condensed, his objections run as follows. Krishnamurti does not want to be in a book with other people, with ideas different from his own. It is not conceit, he says, I may even be wrong, he says, what I have to say may all be "rot," he urges, "but you must realize that what I'm saying is sacred to me." I attempt to reassure him that the book will be dignified, that there will be nothing sensational nor cheap to embarrass him, but he is impatient with these attempts.

For the next forty-five minutes, as I helplessly watch my tape-recorder sit useless in the "off" switch—for which I have by now given Krishnamurti my word—he talks to me. The subjects are varied: incidents from his life that make some special point. Many of these are fascinating and will—I think with pleasure—make marvellous reading. They are autobiographical tales from his past and seem designed to buttress Krishnamurti's refusal to be taped for this book. The theme of each story is the same: fame and worldly goods offered and refused.

Later I begin to set these down for my reader but a strange self-censorship overcomes me as I visualize the vulnerability and innocence of the man who is, at the same time, an impregnable wall of strength, even hardness at times. This, like everything about Krishnamurti, strikes me as ambiguous, but I have long since lived with the fact that these ambiguities cannot be resolved or even understood by an outsider. All the books and articles about Krishnamurti—even those written by his most ardent devotees—unwittingly add to this ambiguity. This perception of ambiguity must account for the surprising ambivalence which many of those who know and respect Krishnamurti seem to feel. Thus, as the urge to protect the enigmatic man I have left wins out, I resolve upon a selective recording of the anecdotes Krishnamurti has recounted.

I content myself with setting down only one such anecdote; unproblematic, it is the most colorful and charming of them in any case, and though Krishnamurti was unaware of it at the time, it fits mysteriously into the theme of this book.

He recounts that once when he was practising yoga in a tiny hut high up in the Indian Himalayas, a large wild monkey with a huge curled tail graced by a puff at its end—a species reputed to be fierce and even dangerous—appeared at the open window and made as if to come in. As a first step, the animal held out its paw inside the open window. Taken aback, Krishnamurti took the monkey's hand and held it for some time. It was, he tells me, a marvellous hand: smooth and pliable, very beautiful, the palm roughened in places to adapt it to climb trees; but after a while Krishnamurti told the interloper aloud, "Look old chap, you can see for yourself that this hut is far too small for us both, so you can't come in," whereupon the monkey, after a further trial and similar admonition, reluctantly left.

This anecdote, with minor variations, is followed by several others: the wild tiger that sat peacefully so near Krishnamurti that he could have stroked it; and the huge cobra which became aware of Krishnamurti's presence behind him and which, having relinquished its prey, a bird, slithered silently out of sight.

Krishnamurti offers these stories without comment or conclusion, but I have been steeped in eastern mysticism long enough to know their import, and draw the conclusion for him.

"You are saying that even wild animals sense the harmlessness in a genuinely peaceful person," I offer.

"Yes, of course," he assents, adding, "I could tell you many more stories like that."

I am long familiar with this possibility. In fact, it ties in with this book through the theory of subtle matter that both eastern philosophy and Bohm propose, with Sheldrake's morphic resonance (the wild animals are tuned in to the sensitive vibratory pattern emitted by the sage), and with the power of compassion that sages like Lama Govinda, the Dalai Lama, and Fr. Bede Griffiths describe and themselves radiate.

Towards the end of this anecdotal part of our discussion, Krishnamurti observes that most people live for security and therefore wind up in constant insecurity—the fear of not holding on to what they have—but that he lives without any idea of security at all and that, consequently, he has real security, "the only security there is." It fits a favorite theme of his public talks, one which always sends a ripple of recognition through his audiences and which can be predicted to make everyone uneasy.

When all the cobwebs about what we are to talk about—the book, recording versus not recording—have been cleared away, Krishnamurti shifts into content. He brings in numerous examples of people he knows who are suffering, and his eyes sadden as he rehearses these painful stories. For millions of years, he says, mankind has suffered, people have been killing one another, there have been few interludes without wars, people have cried—'Have you heard them cry?" he wants to know. "Have you seen people back from the Vietnam war without legs?"

Several times, he shifts from the theme of suffering back to the book and its contents. I had, in connection with the Hawking interview, brought up the Big Bang, and it is on this that Krishnamurti now pounces. What's the point of talking about the Big Bang, he asks me, when the world is in flames, when people are crying, when man is indescribably cruel to his fellows? These things are facts, he says repeatedly, the other is a luxury.

I have risked one more protest, telling him that I have come all this distance to talk about nature and science with him, but he is adamant. Yet the more firmly he puts his foot down, the more gentle—even tender—does his bearing become. As he hammers the point home again and again, he takes my hand as if to soften the blow.

Even in my frustration, I find myself responding to his iron-willed exhortation to get our priorities straight. Is he not right, after all? Is he not one of the few sane people who—seeing the tidal wave of destruction that we are preparing for ourselves—refuses to allow himself to be diverted? Have we, the others, become like Faust, seduced by knowledge at any price, heedless—though aware—of the fact that the price will be global annihilation? Is Krishnamurti the pessimistic, narrow-minded alarmist or is he the visionary prophet sounding the alarm in the face of our inertia and Faustian bargain?

My resolve begins to weaken as I find myself remembering that the Buddha, too, refused to discuss metaphysics—the science of the sixth century B.C.—until, he said, we have solved the problem of suffering. On sheer practical grounds, the Buddha termed all other pursuits vain and misguided.

Even when I attempt to shift the connotation of "science" toward its pure rather than applied meaning, Krishnamurti refuses to hear me out. I utter the word "Einstein," but he waves it aside, repeating that until the basic human problem is resolved, nothing else matters. Again I ponder whether Krishnamurti's position is really different from the Buddha's, who justified his priorities with his famous metaphor of the arrow. Buddha likened the human condition to that of a man with a poisoned arrow stuck in his back and argued that the fundamental human task was to pull the arrow out and help others do the same. I have always admired the boldness and discernment of the Buddha's stand. Why, when Krishnamurti is taking a similar clearsighted and unyielding position, am I fighting him?

Until this moment, I have been the interviewer, fixed single-mindedly on the needs of my book. Now as he evokes the vision of a species bending its talents to probe its stellar origins in the remote past while its very continuity in the present and future lie in doubt, I grow silent. There is only the sound of the rain, falling in a steady, fine downpour. Krishnamurti again takes my hand, and proposes a metaphor that will run like a recurrent refrain through the rest of our conversation.

He suggests that we drop "all our roles;" mine as a professor, his as a "sage or whatever role you've cast me in," and that we "talk together about the basic human problem as two people who have come together by accident to take shelter in the rain." For the rest of the afternoon, science will be abandoned except as the symbol of dubious human priorities.

Krishnamurti's objection to it is twofold. First, it is the siren-song which tempts us away from the world of suffering whose resolution will require our total commitment and intelligence. (I know from past experience that it will not do to point to the medical and technological contributions which have alleviated human suffering, for Krishnamurti feels these outweighed by the dangers that science has unleashed.) Investigating the Big Bang or the inner structure of the atom, he says, have done nothing to change us fundamentally, neither the scientist himself nor our root problem. This, he repeats, can be simply stated: all human beings suffer, all have similar fears and anxieties, all want to be free from suffering. In this struggle, humanity is as one. This is the fact, he says again with great weight.

He also holds scientists responsible for fuelling the war-machine. If they would all stop cooperating with governments, he reminds me, much of the harm could be defused, even though he grants my point that most of the damage is done, our available stockpiles being more than enough to do the job of abolishing ourselves. He offers a joke whose import is that even if we blow ourselves up, leaving only one couple to replenish the species, before long they will have reinvented weapons. This presses home his insistence—prominent in all his talks— that unless mankind dismantles its violence from *within* through radical personal change, outer strategies are doomed to fail.

Over and over Krishnamurti uses the analogy of cancer to describe the human plight. What is the point of exploring the Big Bang, he wants to know, when I am suffering from a life-threatening cancer? I object that this is too absolutist a position, but Krishnamurti will have none of it. "You cannot cut out just half a cancer," he counters. "Is it the right analogy?" I venture, but he holds to it. The scourge of mankind is suffering. "If my son or my brother has just died," he continues,

"I am not going to want to discuss the Big Bang with you. I might say, give me a few days, old chap, but right now I'm crying, I'm in pain, and I'm interested in *this*, not in *that*."

Maybe later, he adds, leaving the door open after all. I come back to my script, nature. He is not against nature, Krishnamurti insists, adding that in his talks he often refers to nature. "Nature is order," he tells me. "And beauty?" I add. "Order, order," he repeats with emphasis, but allows that "there is also great beauty in nature, and where there is beauty, there is love. Love and compassion," he adds. Asked to define these, he answers that when sensation, attachment, and possession are *not*, then love and compassion come into being.

I observe that it seems easier to love nature in that way—a tree or a mountain or an animal—much harder to love a human being that unselfishly. He suggests that the answer to that is very simple: nature does not judge us, threaten us with withdrawal of affection, demand things from us, or lord its power over us as human beings do.

By this time there is almost a dialogue between us. Compared with an hour ago, when Krishnamurti scarcely let me get my sentences finished, things are flowing. He has become more and more gentle, holding my hand whenever he—bluntly and sternly—disagrees about some issue. Each time he wants to underline the point that the far-away glamour of the Big Bang—by now the *bête noire* of the conversation— deflects us from the cancer of human cruelty and ignorance, he says, "I'm interested in *this* right now," as he points to the earth, "not *that*," pointing upwards again.

"It's your responsibility," he says sternly, as his eyes fix mine. "What are you going to do about it?"

We seem to have left behind Krishnamurti's first objection to science, for he now shifts into a second one. I have often heard him pose it during small seminars with scientists and philosophers. It is a far more fundamental and far-reaching objection, for it impugns the power of the human mind ever to penetrate reality. It is this absolute challenge that Krishnamurti now flings at me.

He is not interested in discussing science, he says, because science is knowledge, knowledge is put together by thought, and thought is trapped in the past. Although he does not spell out the rest of the connection for me, he does not need to. Anyone who has heard or read him is quite familiar with his argument. Truth lies in the living present, in *this* moment, and must be discovered afresh in the present, in the eternal *now*. All forms of its accumulation or accretion—thought, memory, knowledge, time—destroy truth. Therefore science, which is cumulative, which is knowledge (a negative term in Krishnamurti's context), is too far removed from reality to pierce to its secrets.

This position is familiar to me through eastern philosophy. It reveals a basic affinity, if not virtual identity, with Advaita Vedanta, a development within Hinduism that is best expressed in the writings of the seventh-century sage Shankara. Although Shankara uses classical Hindu terms which Krishnamurti rejects, both teach that truth cannot be found in the world of nature, but only in the reality that lies behind or beyond nature. The transcendent, not the immanent face of reality is what interests them. All else is dismissed as illusion and distraction, the insignificant mask of the real.

This holds despite Krishnamurti's teaching that reality can be found in *the daily*, if we know how to look for it. But his teaching—and that of Advaita—differs greatly from the spirit of those early religious scientists whose motto was "God is in the details." On balance, both Shankara and Krishnamurti seem to me to devalue the world of nature. Everything—science, philosophy, history—is undercut in favor of the background source that transcends these. At best, the worldly thing is perceived as a representative of "that." Immanence matters only in so far as it reveals what is transcendent.

Therefore, despite the fact that Krishnamurti has evoked Nagarjuna several times during our talk—"now that is genuine Buddhism," he has said with admiration—he strikes me as far closer to Shankara. Both he and Shankara represent a form of mysticism that is interested in nothing but ultimate union.

Our discussion has lasted for close to two hours. Now I throw a longing glance at the tape-recorder, and reproach Krishnamurti once again with, "Krishnaji, all of this is not on tape!"

"No," he replies, "but it's in your head and your heart."

I am resigned by now not to be permitted to use any of this material for my book but—against all expectations—Krishnamurti offers, "You can use it in any way you like. You can write about it, you can put it in the book, you don't have to show it to me, you can do whatever you want with it—I don't need to see it," he reiterates—"as long as it really comes from within you, from here" (he points to my head) "and here" (motioning to my heart).

The switch is so surprising that I am thrown off center, and to regain it I rehearse Krishnamurti's probable reasons aloud. "You don't want me to lean on the tape-recorder because it's vicarious, you feel it's taking a borrowed reality along instead of my own reality, that it will be cheating, that it's depending on something passive rather than actively having it become a part of me." For the first time that afternoon, his eyes light up. "That's just it," he says, obviously pleased. He points to my tape-recorder, still idle before us. "What a horror it is, all such rubbish," he muses.

The image of the endless taping at all of Krishnamurti's lectures, seminars, and conferences over all these years flicks across my mind, and of the long and growing list of his tapes offered in the catalogue by the Krishnamurti Foundation of America that my mail brings each autumn. But politeness forbids my raising the question of consistency that is forming itself. It is also possible, I speculate, that this is a new reaction of his, leading to new policies in the future. Still, I find myself happy for the time he has spent with me, and for letting me use this material as I choose. Unknowingly, I have been part of an historic event, as I learn a few months later, for the 1985 talks are the last that Krishnamurti will give here at Saanen, ending a twenty-five-year-old tradition, apparently in deference to his age.

The afternoon has obviously taxed him, for he now asks me what time it is. When I reply "six o'clock," he appears surprised and, rising, tells me that "the stranger who has taken shelter in the rain with you has to go now, to catch his next train." He smiles, still relishing the metaphor that has shaped our afternoon. I again offer to send him my chapter for approval, but he declines, repeating, "It is yours now, it is in you now," then adds, "but it has taken me two hours to convince you of this."

"Until we meet next time at another station to take shelter in the rain," he says, and sees me to the door.

It is still raining, and a greyish mist has settled over the Rougemont valley. As I walk through the fine summer drizzle toward the little station where I await the Montreux-Oberland-Bern express that will take me back to Saanen, my mood is turbulent and confused. Nothing adds up, no summary is possible, there are only details recounting the afternoon, but I lack any clear conclusion.

Why, I ask myself, must Krishnamurti be in this book at all? Since I cannot find the answer, I settle for a question. Can it be that he represents the absolute mystic, the essence of what is unique to the position of all mystics through the ages?

There is certainly an absolutist stance here that I have come across only rarely. In its own way, it reminds me suddenly of the stance Stephen Hawking had taken when I saw him two weeks earlier. Hawking, too, is an absolutist. He embodies the extreme position of the positivist wing of science as it faces nature: no mysteries, only puzzles, all of them yielding—sooner or later—to the objective method of science, to equations—without the frills of poetic or philosophical translations into "meaning."

The comparison between Krishnamurti and Stephen Hawking, far-fetched at first, gains plausibility as a number of parallels crowd in on me. Hawking and Krishnamurti both are the nay-sayers to the search for synthesis that animates this book (a likelihood of which I have been aware even as I sought them out).

Neither of them is interested in building bridges between science and mysticism. Hawking despises mysticism, Krishnamurti dismisses science. Yet despite their irreconcilable differences, Hawking and Krishnamurti are mirror-images: both are minimalists—"only *this* really matters." More importantly, both revolve—though in opposite ways—around the mystery of time.

Hawking seeks the first moment when time emerged from the timeless void, Krishnamurti seeks—says he has found—the ending of time. For Hawking the key to the puzzle of our being is time, for Krishnamurti it is timelessness. Each is vehement and passionate in this stand, each pursues it to the exclusion of everything else, has spent a lifetime of dedication in its service, each has total integrity, a one-track mind, purity of focus, high intelligence, love for one thing. Both are creators, not followers.

A philosopher's attempt at their reconciliation might be to use Kantian language, suggesting that Hawking tracks the phenomenal world, Krishnamurti the noumenal one. But even as I ponder this move, I reject it.

Hawking and Krishnamurti are not—like the other scientists and sages in this book—the great synthesizers. Hawking, even should he find the one great equation, the wave-function of the universe that he seeks, will leave consciousness and man out of the answer. Krishnamurti will by-pass the contributions of time—cosmic and human—of science, of history. The reconciliation between nature as immanent and nature as transcendent is not their problem.

A question with which I have wrestled recurrently now resurfaces. If a Nobel Prize caliber physicist were at the same time a powerful mystic, familiar with the timeless dimension that mystics inhabit—the scientist and the sage combined in one—could such a person forge a bridge between physics and mysticism, between outer and inner science?

Because each practices his path with the utmost purity of motive and being, this was the question I had hoped to place before Stephen Hawking and Krishnamurti. But it has become very clear by now that the answer—if there is an answer—is not going to come from either of them.

But is there an answer?

Later that night, as I watch the immensity of stars—clear and close without the competition of city lights—my mind wanders back over a dialogue held only a few days earlier at Rikon, in which the scientist and the sage, for two rare hours, come near to embodying the fusion of my fantasied image.

The inquiry into matter can lead us to ask whether there is something beyond matter, or whether matter is so subtle that it is beyond matter as we ordinarily know it.

DAVID BOHM

Once we see our time concept, our way of thinking is an expression of something universal; we find the link without appealing to some kind of external, extraneous mysticism.

ILYA PRIGOGINE

Without a zero we cannot make ten or a hundred. Similarly with emptiness: It is emptiness and at the same time it is the basis of everything.

THE DALAI LAMA

The question is whether matter is rather crude and mechanical or whether it gets more and more subtle and becomes indistinguishable from what people have called mind.

DAVID BOHM

DAVID BOHM, THE DALAI LAMA, AND RENÉE WEBER

13

Subtle matter, dense matter

HIS HOLINESS, THE DALAI LAMA
AND
DAVID BOHM

To put the conclusion crudely - the stuff of the world is
mind-stuff.

EDDINGTON

WITH the exception of the interview in south India with Fr.
Bede, the setting for this dialogue was the most exotic and
culturally rich of all the ones in this book.

The monastery sits high on a hill overlooking Alpine meadows,
amidst stunning scenery near a pine forest which, with its traditional
stupa—a bell-shaped stone monument dating back to early Buddhism,
and consisting of various tiers that symbolize various stages of spiritual
development—has taken on the flavor of Tibet. So has the monastery,
known also as the Tibet Institute of Rikon, which offers courses in the
theory and practice of Tibetan Buddhism. It is a square flat-roofed
white bungalow more typical of Tibetan houses than the slant-roofed
wood-carved chalets found all over Switzerland. Tibetan prayer-flags
flap in the breeze and—together with the glowing variegated flower
beds—add color and a festive air.

The day shimmers in blue and gold; a perfect climate—warm but
dry—the air carries the fragrance of the near-by pine forest, endowing
one with a sense of well-being. As I look out over the meadow directly
behind the monastery, the scene offers a nearly idyllic simplicity: a deep
sloping meadow where cows mill gently about, the bells on their necks
emitting sporadic tinkling sounds that evoke an unhurried world which
has preserved the rhythms of nature. The monastery lies in Upper
Rikon, about three-fourths of a mile from the Tibetan village of Rikon,
twenty miles or so northeast of Zürich. Rikon has a settlement of about
one hundred and fifty Tibetans, roughly one tenth of the ones living in
Switzerland. It is surprising to hear flawless German issue from so
many of these Mongolian faces, especially those of the children, many
of whom have been born here.

In an architectural style unique to Tibet, the upstairs quarters are
reached by outside stairs, a separate entrance being necessary for access

to the downstairs quarters (which in Tibet houses the animals and fodder). Here they serve as an all-purpose room for the monastery, where I observe several large photographs of the Potala, the former residence of the Dalai Lamas in Lhasa.

The ambience at the monastery and indeed all over Rikon is festive since this is to be the first day of the Kalachakra Initiation Ceremony over which the Dalai Lama is to preside immediately following our dialogue. The roads in Rikon have been filled for hours with throngs heading towards the tent where the ceremony is to be celebrated. Earlier I notice that even the forest paths near the monastery are dotted with visitors, silent figures walking about or sitting in meditative postures near the *stupa*. Outside the bungalow, the monastery staff and the people from the Office of Tibet gather and coordinate events; without the staff's careful scrutiny verifying one's invitation, access to the monastery during the Dalai Lama's stay there is hopeless.

But to me their presence outside the house and on the steps signals not only security—although that is a part of their function—but also an added presence of Tibetan culture. In their colorful monk's robes of the Gelugpa Order, these beautiful poised figures serve to enhance the vividness and reality of this unlikely spot as an outpost of the Tibet that is no more.

We tape in the living room, a small room simply furnished with a couch, a few chairs and a long marble coffee table to which the Dalai Lama points throughout the dialogue as an illustration of the world of inert matter, when this turns up in our conversation. Still, the atmosphere is unmistakably Asian. Tibetan colors bursting with life in the deep red and patterned rugs and *tankas*—traditional hand-painted scenes of Buddhist religious life—that adorn the walls in scroll-like hangings. Just outside the room is the proverbial Swiss-style wooden balcony with its superb view.

Inside the Dalai Lama's quarters, this same mix of Europe and Tibet is in evidence. As in all the interviews and small conferences with the Dalai Lama in which I have been involved, the room is teeming with life. This is the result of the complement of people and the exuberant atmosphere that invariably punctuate these gatherings. On this occasion, aside from His Holiness, David and Saral Bohm and myself, there are two translators—Dr. Jeffrey Hopkins (see Chapter 7) and a young Swiss who has become a Tibetan monk now called Sangye Samdrup. There are, as well, a crew from London filming our dialogue for the Office of Tibet, part of a series of conversations that the Dalai Lama has been holding with various scientists, and several other Tibetans.

Our interview is a mixture of intense concentration interspersed with humor. The Dalai Lama often bursts into abandoned laughter, even amidst serious topics, and this is so catching that it soon sweeps over the entire room, to his evident delight. There is of course never a doubt that he cares about the discussion, for he considers each question seriously and at some length, and confers with his translators before answering.

His relationship to David Bohm is quite touching in its combination of affection—which he openly shows—and respect, which manifests as intense interest in what Bohm has to say about physics. This respect and affection are evidently reciprocal, for Bohm seems relaxed and happy in the Dalai Lama's presence. A few months earlier, at Amherst, the Dalai Lama had asked Bohm to teach him some of the fundamentals of quantum physics, and today he again makes the point that each can learn from the other. Tolerant and open-minded, like Buddhism itself, the Dalai Lama remarks on the importance of learning from both these paths—the scientific and the spiritual.

Many in the Dalai Lama's entourage are familiar to me, monks or staff I have met in Illinois and at Amherst. Among the most impressive is Tempa Tsering, his intelligent and efficient secretary, possessed like so many Tibetans of a tranquil and unforgettable face, with its extraordinary handsome cheek-bones, dark eyes and warm smile. As on other occasions, Tempa Tsering is there in the background, gliding gracefully in and out of the room, but firmly reminding the Dalai Lama—towards the end of the interview—that His Holiness must make his way toward Rikon village for the start of the Kalachakra ceremony. The Bohms return to our hotel in Winterthur but—heading for Rikon village on foot—I decide to drop in on the ceremony.

It is held in an enormous rectangular tent, decked out with yellow paper lanterns, green and red flags, garlands everywhere. The wooden platform built for the occasion is bursting with color: *tankas*, candles, flowers, rows of chanting monks flanking each side of a gaily painted seat from where the Dalai Lama reads *The Heart Sutra*, recites the *Three Jewels* and other Buddhist scriptures, and chants and speaks to the audience. At times he is accompanied by the monks, each of whom—a documented but continually stupefying fact—is capable of chanting an entire chord. Dr. Hopkins sits on the stage near the Dalai Lama, translating into English, but many in the audience are wearing headphones through which the teachings are being rendered into German, French, and Italian.

The assembled crowd offers an absorbing variety to delight the eye and imagination. I find the Tibetans, above all, captivating. They are a beautiful people, physically robust and handsome in their carriage, especially the gorgeously gowned children in their Tibetan dresses and aprons. I greatly admire the Tibetans for their combination of calm and high energy, and the joy for which they are well-known and which I have heard the Dalai Lama attribute to their religious outlook. They are intelligent and capable, rooted in this world of practical tasks yet deeply attuned to the spiritual one which forms the enduring background of their daily lives.

Tempa Tsering tells me there are 5400 people attending the ceremony, the start of ten days of activities. Rikon has experienced the largest influx of Buddhists ever assembled in Europe. The Swiss media have given wide coverage to the event, transmitting parts of the Kalachakra ceremony over television. When I catch up with it in Zürich a week later, my TV informs its viewers that about 3000 Europeans—many of them with degrees (the impressed announcer specifies)—have taken part in the ceremony. I watch an interview with the Dalai Lama on the Swiss-German evening news, together with the interviewer's remarkably accurate four-point summary of Buddhism. The precepts he singles out are: that all things are dependent on factors other than themselves, that all things are interdependent, that the central ethical concept is harmlessness (*ahimsa*), which enjoins us not to hurt anything, and that this entails the doctrine of compassion, which requires one to help lessen the suffering of others. I am fascinated to watch the newscaster urge his audience to look for similarities between Buddhism and science—their common search for truth, he says—and to hear him define Buddhism as "a science of the spirit." On August 1st the gathering at Rikon celebrates the Dalai Lama's 50th birthday (which in fact is July 6th).

It is the day I must leave Zürich for New York, but the Rikon experience follows me onto the plane. I summon back its atmosphere as I visualize the details of the day, trying to extract its essential meaning.

All at once the image of a woman brought to our session by a friend returns to my mind. A European intellectual unacquainted with the ideas of the east, this is her first glimpse of Tibetan culture. She tells me that—though she considers herself non-religious—this day has been like a gift for her, "one of the highlights of my life," she calls it.

I share her feeling. Several times during the session, as I watch the spiritual head of Tibetan Buddhism and the scientist who leads the holistic approach to physics earnestly engage each other in the pursuit of these questions, I too am aware of the rarity of this hour.

And I wonder—even as I savor its contents—if the real significance of this dialogue lies not only in what is being said but in the fact that it is taking place at all.

WEBER   In the twentieth century, the whole concept of matter has undergone a fundamental change. David Bohm, for instance, uses terms like subtle matter and dense matter. Can we discuss matter from the perspective of contemporary physics, and also from the perspective of Tibetan Buddhism?

BOHM   Matter, which appears to be dense according to physics, actually is made up mostly of empty space, with a few very small particles moving around like planets, and at high energy other particles pass through what appears to be solid matter. Although the particles themselves might be thought of as more dense, when we study relativity and quantum theory we find that matter also has to be conceived as a field, and the particles as concentrations of the field. This field is universal, and it obeys the laws of quantum theory. I feel that these laws are not really deeply understood by physicists, but we are able to draw some conclusions from them. One of these is that the field is made up of waves of many kinds. Each wave has a certain minimum amount of movement, in discrete forms of quanta. There is a minimum energy possible for each wave, which is not very great, but there are so many waves in empty space that that adds up to an enormous amount. In fact, if we allow waves as short as we please, the energy will be infinite. And if we find some reason to limit this (which we have) at certain places where we expect the theory to break down, then if you estimate the energy it will come out that the energy in one cubic centimeter of empty space is much greater than would be liberated by the disintegration of all the matter in the known universe. That suggests that matter as we know it is a small ripple on empty space. In some sense, space is very dense; in another sense not, because it's a movement, a very complex movement.

Modern cosmology believes that the universe started from a Big Bang, where everything was in one point and then spread out. One could imagine that this concentration of energy spread out like a wave suddenly appearing in the middle of the ocean. From one point of view, that is the whole universe, but from a deeper point of view, it's still just a ripple.

As you probe more deeply into matter, it appears to have more and more subtle properties. I haven't gone into all of them here, but they are not simply particles moving in mechanical ways. In my view, the implications of physics seem to be that nature is so subtle that it could be almost alive or intelligent.

WEBER   Could Your Holiness comment on this from the point of view of Tibetan Buddhism?

THE DALAI LAMA   In Buddhism, there are levels of coarseness and subtlety of particles, and the most subtle of all particles would be the particles of space. These serve as the basis for all of the particles that are identified in Tibetan Buddhism. The particles of space remain forever. What they do moment by moment, I don't have any clear explanation of. In that respect, I feel we could learn from the scientists' work, from their experience and investigations.

BOHM   What about time?

THE DALAI LAMA   If we just speak about time in general as if it were some independent thing it would be difficult to explain, because time is posited relative to and dependent upon other factors.

WEBER   What about the Big Bang, that infinitesimally small beginning that became our universe—is there anything similar to this in Tibetan cosmology?

THE DALAI LAMA   According to Buddhism, there are times when the entire universe forms, remains for a certain period, and then disintegrates and remains empty for a certain period.

WEBER   Dormant or empty?

THE DALAI LAMA   Empty. Buddhism speaks of the formation of a world-system, the abiding of a world-system, the destruction of a world-system, and then a state of emptiness. These four repeat over and over again. There is no explanation of some first original beginning. Buddhism believes that all phenomena which depend on causes are always changing. In all particular things there is a beginning and an end, and there must be a cause in order for them to appear. We speak of many different types of causes, and the topic of karma gets connected with these. When you consider where those karmic predispositions reside, you are led into the topic of the mental continuum of the person. Then you must look for the causes of consciousness, and thus we say there's no beginning to consciousness either. Matter cannot make consciousness.

WEBER   Does nature have a karmic pattern of its own?

THE DALAI LAMA   If persons and sentient beings are the user, then the phenomena are the things that are being used. Among the things that are used by the person, there's one's own body, which is immediate, and as you move out, it includes all of the environment. If we speak about, say, a flower, there will be the matter, which serves as the substantial cause of the flower. When you go back and back, researching what the substantial causes are, you will eventually get back to the particles of space.

BOHM   If we look at nature without man, would you say that it has a cause that is independent of consciousness or does it depend on consciousness?

THE DALAI LAMA   The consciousness and the object which is depending on the consciousness don't need to exist at the same time. It's as if you build a house for somebody: it is somehow dependent on the person who will live there, but he may not yet be in it. The karma of the beings who are going to be born there serves as one of the types of causes shaping the matter. Buddhists believe in limitless rebirths, and in an infinite universe. By being here together at this moment, for example, we accumulate a certain kind of karma. This makes imprints on our consciousness. After trillions of years, due to today's action, at a certain period, new worlds will form physically, on the basis of the empty space-particle. The basic cause is those beings who in the future will use that thing. So the basic creator is their consciousness, their karma.

BOHM   Does something create the particles of space, or are they present when the whole universe has dissolved?

THE DALAI LAMA   The substantial causes are those particles, but what I'm talking about is the cooperative conditions which are our actions.

BOHM   Are the particles eternal in themselves?

THE DALAI LAMA   I don't know about the particular particles, but the continuum of those particles of space goes on forever. What to say about one particular particle is unclear.

WEBER   Can we clarify what is meant by this space-particle? Is that a concept recognizable to modern physics?

BOHM   Because of quantum theory, various people are considering similar ideas. When you apply it to relativity, it becomes very difficult to define various small regions of space. They become ambiguous. Various alternatives exist. One idea is to say there are very small units of space, 10^{-33} cm — which would indeed be extremely small. One can take that as a possible point of view. It is implicit even in some of the work that people like Hawking are doing, and others have considered it explicitly. That's another way of looking at this field with tremendous energy which I talked about. We can think of this field as constituted of a tremendous number of particles of space, with each particle having a very high energy. If a wave is formed on those particles, then matter as we know it begins to emerge.

WEBER   Would that wave that forms out of so-called empty space be equivalent to the eastern concept of *maya?*

THE DALAI LAMA   According to the Buddhist explanation, the ultimate creative principle is consciousness. There are different levels of consciousness. What we call innermost subtle consciousness is always there. The continuity of that consciousness is almost like something permanent, like the space-particles. In the field of matter, that is the space-particles; in the field of consciousness, it is the clear light. These two are something like permanent [sic], as far as continuity is concerned. The clear light, with its special energy, makes the connection with consciousness.

WEBER   Light has been used by the mystic as the symbol of his experience of union. In contemporary physics, light is the great mystery. I have elsewhere discussed with David Bohm why light is so central to both these. Could you further elaborate on what the clear light is?

THE DALAI LAMA   The clear light is positive mainly from the point of view of clearing away the darkness of ignorance. It is like the basic substance that can turn into a consciousness that knows everything. All of our other [kinds of] consciousnesses—sense consciousness and so on—arise in dependence on this mind of clear light.

WEBER   It's an energy, not just a symbol?

THE DALAI LAMA   It's an energy. That's right.

WEBER   It's an actual state of consciousness.

THE DALAI LAMA   Yes, and it's very subtle.

BOHM   Is this personal mind or does it belong to the universe?

THE DALAI LAMA   It is personal. It belongs to each person. If we speak about a particle of stone, that has no life; the flower, which does have life; and then of human beings, that have some further qualities—consciousness or whatever—then does science not draw distinctions with regard to the *nature* of the most subtle particles that compose these? If that is so, then at what point and in what way does, say, this [marble table] come not to have life, that [flower] come to have life, and we ourselves to have a basis for consciousness?

BOHM   You could say that the matter itself contains subtle potentialities that have not been realized. For example, the particles of space may be organized into worlds by subtle consciousness which is yet to come, but we have to ask: Is that subtle consciousness distinct from matter? Is it matter or is it not matter?

DR. HOPKINS   His holiness was not saying that the consciousness yet to come forms it, but that the karma of the beings who will be born there shapes it. Then they are born there and use it.

BOHM   Yes, but even before there were people in the world, there must have been this karma present, unless you believe that people were always there.

DR. HOPKINS   His Holiness was saying that there are many other world-systems, and people making karmas there.

THE DALAI LAMA   Infinite.

WEBER   Without beginning, as counted by *our* time?

THE DALAI LAMA   For a particular world, there is a beginning, but for the cosmos as a whole there is no beginning.

WEBER   And no end?

THE DALAI LAMA   Individually, there is an end, as a whole there is no end—unfortunately or fortunately [laughter].

BOHM   Is there any continuity of identity of the individual person across this process or does he just arise and vanish?

THE DALAI LAMA   There is a *mere* "I" or a mere self of which you can say: "*My* former lifetime, *my* future lifetime." The *mere* I or *mere* self exists in the former lifetime, exists in this lifetime, and will exist in the next lifetime. Yesterday's *I* and today's *I* and tomorrow's *I* are in a sense the same *I*, but in another sense, yesterday's *I* is no more; it is already gone, and tomorrow's *I* is yet to come. But as a whole, the continuum of the *I* moment by moment extends through the whole process.

WEBER   Without that, karma would not be logical, would it? The karma of a thousand years ago that "I" have made and that now bears fruit somehow has to be associated with my constellation and attributable to it.

THE DALAI LAMA But there are more powerful and weaker types of karma. You create a certain karma, an action that is powerful enough to have certain consequences. Under those circumstances, it is as if the results are already planned or made. But another new action may occur the energy of which is more powerful than the previous one, and it can change it.

WEBER So it's not a strict determinism.

THE DALAI LAMA That's right. And it all depends on motivation or intent. So ultimately karma is written in our own hand.

BOHM Therefore you are saying that we have the choice to change.

THE DALAI LAMA Yes. Generally speaking, yes. Karma is not created by some outside forces but by oneself.

WEBER Is there an analogy between karma and what a physicist would call the "world-line of a particle," its energy exchanges up to this present moment?

BOHM There is a sort of an analogy in the sense that everything that happens to the particle depends on what happens to everything in the past. There's a web of interconnections which eventually is infinite. But each particle of course has no choice. In physics, it is simply moving according to the forces which have acted on it and these may eventually extend out to great distances in time. Some factors may become negligible and others more powerful. But you must think of the universe as this web of interrelationships of particles.

In physics, particles can be created out of energy and annihilated by combining with each other. Therefore it is not necessary that particles have a permanent existence, even though they may have a long existence. It is now believed that every particle has a limited time of existence, even the proton, which may be at least a million times the age of the present universe. But every particle and every structure of particles eventually falls apart.

THE DALAI LAMA What about the smallest particle, say the quark, or there's even something smaller nowadays, isn't there?

BOHM Yes, people are looking for something smaller.

DR. HOPKINS Is the quark changing all of the time?

BOHM Yes, but it's very hard to know what it is because it cannot be isolated. One view is that it may not even be a particle. Maybe it's a form that emerges from the vacuum and falls back. But people are considering still far smaller particles, gravitons, which would carry the force of gravity and determine the properties of space. But none of these would be permanent.

DR. HOPKINS His Holiness was not saying that the individual particles of space are permanent, only the whole system.

BOHM   Yes, the presence of the base is always there.

THE DALAI LAMA   Is there in science no permanent, continuous particle?

BOHM   No. People are looking instead for a permanent field, the so-called Unified Field Theory. The particle would be a state of excitation of the field. But they are trying to unify the four fields: the ordinary electromagnetic, the strong and weak fields of nuclear interactions, and the gravitational field. Physicists would like to unite them as different forms of one field. They would say that originally all these fields were the same but that some unbalance has occurred and now they have separated and become different. One view is that the universe expands, contracts out of existence, and then starts up again. But the puzzle is, what happened before time began? I think that present physics cannot go that far. Some physicists say that it was God who started the whole thing. The sort of thing I have in mind is akin to the ocean, where many, many waves are going in different directions and by accident they may come together at a certain point and produce a tremendous wave.

WEBER   Of course it leads to the question: From where do those waves come?

BOHM   From the Buddhist point of view you might argue that those waves are a kind of karma. I think physics at present cannot go any further with that question, maybe later.

THE DALAI LAMA   The earlier question wasn't clarified: whether the three types of particles—the rock, the flower, and something that is able to support consciousness—are all the same. If so, at what point did one become able to support life and the other become able to support consciousness? And if there is such a point, what is its cause?

BOHM   The stone is much more in a hidden order than it appears to be. There is a hidden order in matter which organizes the particles and it may take a long time to show up.

DR. HOPKINS   His Holiness's question is: Even if some potentiality is there from the very beginning, what changes it later so that it becomes manifest to serve as the basis of life?

BOHM   It would depend, first of all, on having the right general conditions. We know that life cannot exist without these, the right chemicals and so on.

WEBER   That wouldn't exactly solve the problem because, after all, the rock stayed inert and the plant didn't. It evolved and we also evolved in a subtler way, and His Holiness's question was: Why? From the point of view of physics, why is there this distinction? Isn't that the question?

THE DALAI LAMA   Yes.

BOHM It's not so simple, because even the rock may contain the rudiments of organisms and we ourselves contain material from all over the world.

WEBER Is the rock conscious?

THE DALAI LAMA No.

BOHM Not directly, but it may have the potential for consciousness.

WEBER At one time you said that even the rock might have a very low-level sort of consciousness. Could you explain that a bit? It would also be interesting what His Holiness would say about it.

BOHM That deals with the question of why the rock should remain a rock and not become something else. Consider how a plant grows: You put the seed in the ground but the material comes from the sun, the air, the water, and the soil. It all gathers together of its own accord and makes a plant. According to modern science, the main thing the seed supplies is information in the form of DNA. Once this DNA supplies this information, it makes a plant. Similarly with an animal. My suggestion is that matter has a kind of proto-intelligence—it's not exactly like ours—that moves according to information of a subtle nature, just as people say the DNA has. But eventually it must be the whole surrounding environment which carries it out, because the material comes from there. Therefore the ability to respond to information must be understood. It may be something akin to intelligence, though not identical with it.

THE DALAI LAMA I believe that without knowledge of consciousness, it is very difficult to have a thorough knowledge of matter. And if you know the modern scientific explanation of matter, this could help to explain consciousness better. We Buddhists believe that there are two forces in reality: matter and consciousness. Of course, consciousness depends very much on matter, and changing of matter also depends on consciousness. So I feel that further research in physics and neurology can lead us one day to find new phenomena. It is also very important and very useful to experiment within one's own physical self: yogic practices, or meditation through which you can gain some non-ordinary experience. There is some energy besides the physical, and through consciousness you can change your physical body. So if we have balanced knowledge, good knowledge about consciousness and good knowledge about matter, I think we will have a better human society.

WEBER Are the mystic and the physicist looking for the same thing without being aware of it, even though the one starts with subtle matter and the other with dense matter?

THE DALAI LAMA Today's physicist has a different attitude from previous ones. In the past, it seems that physicists were looking totally to external matter. Upon discovering that the whole story could not be understood by looking that way, they put much more emphasis on the consciousness that is observing, designating and computing phenomena, whether you call it consciousness or not. We Buddhists call it consciousness, others might call it the observer, you might call it wholeness—in short, you cannot have a completely objective view of reality or of the particle, but you need to involve the whole situation in observing them, therefore also the observer or consciousness. It is some indication that there are other forces besides the particles, besides external things.

WEBER   Are wholeness and *sunya* (emptiness) related?

THE DALAI LAMA   Aren't you speaking of wholeness because it is the case that the individual things cannot stand under their own power? They are not self-sufficient but are interrelated. This lack of independence is *sunya*. Emptiness is the absence of independence. In the Buddhist viewpoint, because the ultimate nature is *sunya*, wholeness comes into being. This interdependence itself is a sign of a lack of independence, so the indication of *sunya* is that we ultimately have to invoke wholeness.

BOHM   Yes, the whole must be taken into account in considering how the parts work. When we see the kind of organization of the whole and the parts that goes on in the cell or in other systems, it seems that there is something which is vaguely similar to consciousness even if it is not the same. It has quite a bit of the features of intelligence. In all matter, the whole actually works in the parts in such a way that there is this kind of proto–consciousness, proto–intelligence. It seems less like a force and more like carrying information—they even use the word "messenger"—from one place to another to carry out instructions to build. So the complexity of the process suggests that although it is not consciousness as we know it, it's a kind of simple intelligence.

Epilogue

TWO eminent scientists are missing from this book who should have been in it. They are George Wald and Barbara McClintock. Both are biologists, both Nobel laureates, both examples of highly intuitive scientists whose work has genuine affinity with the theme of this book. I discovered their writings just after this volume went to press, too late—to my deep regret—to interview them. I am resolved to make at least partial amends for this omission through the following brief sketches.

George Wald is an eminent biologist and philosopher of science who has spent most of his career at Harvard University, where he was Higgins Professor of Biology. Now Professor Emeritus, he still spends much of his time in his research laboratory at Woods Hole in Massachusetts. He was co-recipient of the 1967 Nobel Prize in Physiology and Medicine for his contributions to vision, chiefly the area of electrophysiology, the transmission of nervous impulses from the retina to the brain. Wald is best known for his discovery, in 1933, of the presence of vitamin A in the retina.

The author of dozens of technical papers on vision and biochemical evolution, Wald also wrote *General Education in a Free Society* (1945) and *Twenty Six Afternoons of Biology* (1962). A striking and colorful figure at 78, he is a dynamic speaker whose lectures are characterized by their eloquence and wit. A frequent theme is the unity of man and nature.

In a daring article, "Life and Mind in the Universe" (1984), Wald argues that "mind, rather than emerging as a late outgrowth in the evolution of life, has existed always ..., the source and condition of physical reality." Echoing Eddington's thesis, Wald terms the basis of our physical world "mind-stuff." In this, Wald—like Bohm and Sheldrake—proposes a frankly teleological account of nature. He writes: "It is mind that has composed a physical universe that breeds life, and so eventually evolves creatures that know and create.... In them, the universe begins to know itself." Like Bohm (Chapter 8), Wald extends this view even to the status of mathematics, asking "... what are those

243

equations [i.e. of quantum mechanics], indeed what is mathematics, but mind-stuff?—virtually the ultimate in mind-stuff and for that reason deeply mysterious."

Wald, in fact, argues for the evolution of consciousness—parallel to the evolution of matter—leading to nature's ever-increasing self-awareness. His remarks at Stockholm on receiving the Nobel Prize may well sum up his attitude towards his work: "A scientist lives with all reality. There is nothing better. To know reality is to accept it, and eventually to love it. A scientist is in a sense a learned child. There is something of the scientist in every child. Others must outgrow it. Scientists can stay that way all their lives."

Barbara McClintock was associated with Cornell University during most of her professional life, which she devoted to research on the cytogenetics of maize. (Cytogenetics links the study of the visible structure of the chromosomes with the study of genetics.) Working in virtual isolation for fifty years, and propounding unconventional views that were rejected by her peers, McClintock was finally honored and her contributions acknowledged when—at age 81—she won the 1983 Nobel Prize in Physiology and Medicine.

An individualist who spends much of her time alone, McClintock still pursues her research in her Cold Spring Harbor (New York) laboratory. Her life, person, and work are vividly evoked by her biographer, Evelyn Fox Keller in her superb book, *A Feeling for the Organism* (1983). The phrase captures McClintock's attitude towards the plants with which she has worked for fifty years, and which to her are alive. According to Evelyn Keller, McClintock believes that the scientist must, above all, have "a feeling for the organism" (Keller, p. 198); she speaks of listening to "what the material has to say to you" and of the need for the "openness to let it come to you" (Keller, p. 198). Keller also makes the point that McClintock—without being able to account for it—"has always had an 'exceedingly strong feeling' for the unity in nature." Keller conjectures that this feeling lies behind McClintock's remarkable creativity and that it sustained her during the decades when she was virtually alone in her views. In fact, her biographer says that McClintock "is proud to call herself 'a mystic'," for whom "basically, everything is one" (p. 204). She has studied Tibetan Buddhism and has practised some of its yogic techniques which, surprisingly, she seems to have discovered on her own.

Assessing McClintock's impact on biology, Keller writes: "To those who see in ... recent developments the makings of a new revolution in biology, McClintock's name has become something of a password. Matthew Meselson of Harvard believes that history will 'record her as the originator of new and very much more subtle and more complex genetic theories that are as yet only dimly understood'" (p. xi).

Notes

1 Fritz Kunz, personal communication.

2 Feynman, Richard, *The Character of Physical Law*, Cambridge: MIT Press, 1967.

3 Einstein, Albert, *Ideas and Opinions*, Sonja Bargmann (trans.), New York: Crown Publishers, 1954.

4 Max Planck, *Where Is Science Going?*, New York: Norton, 1932.

5 *Amritabindu Upanishad* in *The Upanishads*, trans. Prabhavananda and Manchester, New York: New American Library, 1957.

6 *Amritabindu and Svetasvatara Upanishads*, ibid.

7 Govinda, Lama Anagarika, *Foundations of Tibetan Mysticism*, New York: Samuel Weiser, 1969.

8 Bohr, Niels, *Atomic Physics and Human Knowledge*, New York: John Wiley & Sons, 1958.

9 Eckhart, Meister, *Sermons*, Raymond B. Blackney, (trans.), New York: Harper Torchbook, 1957.

10 Wilber, Ken (editor's note), *ReVision Journal*, Fall 1982.

11 *Ibid.*

12 In *Teachings of His Holiness, the Dalai Lama* (edited and photographed by Marcia Keegan), New York: Clear Light Publications, Inc., 1981.

13 *Ibid.*

14 Prigogine, Ilya, *Order Out of Chaos: Man's New Dialogue with Nature*, New York: Bantam Books, 1984.

15 *Ibid.*

16 Einstein, Albert, *The World As I See It*, New York: Wisdom Library, 1979, and *Ideas and Opinions*, Sonja Bargmann (trans.), New York: Crown Publishers, 1954.

Bibliography

Aurobindo (Sri), *The Life Divine*, New York: Dutton, 1949.

Bohm, David, *Quantum Theory*, New York: Prentice Hall, 1951.

Bohm, David, *Causality and Chance in Modern Physics*, London: Routledge & Kegan Paul, 1957.

Bohm, David, *The Special Theory of Relativity*, New York: W. A. Benjamin, 1965.

Bohm, David, *Wholeness and the Implicate Order*, London: Routledge & Kegan Paul, 1980.

Bohr, Niels, *Atomic Physics and the Description of Nature*, Cambridge, England: Cambridge University Press, 1934.

Bohr, Niels, *Atomic Physics and Human Knowledge*, New York: John Wiley & Sons, 1958.

Briggs, John P. and Peat, David F., *Looking Glass Universe*, New York: Simon & Schuster, 1984.

Capra, Fritjof, *The Tao of Physics*, Berkeley: Shambhala, 1975.

Chandmal, Asit, *One Thousand Moons: Krishnamurti at Eighty-Five*, New York: Harry N. Abrams, Inc., 1985.

Chatterji, J. C., *The Wisdom of the Vedas*, Wheaton: Quest, 1973.

Dalai Lama, His Holiness, Tenzin Gyatso, The Fourteenth Dalai Lama, *The Buddhism of Tibet and the Key to the Middle Way*, New York: Harper & Row, 1975.

Dalai Lama, His Holiness, Tenzin Gyatso, The Fourteenth Dalai Lama, *The Opening of the Wisdom Eye*, Wheaton, Illinois: Quest Books, Theosophical Publishing House, 1975.

Dalai Lama, His Holiness, Tenzin Gyatso, The Fourteenth Dalai Lama, *My Land and My People*, New York: McGraw Hill, 1962. New York: Potala Corporation, 1978.

Dawkins, Richard, *The Selfish Gene*, Oxford: Oxford University Press, 1976.

Driesch, H., *History and Theory of Vitalism*, London: Macmillan, 1914.

Driesch, H., *Mind and Body*, London: Methuen, 1927.

Eckhart, Meister, *Meister Eckhart*, A Modern Translation by Raymond Bernard Blakney, New York: Harper Torchbook, 1957.

Eddington, Arthur, *The Nature of the Physical World*, London: Dent, 1935.

Einstein, Albert, *Essays in Science*, New York: Philosophical Library, 1934.

Einstein, Albert, *Ideas and Opinions*, Carl Seeling (ed.), New York: Dell Publishing Co., 1973.

Evans-Wentz, W. Y., *Tibetan Yoga and Secret Doctrines*, Oxford: Oxford University Press, 1935.

Evans-Wentz, W. Y., and Lama Kazi Dawa-Samdup (eds.), *The Tibetan Book of the Dead*, Oxford: Oxford University Press, 1957.

Govinda, Lama Anagarika, *The Psychological Attitude of Early Buddhist Philosophy*, London: Rider, 1961.

Govinda, Lama Anagarika, *Foundations of Tibetan Mysticism*, New York: Samuel Weiser, 1969.

Govinda, Lama Anagarika, *The Way of the White Clouds: A Buddhist Pilgrim in Tibet*, Boulder: Shambhala, 1970.

Govinda, Lama Anagarika, *Creative Meditation and Multi-Dimensional Consciousness*, Wheaton: Theosophical Publishing House, 1976.

Griffiths, Fr. Bede, *Return to the Center*, Springfield, Illinois: Templegate Publishers, 1977.

Griffiths, Fr. Bede, *The Golden String*, Springfield, Illinois: Templegate Publishers, 1980.

Griffiths, Fr. Bede, *The Marriage of East and West*, Springfield, Illinois: Templegate Publishers, 1982.

Griffiths, Fr. Bede, *The Cosmic Revelation*, Springfield, Illinois: Templegate Publishers, 1983.

Griffiths, Fr. Bede, *Christ in India*, Springfield, Illinois: Templegate Publishers, 1984.

Hawking, Stephen, "The Existence of Cosmic Time Functions," *Proc. Roy. Soc. A308*, 1968.

Hawking, Stephen and Ellis, G. F. R., *The Large Scale Structure of Space-Time*, Cambridge: Cambridge University Press, 1973.

Hawking, Stephen and Carr, B. J., "Black Holes in the Early Universe," *Mon. Not. Roy. Astr. Soc. 168*, 1974.

Hawking, Stephen and Gibbons, G. W., "Cosmological Event Horizons, Thermodynamics and Particle Creation," *Phys. Rev.D 15*, 1977.

Hawking, Stephen, "Spacetime Foam," *Nucl. Phys. B. 144.*, 1978.

Hawking, Stephen and Israel, W. (eds.), *The Path Integral Approach to Quantum Gravity, General Relativity: An Einstein Centenary Survey*, Cambridge: Cambridge University Press, 1979.

Hawking, Stephen, "Is the End in Sight for Theoretical Physics?" Inaugural Lecture, Cambridge: Cambridge University Press, 1980.

Hawking, Stephen and Rocek, M., (eds), *Superspace and Supergravity*, Cambridge: Cambridge University Press, 1981.

Hawking, Stephen and Hartle, J. B., "Wave Function of the Universe," *Phys. Rev. D. 28*, 1983.

Hawking, Stephen, "The Edge of Spacetime," *Am. Sci.*, July-Aug., 1984.

Hawking, Stephen and Halliwell, J. J., "The Origin of Structure in the Universe," *Phys. Rev. D31*, 8, 1985.

Heisenberg, Werner, *The Physicist's Conception of Nature*, Arnold J. Pomerans (trans.), New York: Harcourt Brace & Company, 1958.

Heisenberg, Werner, *Physics and Philosophy*, New York: Harper Torchbooks, 1958.

Heisenberg, Werner, *Physics and Beyond*, New York: Harper & Row, 1971.

Huxley, Aldous, *The Perennial Philosophy*, New York and London: Harper & Brothers, 1945.

Jantsch, Erich, *The Self-Organizing Universe: Scientific and Human Implications of the Emerging Paradigm of Evolution*, Oxford: Pergamon Press, 1980.

Jeans, James, *The Growth of Physical Science*, Cambridge: Cambridge University Press, 1951.

Keller, Evelyn Fox, *A Feeling for the Organism: The Life and Work of Barbara McClintock*, New York: W. H. Freeman, 1983.

Koestler, A. and Smythies, J. R. (eds.), *Beyond Reductionism*, London: Hutchinson, 1969.

Krishnamurti, *Freedom From the Known*, New York: Harper & Row, 1969.

Krishnamurti, *The Urgency of Change*, Mary Lutyens (ed.), New York: Harper & Row, 1970.

Krishnamurti, *The Awakening of Intelligence*, New York: Harper & Row, 1973.

Krishnamurti, *Truth and Actuality*, New York: Harper & Row, 1978.

Krishnamurti, *The Wholeness of Life*, New York: Harper & Row, 1979.

Krishnamurti and Bohm, David, *The Ending of Time: Thirteen Dialogues between J. Krishnamurti and David Bohm*, San Francisco: Harper & Row, 1985.

Kuhn, Thomas S., *The Structure of Scientific Revolutions*, Chicago: Chicago University Press, 1962.

Kunz, Fritz L., "The Reality of the Non-material," *Main Currents in Modern Thought*, December, 1963.

Kunz, Fritz L., "On the Symmetry Principles," in *Order in the Universe*, New York: The Foundation for Integrative Education, 1967.

Margenau, Henry, "Fields in Physics and Biology," *Main Currents*, 1972.

Margenau, Henry, "The Method of Science and the Meaning of Reality," *Nature, Man, and Society*, New York: Nicolas Hays, 1976.

Monod, Jacques, *Le Hasard et la nécessité*, Paris: Editions du Seuil, 1970.

Murti, T. R. V., *The Central Philosophy of Buddhism*, London: Allen & Unwin, 1955.

Otto, Rudolf, *Mysticism: A Comparative Analysis of the Nature of Mysticism*, Bertha L. Bracey and Richenda C. Payne (trans.), New York: Meridian Books, 1960 (4th printing).

Popper, Karl, *The Logic of Scientific Discovery*, New York: Harper Torchbooks, 1959.

Popper, Karl, *Conjectures and Refutations*, London: Routledge & Kegan Paul, 1969.

Prigogine, Ilya, *From Being to Becoming: Time and Complexity in the Physical Sciences*, San Francisco: W. H. Freeman & Co., 1980.

Prigogine, Ilya and Isabelle Stengers, *Order Out of Chaos: Man's New Dialogue With Nature*, New York: Bantam Books, 1984.

Schroedinger, Erwin, *What is Life?* and *Mind and Matter*, Cambridge: Cambridge University Press, 1967.

Shankara, *Crest-Jewel of Discrimination*, Swami Prabhavananda and C. Isherwood (trans.), New York: New American Library, 1970.

Sheldrake, Rupert, *A New Science of Life: The Hypothesis of Formative Causation*, Los Angeles: J. P. Tarcher, 1981.

Stace, W. T., *The Teachings of the Mystics*, New York: New American Library, 1960.

Suzuki, D. T., *Essays in Zen Buddhism* (3 volumes), London: Rider, 1953.

Thompson, D'Arcy W., *On Growth and Form*, Cambridge: Cambridge University Press, 1942.

Wald, George, "Life and Mind in the Universe," *International Journal of Quantum Chemistry*, 11, 1984. New York: Wiley & Sons, 1984.

Weber, Renée, "The Reluctant Tradition: Esoteric Philosophy East and West," *Main Currents in Modern Thought*, 31, March-April, 1975.

Weber, Renée, "The Good, the True, the Beautiful: Are they Attributes of the Universe?" *Main Currents in Modern Thought*, 32, Nov. 1975.

Weber, Renée, "The Tao of Physics Revisited," A conversation with Fritjof Capra, *ReVision Journal*, 4, 1, Spring 1981.

Weber, Renée, "The Physicist and the Mystic – Is a Dialogue between them Possible?" Interview with David Bohm. *ReVision Journal*, Spring, 1981.

Weber, Renée, "Reflections on David Bohm's Holomovement: A Physicist's Model of Cosmos and Consciousness," Chapter 5 in ed. R. Valle and R. von Eckartsberg, *The Metaphors of Consciousness*, New York: Plenum, 1981.

Weber, Renée, "What is Insight?" An interview with Krishnamurti, *ReVision Journal*, Spring 1980 and in P. Jayakar and S. Patwardhan (eds), *Within the Mind*, Madras: Krishnamurti Foundation of India, 1982.

Weber, Renée, "Field Consciousness and Field Ethics," in Wilber, Ken (ed.), *The Holographic Paradigm and Other Paradoxes*. Boulder: Shambhala, 1982.

Weber, Renée, "Meaning as Being in the Implicate Order Philosophy of David Bohm," *David Bohm: Quantum Physics and Beyond*, Basil Hiley and David Peat (eds), London: Routledge & Kegan Paul, 1986.

Weizsäcker, Carl Friedrich von, "Platonic Natural Science in the Course of History," (trans. Renée Weber), *Main Currents in Modern Thought*, 29, Sept.-Oct. 1972.

Weizsäcker, Carl Friedrich von, *The Unity of Nature*, Francis J. Zucker (trans.), New York: Farrar, Strauss & Giroux, 1980.

Whitehead, Alfred North, *Science and the Modern World*, Cambridge: Cambridge University Press, 1928.

Whitehead, Alfred North, *Modes of Thought*, New York: Macmillan, 1968.

Whyte, Lancelot L., *The Unitary Principle in Physics and Biology*, London: Cresset Press, 1949.

Wilber, Ken, *The Spectrum of Consciousness*, Wheaton, Ill.: Quest, 1977.

Wilber, Ken, *No Boundary: Eastern and Western Approaches to Personal Growth*, Boulder and London: Shambhala, 1981.

Wilber, Ken (ed.), *The Holographic Paradigm and Other Paradoxes*, Boulder: Shambhala, 1982.

Wilber, Ken, *Eye to Eye: The Quest for the New Paradigm*, New York: Doubleday, 1983.

Wilber, Ken, (ed.), *Quantum Questions: The Mystical Writings of the World's Great Physicists*, (includes "Beyond the Cave" and "Of Shadows and Symbols"), Boulder: Shambhala, 1984.

Index